Justice Imperiled: The Anti-Nazi Lawyer Max Hirschberg in Weimar Germany,
  Douglas G. Morris
The Heimat Abroad: The Boundaries of Germanness, edited by Krista O'Donnell,
  Renate Bridenthal, and Nancy Reagin
*Modern German Art for Thirties Paris, Prague, and London: Resistance and
  Acquiescence in a Democratic Public Sphere,* Keith Holz
*The War against Catholicism: Liberalism and the Anti-Catholic Imagination in
  Nineteenth-Century Germany,* Michael B. Gross
German Pop Culture: How "American" Is It? edited by Agnes C. Mueller
Character Is Destiny: The Autobiography of Alice Salomon, edited by Andrew Lees
*Other Germans: Black Germans and the Politics of Race, Gender, and Memory in
  the Third Reich,* Tina M. Campt
State of Virginity: Gender, Religion, and Politics in an Early Modern Catholic State,
  Ulrike Strasser
Worldly Provincialism: German Anthropology in the Age of Empire,
  H. Glenn Penny and Matti Bunzl, editors
Ethnic Drag: Performing Race, Nation, Sexuality in West Germany, Katrin Sieg
Projecting History: German Nonfiction Cinema, 1967–2000, Nora M. Alter
Cities, Sin, and Social Reform in Imperial Germany, Andrew Lees
The Challenge of Modernity: German Social and Cultural Studies, 1890–1960,
  Adelheid von Saldern
Exclusionary Violence: Antisemitic Riots in Modern German History,
  Christhard Hoffman, Werner Bergmann, and Helmut Walser Smith, editors
Languages of Labor and Gender: Female Factory Work in Germany, 1850–1914,
  Kathleen Canning
That Was the Wild East: Film Culture, Unification and the "New" Germany,
  Leonie Naughton
Anna Seghers: The Mythic Dimension, Helen Fehervary
*Staging Philanthropy: Patriotic Women and the National Imagination in Dynastic
  Germany, 1813–1916,* Jean H. Quataert
Truth to Tell: German Women's Autobiographies and Turn-of-the-Century Culture,
  Katharina Gerstenberger
The "Goldhagen Effect": History, Memory, Nazism—Facing the German Past, Geoff
  Eley, editor
Shifting Memories: The Nazi Past in the New Germany, Klaus Neumann
Saxony in German History: Culture, Society, and Politics, 1830–1933,
  James Retallack, editor
*Little Tools of Knowledge: Historical Essays on Academic and Bureaucratic
  Practices,* Peter Becker and William Clark, editors

Social History, Popular Culture, and Politics in Germany
Geoff Eley, Series Editor
(Continued)

OTHER GERMANS

OTHER GERMANS

BLACK GERMANS
and the Politics of Race, Gender,
and Memory in the Third Reich

TINA CAMPT

The University of Michigan Press
ANN ARBOR

First paperback edition 2005
Copyright © by the University of Michigan 2004
All rights reserved
Published in the United States of America by
The University of Michigan Press
Manufactured in the United States of America
⊗ Printed on acid-free paper

2008   2007   2006   2005   5   4   3   2

A CIP catalog record for this book is available from the British Library.

Library of Congress Cataloging-in-Publication Data

Campt, Tina, 1964–
Other Germans : Black Germans and the politics of race, gender,
and memory in the Third Reich / Tina Campt.
p.   cm. — (Social history, popular culture, and
politics in Germany)
Includes bibliographical references and index.
ISBN 0-472-11360-7 (cloth : alk. paper)
1. World War, 1939–1945—Blacks—Germany.   2. Blacks—Race
identity—Germany—History—1939–1945.   3. Africans—Germany—
History—1939–1945.   4. Germany—Race
relations—Political aspects.   I. Title.   II. Series.

DD78.B55 C36 2004
943'.00496—dc22   2003015703

ISBN 0-472-03138-4 (pbk. : alk. paper)

FOR FASIA AND HANS,
THAT OTHERS MIGHT KNOW . . .

ACKNOWLEDGMENTS

This project was initiated many years ago through an unexpected exchange with an Afro-German man at a street fair in 1988 in Bremen, Germany. It began with his greeting, "Hello, Sister," and ended with his telling me the very personal story of how he came to call himself Afro-German. I sat on a doorstep and listened in fascination. It was an anonymous encounter, for we never exchanged names and never saw each other again. I never imagined that fifteen years later that conversation would result in this monograph. It is the product of numerous enriching cultural and intellectual exchanges and the generosity of many people who shared their very different stories with me. For this I must thank this anonymous Afro-German man as well as many other individuals and institutions.

The interviews and archival research that form the basis of this study were funded by grants from the Social Science Research Foundation and the Volkswagen Foundation through the Berlin Program for Advanced German and European Studies. I received additional funding for this research from the German Academic Exchange Service (DAAD). The Luigi Einaudi and Beatrice Brown Foundations provided much-needed funding for recording equipment and the transcription of my interviews. The follow-up research and writing of the book was enabled by a sabbatical leave from the University of California, Santa Cruz, and the generous financial support of the American Association of University Women, the Leverhulme Trust, and the Center for German and European Studies at Georgetown University. The Center for European Studies at the University of California, Berkeley, and the University of California's Committee on Research provided travel grants that allowed me to conduct follow-up interviews with some of my informants.

As with all scholarly work, this study is the product of many dialogues and revelatory exchanges. For those moments of insight and inspiration over the course of the many years I have worked on this project, I am grateful to Yara-Colette Lemke Muniz de Faria, Pascal Grosse, Carla Freccero, Jacqueline Nassy Brown, Saidiya Hartmann, Roger Chickering, Jeff Peck, Sara Lennox, Atina Grossmann, Clare Hemmings, Nikolas Rose, Chetan Bhatt, Barnor Hesse, Sabine Hark, Ilona Pache, and Christina Thürmer-Rohr. My colleagues and friends in the UCSC Women's Studies Department have been marvelous mentors who have advised and consoled me through the highs and lows of my writing. I benefited greatly from comments and suggestions made by faculty and graduate students during my residencies at the Center for German and European Studies at Georgetown University and in the Sociology Department at Goldsmiths College in London, where I presented early versions of chapters of the book. The book has benefited immeasurably from the editorial attention given to different versions of the manuscript by Zoe Sodja and Olga Trokhimenko.

I must also acknowledge some of the many individuals whose support was neither material nor quantifiable but was nonetheless essential to the realization and completion of this project. Dagmar Schultz, Ika Hügel-Marshall, Ilona Bubeck, Sarah Schnier, and all of the present and former women of Orlanda Frauenbuchverlag supported me and my work from what feels like the moment I began it. Christel Priemer put me in contact with the two most inspiring individuals I have ever met—after having known me for less than an hour. And May Ayim encouraged me for as long as I had the privilege of knowing her.

Finally, there are those whose influence on both me and my work is immeasurable. My father, Yara, and Derek have been tireless emotional cheerleaders, nurturers, and comforters. But without Fasia and Hans, this book would not have happened. I thank them for never treating me like a stranger and for being the bravest people I have ever known.

CONTENTS

INTRODUCTION
RACE, MEMORY, AND
HISTORICAL REPRESENTATION

Contextualizing Black German Narratives

of the Third Reich

QUESTIONS OF CONTEXT: RACE,
GENDER, AND HISTORIOGRAPHY

The most difficult part of beginning any story, any project, or any study but especially any history lies in the choices and decisions we make with regard to context. How and why do we situate the stories we want to tell in the ways we do? What information needs to be known so that our stories make sense? Against what backgrounds and in what frameworks do we want our stories to be understood? What other stories do our tales cite or reference, and what differentiates our stories from those of others? Contexts—both discursive and sociohistorical— are the possibility of existence and intelligibility of our stories as well as the ultimate limit of how they are read. At times, contexts even constitute the source of the misreading or unraveling of the very stories they seek to construct. In this way, contexts can be as problematic as they are illuminating.

This book tells the story of a group of individuals that is frequently left out of numerous stories, histories, and historiographies. However, this volume is in no way the definitive or comprehensive telling of this story. It offers instead a partial account of how, in the first half of the twentieth century, German Blacks were constituted as particular kinds of raced and gendered subjects in Germany under the Nazi regime—a regime that is most often considered primarily for its profoundly destructive capacity. Breaking with this tendency, this work examines the generative effects of this totalitarian government and the processes of racialization and gendering that constituted its fundamental organizing techniques and practices. This book does so by looking at a population that is not popularly seen as the primary target of this regime's racial ideology—Germany's Black citizens. This book examines the historical discourses that preceded and enabled the emergence of a Black German subject and analyzes how the processes of racial and gender formation designed by National Socialism to purge non-Aryans from the landscape of German society contributed in paradoxical ways to the production of some of the subjects it sought to expunge. In this way, this work seeks to theorize and understand racial and gendered subject formation as a historical as well as social process. I construct this account through an analysis of the memory narratives of two Black Germans whose status as German subjects was shaped by this regime in profound ways. In this way, the book uses memory as both a lens for theorizing and a site for analyzing this regime's effects on these individuals.

The challenge of contextualizing the history of Black Germans in the Third Reich lies in recognizing both the productive and delimiting implications of some of its most pertinent historiographical contexts. The history of this population opens up alternative ways of conceiving of racial and gender formation and adds new levels of complexity to interpretations of race and gender in the historiography of German colonialism, the Holocaust, and National Socialism as well as for theorizing memory, oral history, and the African diaspora. Yet it is equally important to acknowledge the limitations of reading this history solely through any one of these contexts.

Although the contextualization of one's object of study is always a central part of any scholarly analysis, the stakes of this project are particularly high with respect to representing the history and experiences of a population such as Afro-Germans. Because of the late emergence of this group in the larger narrative of German history, the context in which their accounts are placed is that much more significant, particularly with regard to how this book is situated in the historiography of the Holocaust. An anecdote may help to more clearly illuminate some of the issues involved here. A few years ago, while I was researching parts of this book at the United States Holocaust Memorial Museum

(USHMM), I received an unexpected inquiry from one of the museum's archival staff—a request to donate materials I had collected on Afro-German history (specifically, oral histories I conducted) to the museum's archive. Indeed, it was quite a straightforward and affirming request: straightforward because it would appear that the question of whether I would want to have the life histories of the courageous and inspiring individuals whom I interviewed preserved in one of the finest archives of German history in the United States would seem a no-brainer; affirming, I believe, because despite criticism to the contrary, the interest shown by the USHMM in the history of Afro-Germans in the Third Reich is a sincere expression of the museum's conception of the Holocaust as a phenomenon by no means restricted to the persecution of European Jews but rather one fundamentally centered on the larger question of race.

But from another perspective, this question is not a straightforward one. From this question arises a series of other questions, each of which reflects the profound implications of context and memory in the constitution of identity, community, and history. On the one hand, what does it mean to deposit in an American archival collection dedicated to the study of the Holocaust some of the few recorded memories of a group of people whose history has begun to be written only in the last twenty years? As inclined as I am to have these materials preserved in the hands of an institution as respected as the USHMM, it is nevertheless necessary for me to acknowledge the fact that to place them in this collection is also to insert these narratives into a particular historical context. At the same time, to have these voices enter into history framed by this particular context is also to be aware of the ways in which this framework influences, shapes, and necessarily limits how these memories might be read—for example, as stories of victimization and persecution rather than as narratives of affirmation and resistance.[1]

One example of this can be found in David Okuefuna and Moise Shewa's excellent documentary, *Hitler's Forgotten Victims: Black Survivors of the Holocaust.*[2] The film is invaluable for the wealth of new material it provides—in particular, the documentary footage and still photographs of Black GIs and Africans in Nazi Germany as well as the Afro-German oral history testimony that serves as the film's core. But the film presents these individuals' testimony and the supporting historical source material in an extremely narrow context: Afro-Germans are essentially rendered one-dimensionally, solely as victims of Nazi persecution. Even at obvious moments in the film, when narrators offer fascinating accounts of their lives in the Third Reich—recounting, for example, their membership in the Hitler Youth or military service (the implications of which will be discussed at length in chapter 3)—the ways in which such accounts complicate the status of victimhood are left wholly unexplored.

The stakes of contextualizing the history of Black Germans in the Third Reich are similarly high with regard to how these individuals' narratives are situated in the larger context of the African diaspora. Indeed, some renderings of the experiences of Afro-Germans have shown a worrisome tendency to overlook the complexities of the contradictory and ambivalent ways in which members of this population have been positioned historically in German society. This tendency can be observed in the collection *The African-German Experience,* edited by Carol Aisha Blackshire-Belay. With noteworthy exceptions, the essays collected in this volume contextualize Afro-German history and articulations of identity in relation to African-American history and community formation. In this way, Afro-German identity and the history of this community are often rendered in an almost patronizing manner, in what amounts to a portrayal of them as a group of individuals at the beginning of a long journey toward "real" or "true" Black consciousness, a model assumed to be exemplified by the African-American community.[3]

Such contextual considerations provoke a reformulation of the more general questions posed here regarding the stakes of framing and historical context. Specifically, in what contexts are we to read the history of this population? How does the history of Black Germans broaden our understanding of ongoing historical and theoretical debates? In short, where does this history fit into a larger scholarly project? The two most obvious contexts in which this study of Black Germans in the Third Reich must be located are historical interpretations of the Holocaust and National Socialism. Yet it is perhaps as important to outline what my analysis will not undertake in this context as it is to emphasize how the history of Black Germans in this regime adds and shifts within this historiography.

First, this book will not examine the set of questions posed under the rubric of the *Historikerstreit* regarding the uniqueness or singularity of Nazi genocide. Despite the fact that this debate continues to produce fruitful analyses, it is not my primary concern here. Although this book discusses the forms of Nazi victimization and persecution of some members of the Black German population, I do so in ways that challenge a conception of this regime's response to this group as a systematic or coherent state policy. Indeed, the contradictory and uneven effects of Nazi racial policy on the Black German population will demonstrate not only the extent to which the National Socialists seemed unable to fit Black Germans neatly into their racial ideology but also that Black Germans were a highly diverse group of individuals whose status and fate within this regime was quite different from and thus cannot be subsumed in historical accounts and explanations of other "non-Aryan" groups such as Jews and "Gypsies." I will engage race as the foundational discourse that motivated and propelled this regime but also paradoxically presented the ultimate impossibility of fully realizing a racial state.

Rather than placing anti-Semitism at the center of my analysis of National Socialist (NS) racial policy, I recenter the concept of race that formed the true basis of this regime's fundamental organization as well as its authorizing discourse. I ask how race worked in the Third Reich by looking at its Black rather than its Jewish community. Hence, I focus on a very different question than that posed by many studies of Nazi Germany and the Holocaust: What happens when we view the Holocaust not through the history of anti-Semitism and the persecution of the Jews but through the ideology of racial purity? In this way, I emphasize how, in the service of racial purity, this regime produced the same subjects it regulated, administered, and indeed ultimately sought to destroy.

This approach to understanding National Socialism's effects also means that this book does not attempt to assess or address the status of this regime as a particular kind of fascist or totalitarian state. Rather, this work looks at how in the Third Reich, power worked through racialization and gendering to produce different forms of both docile and resistant subjects in ways that at times worked against the grain of and in contradiction to the regime's aims. This emphasis on subject formation among Black Germans is intended to highlight the extent to which these individuals were interpellated by this racial state in ways that both constrained and enabled their constitution as German subjects. In the societies in which they lived, the categories of Blackness, Germanness, and gender were both internally contradictory and contradicted each other; thus, Afro-Germans' accounts of their experiences within the Reich vividly reflect their negotiation of these contradictions. The racial and gendered technologies of subject constitution that these people experienced within the Third Reich were productive in that they quite literally brought these individuals into being as particular kinds of differentially valued and devalued German subjects, both with and without certain kinds of possibilities. Thus, these technologies enabled and constrained them as the raced and gendered parameters of their intelligibility yet they lacked the capacity to ever completely define or fully contain those parameters and possibilities.

An equally significant context for understanding Black German subject formation is Germany's colonial history. Connecting the Nazi ideology of racial purity and public discourse on Black Germans to earlier discourses on Black Germans both within and beyond the boundaries of the German nation in the years preceding the establishment of the NS state plays a crucial role in explaining the power and efficacy of such discourses within the Third Reich. This study supports the contentions of several key texts in the emerging historiography of the German colonial experience. In particular, the keen analyses of Susanne Zantop, Sarah Friedrichsmeyer and her coeditors, Pascal Grosse, and Lora Wildenthal have recently broken new ground through their focus on the mutually reinforcing interplay between metropole and colony that connects colonial discourses of race and gender to their implications and consequences within the metropole, and vice versa.[4] This book draws on these scholars' work to emphasize the links between colonial discourses on miscegenation and citizenship and their influence on parallel and subsequent debates on the status of Black Germans within the Reich. Moreover, this volume supports this work by underlining the fact that despite its truncated colonial history, Germany depended as much as any other European nation on the distinction from non-European populations in the constitution of national identity.

Throughout this book, it is important not to view the links between the historical periods examined here as cumulative or inevitable in their relation. Nor should the developments documented with regard

to the public discourse and response to Black Germans be read as cul-
minating in the Nazi sterilization of Black Germans. On the contrary,
I seek to paint a far more complex picture. In fact, I try strenuously
and carefully to resist a convenient or predictable teleology of Nazi
persecution by focusing instead on a nuanced notion of historical
"echoes" and "specters." What is most remarkable about the relationship between discussions about and discourse on Black Germans in the
colonies following World War I and in the Third Reich is the discursive
echoes that recurred in each context. These echoes of the dangerous
specter posed by a Black German population link the very different
historical events of each of these periods and demonstrate the resilience
of the perceived threat of racial mixture. At the same time, these echoes
show how the discourse of nation was and remains an inherently gendered and racialized discourse that relies on gender and race to incite
and sustain its efficacy. Overdetermining the links between these events
and epochs would in my view be a mistake that denied and occluded
the complicated ways that race and gender historically have worked
together, with powerful social and political effects. This volume moves
in a different direction by connecting and historicizing the discourses
that incite and enable historical events—that is, not necessarily by connecting and historicizing the events themselves. In this way, placing the
history of Black Germans in the Third Reich in the context of Germany's colonial legacy underlines not only continuities in how Black
Germans were perceived but, more importantly, continuities in the
stakes and salience of a conception of national purity as racial purity.

In the same way that this book speaks to some of the central questions of Holocaust and NS historiography from an alternative vantage
point, it also approaches the question of the relation of Black Germans
to the African diaspora from an oblique perspective. The second half
of this book examines from an unconventional viewpoint some of the
debates and questions central to the study of the African diaspora, asking, for example, how the African diaspora is constituted by looking at
Germany rather than at Africa or the Americas. Instead of focusing on
the implications of displacement, migration, or settlement from the
African continent to sites elsewhere, I explore the thorough emplace-
ment of the Black German community. Hence, this study is situated
firmly in Europe, albeit in a part of Europe that usually falls out of the
traditional cartography of the African diaspora. My analysis of the

narratives of my Black German interview partners contests both the
centrality of triangulation that characterizes many conceptions of the
African Diaspora and the crisscrossing trajectory of movement
mapped by the model of the Black Atlantic. Rather than normalizing
any assumed affinities among Black peoples, this book theorizes our
stakes and investments in the links postulated by academics and
nonacademics as constitutive of the relations between different Black
communities transnationally. In this way, this book is strategically
located between two directions in the study of Black European cultural
formations. It builds on the work of scholars of German history and
German studies on the nexus of race, gender, and sexuality in the history of Blacks in Germany as early as the sixteenth century.[5] At the
same time, this work takes up theoretical impulses set out by scholars
of Black British cultural studies, who redefined the concepts of race,
cultural identity, and diaspora to take into account the realities of contemporary Black European communities, particularly in the United
Kingdom.[6] This book uses these theoretical models to think through
the ways in which articulations of Black German identity contest both
German and European national and cultural identities, which have
traditionally been constituted "racially" as white. Here it is useful to
consider another important context—that of the genealogy of the
terms *Afro-German* and *Black German.*

Afro-German (*Afro-deutsch*) is a term of identification that emerged
in the mid-1980s among Germans of African descent to describe their
mixed ethnic and racial heritages. As the Afro-German movement has
evolved and come to include individuals of more diverse cultural backgrounds (individuals of Indian, Arab, and Asian heritage, for example), the term *Black German* (*Schwarze Deutsche*) has also come to be a
widely accepted term of identification among members of this community. *Afro-German* is both a consciousness-raising provocation and an
articulation of the German and Afro-diasporic heritages of this population. At the same time, *Black German* emphasizes the constructedness of blackness in German society and the fact that public perception
of blackness in Germany is not restricted to the attribute of skin color.
Both these terms pose the questions of what or who is Black in German
society and how blackness comes to be defined in this context.
Throughout this text, the German populations of African descent that

are the subjects of this investigation are referred to as either *Afro-Germans* or *Black Germans.* My use of these contemporary terms of identification is not intended retrospectively to attribute to these individuals a form of Black identity or consciousness that they may or may not have had. On the contrary, my usage grows out of the descriptive necessity of finding a term with which to refer to a group of people for whom there existed no positive term of reference as individuals of both Black and German heritage. *Black German* and *Afro-German* are appropriate terms of reference in that they give voice to one of the central phenomena explored in this study: how individuals of African descent were constituted as Blacks in German society on a number of levels, regardless of any personal identification with blackness. Indeed, the extent to which Blacks have identified as "Black" has never been of any consequence in the perception or treatment of them as such. Furthermore, this work attempts to unsettle prevalent notions of racial identity that proscribe a dichotomous, either/or choice between blackness and whiteness, revealing both the constructedness of racial categories and the stakes involved in their definition.

The final context in which this book must be understood is in relation to the methodology of oral history. Throughout this work I refer to the accounts of my Black German interview partners as "memory narratives." My use of this alternative terminology is not meant to imply that the interviews from which these accounts are derived are not oral historical texts. The methodology of oral history quite literally provides the structure of these accounts, and these interviews emerged from an active and critical engagement with oral history, ethnography, and qualitative research methodologies.[7] Yet I will be reading these accounts as narrative texts rather than strictly as documents. Although my analysis aims to mine these accounts' valuable insights into the historical settings that are rendered, I resist seeing the interviews as direct presentations of the past "as it really was." My interest lies in reading these narratives "symptomatically," as Ronald Grele proposed in his often-cited adaptation of Louis Althusser's notion of "symptomatic reading." Like Althusser, Grele envisions the goal of oral history analysis as unearthing the submerged levels of meaning within these narratives—or, in Althusser's formulation, their "problematic." As Grele writes,

If read properly, [oral history interview texts] do reveal to us hidden levels of discourse—the search for which is the aim of *symptomatic* reading. If read (or listened to) again and again, not just for facts and comments, but also, as Althusser suggests, for insights and oversights, for the combination of vision and nonvision and especially for answers to questions which were never asked, we should be able to isolate and describe the problematic which informs the particular interview. It is at the level of this problematic—the theoretical or ideological context within which words and phrases, and the presence or absence of certain problems and concepts, is found—that we find the synthesis of all the various structural relationships of the interview, as well as the particular relation of the individual to his vision of history.[8]

Grele's adaptation of Althusser has greatly influenced my approach to reading oral history texts. Moreover, similar to Freud's observations on dream work, my analysis of my informants' accounts is premised on the notion that the associations my informants make in their accounts should not be read as contingent or random. Rather, these associations reveal deeper underlying meanings and are fundamental to understanding the historical production of their subjectivities as raced and gendered individuals. Hence, their direct utterances as well as the gaps in articulation within their narratives become revealing sites of analysis. My readings of these accounts aim to push the limits of contemporary uses and interpretations of oral history narratives by engaging the dynamic interaction of memory, speech, and articulation in the writing of history. The foregrounding of memory in my conception of these complicated narrative accounts is an approach to interpreting oral testimony that I share with such scholars as Lawrence Langer, Geoffrey Hartman, Shoshana Felman, Dori Laub, James Young, Luisa Passerini, Michael Frisch, and Alessandro Portelli, whose work on memory, oral history, and the Holocaust has significantly influenced mine.[9] My interpretative approach emphasizes the dialogical character of these narratives, which I conceive not as monologues but rather as polyphonic texts that invite historians to probe the multiple, overlapping, and often contradictory voices therein. Reading both speech and silence in these texts and in these individuals' descriptions of the physical and ideological "spaces" they occupied in this society, my analysis reveals the complex manner in which race and gender structured the lives of Afro-Germans and social interaction more generally in the Third Reich—for both "Aryans" and "non-Aryans" alike.

Unlike many analyses of oral historical accounts, this book will not offer readers a complete biographical portrait of either of my informants. My interest is rather in these individuals' recollections of how National Socialism affected their lives and in the forms of subjectivity that were made available to and created by them during that time. This is not to say that their accounts will be treated as snapshots of their lives in the past, rendering photographically "accurate" representations of this period. Instead, these accounts will be treated as complicated texts of memory. Paradoxically, this conception means relinquishing some of the expectations we often take for granted about oral histories. One of these is an expectation of a kind of "knowledge" of the individuals whose accounts are being presented. Although one product of this volume will certainly be some sense of the personae of these individuals, I will provide only a very partial picture of these complex people. One will also not get a sense of who these individuals became after the war, in the wake of the demise of the Nazi regime. In particular, I will not attempt to assess or describe the very personal ways in which they came to terms with the effects of National Socialism in their later lives or what their individual processes of *Vergangenheitsbewältigung* ("coming to terms with the past") looked like. Although such an analysis might well have yielded compelling results, my informants did not allow me access to these aspects of themselves or their psyches, and their invocation of this prerogative is one that I wholeheartedly respect. Sadly, neither individual lived to see the publication of this book, and thus they no longer can provide these potentially valuable insights. However, my objective in examining their testimony was to construct an account of racial and gender formation in the Third Reich. For this reason, I have chosen not to include an extensive postwar analysis.[10] Such an analysis will have to be the subject of a future project.

Consequently, many questions will necessarily remain open about the very rich lives of the individuals presented in this study, and readers of this text may want to know much more about them. I sincerely hope this is in fact the case, for I would be gratified if this book provoked others to fill in the many gaps that remain in the history of the Black German community. Neither a community history nor a study of collective memory, this book seeks instead to use memory as a way of prying into the crevices of the Third Reich to examine how the Nazis contended with a group of people whose status and existence challenged some of the most basic premises of National Socialism. Memory offers a powerful historiographical tool for understanding this regime, a tool that will be utilized and exploited to its utmost potential in this book.

QUESTIONS OF MEMORY: HISTORY, TECHNOLOGY, AND REPRESENTATION; OR, TOWARD A SOCIAL TECHNOLOGY OF MEMORY

A preoccupation with how best to engage the memories of my Afro-German interview partners prompted me initially to recognize the necessity of exploring the complexities of memory in writing the history of this group of individuals. This process is best understood by means of what I have come to conceive as the social technology of memory. My reference to the notion of technology is borrowed in at least two senses. First, it is borrowed from the field of technology studies and its conception of technology as practical and material techniques of production. The notion of technology is borrowed in a second sense from scholars such as Teresa de Lauretis's feminist theoretical appropriations and adaptations of Michel Foucault's conception of technologies as sets of socially constructed techniques that produce specific forms of meaning in society—for example, "the technology of gender" or the "technology of sex."[11] Applying these two complementary understandings of technology to the functioning of memory as it relates to the writing of history, one might conceive of a technology of memory that operates on at least two levels.

In the first sense, the technology of memory functions as the material techniques of recording memories and transforming them into public texts accessible to interpretation—what Pierre Nora refers to as "history." In his seminal 1989 work "Between Memory and History: *Les Lieux de Mémoire,*" Nora contends that what is currently called memory is in fact not memory but is already history. As he writes,

Modern memory is, above all, archival. It relies entirely on the materiality of the trace, the immediacy of the recording, the visibility of the image. What began as writing ends as high fidelity and tape recording. . . . Hence the obsession with the archive that marks our age, attempting at once the complete conservation of the present as well as the total preservation of the past. . . . Memory has been wholly absorbed by its meticulous reconstitution. Its new vocation is to record; delegating to the archive the responsibility of remembering, it sheds its signs upon depositing them there.[12]

Thus conceived, the technology of memory corresponds to a process Nora calls the materialization of memory, involving material techniques of archiving in the broadest sense—processes of recording, preserving, and reproducing memories. These include but are not limited to what he describes as the material, bureaucratic, symbolic, and functional modes of recording and preserving memory, such as collecting, writing, audio and visual recording, and commemorating.

In the second sense, as a set of techniques that produce and inscribe meaning in society, the technology of memory functions as a mode of articulation and construction of identity, experience, events, and history and as a crucial apparatus through which these meanings and understandings are transported, absorbed, and preserved by and among individuals in society. Indeed, both levels of the technology of memory emphasize the fundamentally social character of memory argued consistently by scholars of memory, most prominently by Maurice Halbwachs. As Halbwachs writes in *On Collective Memory,*

The past is not preserved but is reconstructed on the basis of the present. . . . The collective frameworks of memory are not constructed after the fact by the combination of individual recollections; nor are they empty forms where recollections coming from elsewhere would insert themselves. Collective frameworks are, to the contrary, precisely the instruments used by the collective memory to reconstruct an image of the past which is in accord in each epoch, with the predominant thoughts of the society. . . . One may say that the individual remembers by placing himself in the perspective of the group, but one may also affirm that the memory of the group realizes and manifests itself in individual memories.[13]

Yet there is an additional dimension of the technology of memory that necessarily overlaps both of these two domains. This third element of the technology of memory involves what I have previously only hinted at, situated in the gaps (or what de Lauretis calls "the interstices") of these representations.[14] It is that which always exceeds representation, located in the space(s) these representations leave out, bracket, or overlook but at the same time imply. Representation can never fully encompass all meaning; for this reason, some residual or "leftover" will always exceed and at the same time contest the claim of any representation to render its referent comprehensively or with complete accuracy or veracity.

It is in the spaces between representations and in excess of them, de Lauretis locates the terms of alternative constructions of gender and the potential challenge they pose to dominant forms of meaning and representation.[15] By the same token, the representation of memory—and, for that matter, history—will and can always only be partial in its presentation of the past. Moreover, the particular representations of memory and history that have come to be institutionalized as narratives of "official history" and national or collective identities not only leave out alternative forms of memory that have yet to be recorded (memory technologies in the first sense) but also, by definition, render them invisible and unrecognizable by virtue of the fact that they are seen as unintelligible in relation to these "official histories." In this way, recording and preserving the memories (and thereby beginning the process of writing the history) of Afro-Germans is in no way a simple matter of getting the story of "what really happened" and assuming that, as a result, these individuals will enter into the official historical narrative.

As highly textured accounts of race, memory, identity, and history, Afro-German narratives of the Third Reich constitute complicated texts of "experience." *Experience* here is understood in the most complex of terms, as a process that produces and constructs subjectivities.[16] As such, these narratives are always in need of contextualization and analysis. As Joan Scott reminds us, "Experience is at once always already an interpretation *and* in need of interpretation."[17] In this way, recording the memories and life histories of Afro-Germans is only a first step in beginning to write their history, a project that requires critical analysis. In the readings that follow, these accounts will not be treated as factual presentations of "experience" (for we can never gain access to the experience of others in any direct form) in the sense of "what *actually* happened." Rather, they will be approached as representations of history rendered through the lenses of different memory technologies. Thus, to adapt James Young's formulation, the value of such narrative accounts will be less a question of their "factuality" than of the interpretation of their "actuality."[18] That is, what is significant is their capacity to document not necessarily the "experiences" they relate but rather the interpretations that underlie these experiences, or what Young terms "the conceptual presuppositions through which the narrator has apprehended experience."[19] And it is at both levels of interpretation that this study is aimed.

Particularly with regard to the Nazi period and the Holocaust, narrative accounts must be viewed critically as mediated representations of the events they recount and must necessarily be consciously used and interpreted as such. Yet this in no way diminishes or compromises their value as sources. As Young astutely points out,

> Rather than coming to the Holocaust narrative for indisputably "factual" testimony, . . . the critical reader might now turn to the manner in which these "facts" have been understood and reconstructed in narrative: as a guide both to the kinds of understanding the victims brought to their experiences and to the kinds of actions they took on behalf of this understanding. . . . Instead of damaging the credibility of these works, this critical approach might affirm the truth of interpretation and understanding that attends every narrative of the Holocaust.[20]

The inherent partiality of representing memory in historical analysis underlines the issue of the more general limits of representation and of the gaps and excesses these limits intrinsically imply. This study of Afro-Germans in the Third Reich addresses this issue not only at the obvious level of researching and unearthing the memories of a group of Germans who only in the past two decades have come to be acknowledged as having had a history, let alone come to be included in the historiography of Germany. In addition, the narratives of Afro-Germans in the Third Reich also pose the question of the limits of representation in the form of both an excess and a gap.

Perhaps the notion of a simultaneous gap/excess of representation appears a contradiction in terms. In his essay "Trauma and Transference," Saul Friedländer comments on this paradox in relation to the difficulties encountered by historians attempting to represent the Holocaust in historical analyses. This paradox has led Friedländer to describe much historical representation of the Holocaust as characterized by either "surplus meaning or blankness with little interpretive or representational advance."[21] Through his emphasis on the necessity of self-awareness for the historian of the Nazi period and the equal importance of the continual reintroduction of individual memory into the representation of this troublesome epoch, Friedländer calls for the integration of critical commentary by the historian as an essential part of a responsible historical representation of the Holocaust. However, Friedländer also acknowledges the limits of this representation with regard to the project of presenting the Holocaust in historical analysis. As he writes, "The Shoah carries an excess and this excess is the 'something [that] remains to be phrased which is not, something which is not determined.'" Here, Friedländer invokes an evocative formulation by Jean-François Lyotard to articulate the significance of this conundrum.

> The *silence* that surrounds the phrase "Auschwitz was the extermination camp" is not a state of mind, it is *a sign* that something remains to be phrased which is not, something which is not determined.[22]

Lyotard describes silence as a sign of something left over, in excess of or escaping representation, something that remains to be articulated, though not necessarily unspecified, unsaid, or unexpressed. Silence here is a gap or lack and at the same time functions as an excess of meaning. Later in his essay, Friedländer offers an even more eloquent and sophisticated way of understanding this subtle relation by drawing on Maurice Blanchot's notion of absent meaning. In fact, the simultaneous existence of gap and excess is in no way a contradiction but rather constitutes a crucial element of the question of the limits or boundaries of representation. The limits and intrinsic partiality of both memory and history imply that which exceeds them. Indeed, limits and boundaries of any kind in and of themselves function to define spaces within spaces and in this way always suggest something beyond themselves.

I would expand on Friedländer's characterization of these limits and excesses. Such phenomena are not necessarily unique to the Holocaust but are excesses that arise from the concept of race as a category that poses similar problems of limits, gaps, and excessive meaning. Like the category of gender, race is a category both lacking any essential meaning and overdetermined by the meanings attributed to it in society. These attributions (which have historically claimed the status of essential, biological, or natural attributes) lend race the semblance of excessive meaning. In this way, race often comes to overdetermine an individuals' meaning and status in society. By the same token, the representation of the Holocaust, both in narrative accounts and historical analyses, can be read as having a similar plurality of meanings because it is a phenomenon of race par excellence.

In their accounts of life in the Third Reich, Afro-Germans confront both the limits of representation and the proliferation of meaning of the category of race in ways that recall those described by Friedländer and Lyotard. Here, the issue of silence is central. Like Friedländer and Lyotard's characterization of silence as a sign of something left out or left over, in excess of representation though not necessarily unsaid, certain silences in the narratives of Afro-Germans can similarly be read paradoxically as "loud" articulations and forms of indirect speech that reveal important levels of submerged meaning.

In my conversations with members of this particular generation of Black German men and women, I was often confronted with the challenge of interpreting not only speech but more significantly silence. In many instances, "speaking" of race was at least initially characterized less by speech than by silence. Moreover, methodologically, in life history narratives, silences often speak as loudly as speech. In relation to the concepts of race and gender, silence is a powerfully polyvocal signifier that often defers and complicates our understanding of the meaning and function of racialization and gendering—and demands critical analysis and interpretation. In my readings of Afro-German narratives of the Third Reich, silence functions as a complex form of representational excess, crossing the limits of representation on a number of different levels. Focusing on ways of reading different types of silence I have encountered in the testimony of Afro-Germans on the issue of race, I examine silences that are not so much moments of quiet or narrative pause; rather, reading these silences as provocatively filled expressions, I engage them as a narrative phenomenon I call "loud silence." Instead of seeing silences as a lack or a void, my analysis explores how they "speak," what they in fact "say," and how they often "race" rather than "erase" the life histories of my Afro-German narrators.

The richness of oral history texts lies in the interpretation of both speech and silence. Similarly, the challenge of analyzing and interpreting the effects of race and gender in these texts lies in interpreting their simultaneous and mutually constitutive effects. Ironically, in the two narratives of Afro-Germans presented in this book, many of these effects are articulated perhaps most clearly through silences. Silence often functioned as an interstitial space between these individuals' words and statements, framing their articulations by outlining the effects of race and gender and setting them in stark relief.

Perhaps it is most instructive for us to use the notion of interstices not only as a way of understanding the function of silence in these narratives but also as an equally productive way of conceptualizing the excesses of representation. Instead of focusing on the limits of representation as that which is unrepresentable, it might be more constructive to read these limits as always implying an excess in need of alternative forms of both representation and interpretation. Moreover, the spaces between existing historical representations and interpretations insist on such rearticulation and revision. In the narratives of Afro-Germans presented here (accounts situated in precisely these interstitial spaces), interpreting their memories of the Third Reich may eventually become the stuff of such historical revision, an important site for thinking through the excesses of representation and the potential of individual memory for expanding and enhancing the historigraphical project.

CHAPTER OVERVIEW

My inquiry into the history of Afro-Germans in the Third Reich begins with an examination of one of Germany's earliest confrontations with its Black German population. Part 1 of the book, "Echoes of Imagined Danger—Specters of Racial Mixture," traces the trajectory of what I term "echoing specters of racial mixture"—a trope that conceived of racial mixture as a threat to the future of the white race. The two chapters in this section argue that German society's first public responses to this population were articulated through a discourse of purity and pollution that constituted Black Germans as a danger to the German body politic. The specter of racial mixture associated with the Afro-German population evoked a dire sense of endangerment that can be seen to have "echoed" or recurred repeatedly in German history. The chapters in part 1 examine three significant historical contexts in which this was the case. Chapter 1, "'Resonant Echoes': The Rhineland Campaign and Converging Specters of Racial Mixture," explores the discourse of racial endangerment enunciated in the German colonies of the Kaiserreich during the debates on the status of racially mixed marriages and their Afro-German progeny. The chapter links this discourse with a second recurrence of the specter of racial mixture in the Weimar Republic. Setting the colonial *Mischehe,* or mixed-marriage debate, in relation to one of Germany's dominant and most resilient representations of a Black German population, the figure of the "Rhineland Bastard," this chapter ends by reconstructing the emergence of this figure in the post–World War I propaganda campaign protesting the French use of Black troops in the occupation of the Rhineland. This image would have a lasting impact on German perceptions of Afro-German populations, particularly during the Nazi period.

Chapter 2, "Confronting Racial Danger, Neutralizing Racial Pollution: Afro-Germans and the National Socialist Sterilization Program," continues to trace the echoes of the discourse of racial endangerment, taking up the enduring influence of the specter of the Rhineland Bastard in the Third Reich. As the "Black Horror" receded from the arena of public debate and into German collective memory, this figure became more diffuse but nonetheless remained present. As a concretely embodied specter of racial mixture, the figure of the Rhineland Bastard was the decisive image motivating the NS initiative to sterilize the Black children of the Rhineland occupation. Looking at the genesis and execution of this program, chapter 2 assesses Nazi attempts to neutralize this domestic racial threat, concluding with an analysis of the implications of the regime's decision to deal with this "problem" through a program of "internal containment" (sterilization) rather than through disenfranchisement, exportation (deportation), or productive maximization (work camps)—options that the regime considered and pursued for other groups of *Fremdvölkische* in the Reich.

Whereas part 1 focuses on an evaluation of German responses to Afro-Germans as articulated in primary and secondary source material, part 2 places oral sources at the center of its analysis, using them to construct an account of Afro-German memories and recollections of their lives in this period. These three chapters juxtapose two case studies of Afro-Germans in the Third Reich. Chapter 3 focuses on the testimony of a male member of the Rhineland group, analyzing a complex series of events in his biography: his childhood in the Saarland during National Socialism, his experience as a member of the Hitler Youth, his sterilization at age thirteen, his subsequent induction into the Wehrmacht as a young adult, and his later internment as a German prisoner of war in Russia. Chapter 4 examines the testimony of a female Afro-German, who, although a contemporary of the man who is the focus of chapter 3, has a biography wholly unrelated to the Rhineland occupation. This chapter considers the complicated landscape of her life history: growing up in a communist household in Hamburg, being forced to end her early training as a dancer because of her non-Aryan heritage, and perhaps most significant, the paradoxical experience of being required to work as a cook for a concentration camp where she was not interned but rather was allowed to return home each evening after a grueling twelve-hour shift. Contrasting her life history with that of a male member of the Rhineland group, the chapter allows us to see some of the gendered implications of National Socialism for Black German women and men while evaluating the significance of the figure of the Rhineland Bastard for Afro-Germans who did not belong to this group. The testimony of these individuals raises the issue of the status of Afro-Germans in Nazi racial legislation. Each of these accounts problematizes the tensions within NS racial policy, its implementation, and their effects on the constitution of Black Germans subjects within this regime.

Part 2 argues that the bureaucratic nature of National Socialism allowed many Afro-Germans to exist in a "gray zone" of German society. Because German conceptions of Black Germans in this period were so profoundly shaped by one very specific, though much publicized, segment of this population—the six to eight hundred children of the Rhineland occupation—other individuals who did not belong to this group could to some extent escape Nazi scrutiny. As the testimony of these two individuals shows, it was indeed possible for some Black Germans to become integrated into local community networks in German society. These tightly knit social structures, particularly in smaller communities, often proved resistant to NS racial ideology and in this way sheltered those Afro-Germans who were seen as part of the fabric of these communities. Yet in the Third Reich, social integration guaranteed neither security nor safety for an individual. This book reveals one of the paradoxical effects of this racial state—some Afro-Germans could maintain their inferiority to their regime and enjoy some of its privileges while simultaneously suffering discrimination and persecution. This volume seeks to show how the life histories of Afro-Germans highlight such paradoxes in the racial politics of the National Socialist regime, for the functioning of its power in the NS state was rife with contradictions.

Moreover, as a feminist, the goal of my work on Black Germans in the Third Reich is not only to bring feminist and critical theory methodologies to bear on the study of female members of this group. In fact, women are neither the site nor the object of my analysis. My focus instead is on the larger impact of gender and race within the Nazi regime. Specifically, my interest lies in explaining and understanding the simultaneity and inextricability of the processes of racialization and gendering that were central to the National Socialist state and fundamental to its most catastrophic effects. Rather than seeing racialization and gendering as separate, distinct processes or as overlapping or intersecting vectors of social formation, I view these phenomena as part of a single larger whole. What was perhaps most crucial to this regime's power over both women and men was its ability to produce different forms of legitimate and illegitimate raced and gendered subjects and its success in regulating the lives of these subjects through the differential value placed on human lives. Black German memory narratives of the local are an important site for engaging these effects. What a feminist theoretical analysis brings to bear in my readings of the impact of National Socialism on its Black German subjects is an emphasis on the fact that not only did this system work through race in its administration of individual lives but also, perhaps more reveal-

ingly, that race necessarily worked through gender and gender necessarily worked through race. This mutual constituency—this inextricability in the production and regulation of individual subjects and the
contradictions that arise from a system that attempted to reduce all
individuals to their essential, biological traits—serves as the focus of
my inquiry into the effects of this regime on this small population.

Like the "Black folk" whose "souls" W. E. B. Du Bois described in
his celebrated volume *The Souls of Black Folk,* most Black Germans
also grow up with a kind of "double consciousness." Contrary to
DuBois's formulation, for my Afro-German interview partners—
members of a generation who came of age during the totalitarian
regime of the Third Reich—this tension was not necessarily experienced as one of absolute duality or "twoness." Rather, it was a contradictory and complexly textured form of identity that forced them to
reconcile these two supposedly incompatible aspects of their identity.
The absence of a Black community for most Afro-Germans, and for
my interview partners in particular, did not diminish the intensity with
which they experienced the tensions of Black identity that DuBois
describes. This lacuna did, however, render my interview partners
qualitatively different from African-Americans, in ways specific to the
German context. Until recently, for example, most Afro-Germans did
not have the option of choosing between a Black community or identity and a German identity. As the testimony of these individuals
shows, they were often forced to occupy a position between a conception of German identity that excluded blackness and a conception of
blackness that precluded any identification with Germanness. This in-
between position (or positioning) is emblematic of the history and
experiences of the generation of Afro-Germans examined here. The
strategies developed by the individuals discussed in this volume for living this in-between position were not approaches of resignation or
defeat. On the contrary, their responses to the challenges of constructing an identity were most often creative and self-affirming, even in the
midst of one of the most repressive of totalitarian regimes. In this way,
these individuals' accounts raise difficult questions about the construction of Black identity in the European context. Specifically, these stories point to the question of the necessary distinctions that must be
made between and among different Black populations and communities in Europe and abroad, particularly with regard to the dominance

of African-American and Black British paradigms for understanding Black identity and Black cultural formations.

The final chapter of the book, "Diaspora Space, Ethnographic Space—Writing History between the Lines," offers a meditation on complicated questions of relation and distinction among and between different Black communities within the African diaspora. This postscript attempts to link the comments of my informants to contemporary discourses of diaspora and examines the ways in which these testimonies challenge and contest key elements of this discourse and the important insights my interview partners provide into the dynamics of transnational Black relations. This chapter explores how these relationships were enacted and negotiated in compelling ways within the ethnographic space of the interview. I argue that both the space of diaspora and the space that constitutes the ethnographic exchange of our interviews are highly constructed sites of projection and desire. At the same time, they are places in which the connections and differences between different communities are played out in ways that reflect broader implications of culture, politics, and power.

Focusing on moments of difference, discrepancy, and translation among Black communities in the diaspora, it uses the comments of my Black German informants to challenge notions of similarity and unity that often anchor dominant modes of theorizing the diaspora and its relations. Placing difference, translation, and interpellation at the center of analysis as constituent elements of the African diaspora, the final chapter tries to unpack the diversity of the diaspora, conceiving of it as a vibrant site of analysis, investment, and aspiration. In this way, the chapter serves as an appropriate coda to the book by enacting the tensions of difference within the diaspora that the larger historical analysis of Black Germans in the Third Reich invites us to consider. Setting these final theoretical reflections in dialogue with this part of this community's history offers fertile ground for continued debate and inquiry into the dynamics of race, nation, and place in the African diaspora.

PART I ECHOES OF IMAGINED DANGER — SPECTERS OF RACIAL MIXTURE

I knew that my father was Algerian, but we never talked about it. It was
just sort of mentioned in conversation: "You can't deny your heritage"—
which was not at all meant to be mean. I couldn't imagine that Algerians
were different. I didn't even know what that meant. I came to understand it
much later. . . . The neighbors' kids taught me that soon enough. . . .
I was insulted and verbally abused about my father's heritage.
That was just after the war. The fathers of all the other kids were
German soldiers. And mine was the enemy.
—HANS (JOHANN) HAUCK, BORN IN FRANKFURT, 1920
SON OF A GERMAN MOTHER AND AN ALGERIAN FATHER[1]

In the above quotation, the speaker describes growing up in Germany
as the son of an Algerian soldier conceived during the post–World War
I French occupation of the Rhineland. Through the comments of others, this man came to think of his Algerian heritage as something that
differentiated him from other German children. The topic of his mixed
heritage and illegitimate birth was taboo in his family and thus was an
issue that was not discussed with or around him. The direct and indirect remarks about his father conveyed to him a particular conception
of Blacks and blackness. During the speaker's youth in Germany during the 1920s and '30s, this conception was strongly influenced and
shaped by the presence and later the memory of the French occupation
troops and by the accompanying mythology of marauding Black soldiers. The image of the "Rhineland Bastard," a term that was coined
during a 1919–22 newspaper campaign, came to embody the children
these soldiers left behind as a complex representation of the manifold
tensions of the occupation.

In the campaign protesting the use of Black occupation troops, at least four powerful discourses converged to create this early and perhaps most enduring image of a Black German population. The first of these was a scientific discourse of race as a biologically immutable category of human difference. The authority of this essential notion of race lie in its value as a means of differentiating among individuals and the social and political implications these distinctions were imputed to have. What were seen as the significant genetic consequences of racial mixture—as postulated in the work of turn-of-the-century geneticists and eugenicists—made this a second particularly potent discourse in these debates. The threat that racial mixture was seen to pose within these essential discourses of race was articulated as a form of endangerment and violation of the boundaries that constituted German national identity. During the Kaiserreich, these discourses came together with a third, equally compelling, colonial discourse on racial mixture—specifically, the legacy of prewar debates on mixed marriage in the German colonies. Together, these three factors significantly shaped German responses to the presence of a Black population, in both pre- and interwar Germany. Finally, a discourse of German victimhood combined with these discourses of race in the Rhineland protest campaign to transform German defeat into a larger narrative of German victimhood. In this narrative, Germany was only the first and most innocent victim of a racial conspiracy/pollution that would ultimately unite it in victimhood with its former enemies, in the process recasting defeat as heroic martyrdom. It was through these discourses that German responses to Blacks and Afro-Germans were articulated, and in their terms that Black Germans came to take on meaning.

The two chapters in this section examine three important events in the history of a group of individuals whose experience constitutes one of the dominant historiographical paradigms of the Afro-German experience in the twentieth century. The Black German children of the Rhineland occupation are without a doubt one of the most well documented groups of Germans of African descent. Although the experiences of this group are in no way representative of those of other Afro-Germans in either the Weimar Republic or the Third Reich (for example, the children of Black immigrants from Germany's former African colonies or those of other African and African-American immigrants to Germany during this time), the events discussed in chapters 1 and 2 had an indelible impact on the lives of Afro-Germans through the representations they engendered in each of these periods.[2] The events to which I refer are the 1912 debates on mixed marriages (*Mischehe*) in the German colonies, the 1919–22 campaign against the use of a Black occupation force in Germany, and the Nazi sterilization program carried out on the Afro-German children fathered by these troops. Each event is crucial to understanding the history and recollections of Black Germans in the Third Reich.

In this trajectory, the Rhineland campaign plays a pivotal role because it articulates the central elements of a specter of the imagined danger of racial mixture that can be found in German public discourse both before and after World War I. Reading the discourse of this campaign in relation to that of its historical antecedent, the 1912 Reichstag debates on colonial *Mischehe,* reveals important resonances and continuities between these two incidents as sites where the danger posed by racial mixture became the focus of political agitation. The Nazi sterilization of the Black children of the Rhineland occupation represents one of the most extreme consequences of the discourses of race and racial purity that converged in the Rhineland campaign as well as the most concrete response to the threat posed by this imaginary specter. The contradictions in the discussion, planning, and implementation of these sterilizations, together with similar tensions in the broader Nazi response to Afro-Germans in the Third Reich (examined in chapters 2, 3, and 4), reveal interesting fissures in National Socialist racial politics. At the same time, Nazi policy toward Afro-Germans reflects the influence of representations of Afro-Germans articulated both in the Rhineland campaign and in the *Mischehe* debate, as well as how these representations were in turn shaped by scientific and colonial discourses of racial mixture and the dangers of pollution that racial mixture was seen to pose.

The French use of African colonial troops in the occupation of the Rhineland following World War I is important not only as a site of confrontation between myth and reality (what Sander Gilman describes as "the first major confrontation between the German image of blackness and the reality of the Black").[3] It is also a location that witnessed the emergence of a figure of the Black that synthesized and rearticulated many of the images of Blacks and blackness that had developed in the preceding centuries. In this way, the significance of the Rhineland campaign should not be underestimated: the discourse on Blacks and Black Germans articulated during this campaign represents an important turning point, when public discussions of the implications of Blacks and Black Germans shifted from a focus on external concerns to a focus on internal concerns. Unlike the stereotypes that preceded it (for example, in the colonies or with regard to African colonial troops), the Rhineland Bastard is the first representation of a domestic, German-born Black native. Contrary to the "mirage of blackness" described by Gilman, this trope emerged simultaneously with the people it represented and eventually would eclipse it as a particularly imposing threat posed from *within* the boundaries of the German nation.[4] Notwithstanding this newer incarnation of the German image of the Black, it nevertheless remains important to emphasize the links between the Rhineland Bastard and the prewar constructions of race, blackness, and racial mixture, for these discourses enabled the figure's emergence. Indeed, as an echo of the specter of racial mixture, the trope of the Rhineland Bastard resonates with and at the same time rearticulates both biologistic constructions of race and racial mixture and colonial conceptions of the social and political consequences of racial mixture that historically had been seen as posing a dire threat.

Each of these discourses contains historical echoes and resonances of a recurring specter that in each context figured racial mixture as a threat to the German nation, German identity, and, by implication, the purity of the white race. In the first case, the specter was a genetic one that transmitted the negative traits of an "inferior race" to contaminate and degrade the genetic pool of the pure and thus superior white race. In the second case, the specter of a mixed-race colonial citizen with a claim to the rights of legitimate political subjecthood posed a threat to the German body politic through the prospect of racial parity symbolized by a mixed-race, Black German citizen. In the post–World War I occupation, this specter returned in the form of the Rhineland Bastard (a term coined during the protest campaign that eventually came to represent the Black German children left behind by these soldiers) as a threat both to the purity of the German nation (read *body*) and to the postcolonial balance of power in the former colonies—a threat posed from within the boundaries of the Reich itself. The echoes of this imagined danger eventually came together in the Third Reich with the vision of a National Socialist racial state and led to the sterilization of members of this group of Afro-German children as the most concrete embodiment of this fantastic threat to the purity of the Aryan race. In this trajectory, the Rhineland campaign is particularly salient because (though not necessarily the first such site) it articulates the central elements of a specter of racial mixture expressed through a language of pollution and endangerment—a specter that recurred repeatedly both before and after World War I.

CHAPTER I "RESONANT ECHOES"

The Rhineland Campaign and
Converging Specters of Racial Mixture

FRENCH *TIRAILLEURS* AND THE POST–WORLD WAR I
OCCUPATION: DIPLOMATIC AND POLITICAL
ORIGINS OF THE RHINELAND CAMPAIGN

I was born in Frankfurt [in August 1920]. Since my mother had a very hard time here when they saw she was pregnant, she went to Frankfurt. My father had been transferred to Frankfurt. Even though they weren't married, she had nobody else, so she followed him there. . . . Sure, there were problems, according to the statements of neighbors who are still alive. . . . Problems—with an occupation soldier, with a *colored* occupation soldier, you have to emphasize that. And then in a good Catholic family—first off, just the stigma of illegitimacy and then, along with that, the worst, with "one of them," with a colored. Back then that was really bad.[1]

France's recruitment of approximately 190,000 African soldiers (*la force noire*) before and during World War I was motivated by strategic military considerations aimed primarily at offsetting deficits in the French army that dated back to the mid–nineteenth century and resulted largely from demographic stagnation and a declining French birthrate.[2] The government initially began recruiting soldiers from French West Africa in an effort to build a stabilizing force to be deployed in North Africa, particularly in Morocco. The conflict that became the Moroccan Crisis of 1912 played a prominent role in the decision to create a Black military force for use as a colonial army, as such operations could free up French troops for European operations. Yet even in its recruitment and eventual use of African soldiers, French officials were concerned with striking a delicate balance between arming and training its colonial subjects as instruments of war and maintaining the country's position of dominance over these subjects within the colonial hierarchy. The French government was well aware of the fact that this new military force presented a potential threat to the balance of power within its colonies because these troops could quickly be redirected at the colonizing nation.

The question of why France chose to include its African colonial troops in the post–World War I occupation force is complex. Keith Nelson argues that there were both strong practical reasons for France's use of these troops and more subtle motivations related to the devastation France suffered during the course of the war. Citing the papers of Major Paul Clark, an American liaison officer, and the remarks of the commander of the French occupation forces in the Rhineland, General Charles Mangin ("the father of the Black forces"), Nelson explains,

> At least in the beginning, it was likely that the morale of these troops would have suffered if they as a group had been deprived of what was widely considered to be the reward for hard fighting. In addition, because a renewal of hostilities was always possible during the armistice period, the victors clearly ran a certain risk in deviating from the manpower practices which had won the conflict. Furthermore, if only French *national* troops had advanced into the Rhineland in 1918–19, the effect would have been to increase the proportion of colored forces in the reserve areas behind the French frontier.[3]

As both Nelson and Pascal Grosse contend, another motivation for using Black troops in the occupation was France's belief in the strategic psychological effect of these troops on their military adversaries. Indeed, Nelson maintains that the French government was engaged in a "subtle kind of psychological warfare against the Germans."[4] France's original motivations for recruiting these troops also explain in part some of the reasons for the decision to deploy them in Germany after the war. The issue of the particular qualities attributed to

Africans played a central role because the racial/anthropological traits associated with Africans were seen as making them especially well suited to contemporary warfare and an invaluable source of military manpower. Mangin introduced the plan to recruit *la force noire* as early as 1910, explicitly emphasizing the qualities that made Africans particularly desirable soldiers:

> They have exactly the traits demanded for the long struggles of modern war: robustness, endurance, tenacity and instinct for combat, an absence of nerves, an incomparable power to shock [intimidate] their enemies. Their appearance on the battlefield will produce a considerable moral effect on their adversary. Precisely these valuable assets regarding their quantity and traits are significant factors that will manifest themselves from their first battle. But if the battle should be prolonged, our African troops offer us almost immeasurable reserves whose source is well beyond the reach of the opponent, and which allows us to continue the battle through to our first success, and once this success has been attained to continue through to victory.[5]

Grosse emphasizes that this conception of the African troops relied on a eugenic interpretation of their innate physical capacities and aptitude for war that attributed these qualities to Blacks and Africans on the basis of an essential, biological construction of their race. As Grosse contends,

> French military strategists relied here first and foremost on "natural capacities," which in the European mind compared less civilized peoples to frail and nervous European men in military conflicts. This construction was based on the opposition of nature peoples to cultured peoples, where European cultural development had succeeded in domesticating natural instincts, including aggressive tendencies. A German commentator on French military affairs affirmed this perception, according to which he asserted that "the West African Negro is more suited than the overworked urban adult European to the craft of the soldier through his . . . primal strength and the hereditary warrior's predisposition he has retained."[6]

The French military relied on these racial stereotypes in hoping and planning that these troops would have a negative psychological impact on their opponents in battle. In point of fact, these soldiers had already elicited precisely this response in prewar Germany. As Grosse's study shows, long before the occupation of the Rhineland, Germany had responded to the project of *la force noire* through the trope of the *schwarze Gefahr* (Black threat). This xenophobic construction, along with the related tropes of the *slawische Gefahr* (Slavic threat) and the *gelbe Gefahr* (yellow threat), demonized each of these groups on the basis of a racialized threat to German culture and civilization. As Grosse explains,

> This demonization of the potential enemy is much more to be understood in the context of a psychological preparation for war. The "Black threat" thus became the symbol of the anticipated brutality of the coming war. . . . The discursive brutality that the characterization of the "Black threat" evoked anticipated projected the violent potential of war into an image of dehumanized French colonial troops as its eventual source. In this way, a war-ready German *Volk* (or, in other words, "the white race") could stylize itself as the sole true protectors of European culture that saved "the dignity of Europe from . . . African barbarians" and prevented a return to the era of the Thirty Years War.[7]

It seems clear that France was aware of and consciously chose to disregard Germany's discomfort with the idea of "colored" troops: German fears about these troops were already apparent and could thus be exploited by the French government. It is quite plausible that French military commanders such as Mangin, Obissier, and Marceau supported the use of these troops in the occupation precisely because of their awareness of the negative response such a deployment would provoke. Indeed, the older arguments justifying the recruitment of African colonial troops were based on this positive strategic assessment of the value of the racial attributes of Africans. As Hans-Jürgen Lüsebrink points out, following the war the Rhineland propaganda campaign employed much of the same anthropological discourse used by the French military ten years earlier. However, the biologistic argumentation that the French had employed in a positive sense was turned on its head by the Germans in the Rhineland campaign.

In the context of the German campaign against the "Black Shame," the descriptive attributes Mangin had used, such as "l'obéissance aveugle," "l'agressivité innée," "penchant matériel pour la guerre," among others, as well as the "uncivilizedness" of the African soldiers, took on a radically different meaning. Instead of being regarded as positive character traits—as in the colonial anthropology of prewar France—these "grands enfants" and "âmes simples," who were previously regarded as subjects to be educated, were transformed in the German public into symbols of barbarous savagery.[8]

France's decision to deploy these troops in the occupation of the Rhineland provoked a concrete response from Germany as early as 1918, when the German Foreign Minister Wilhelm Solf urged his representative at the armistice negotiations to prevent German territory from being occupied by Black French or U.S. soldiers.[9] In April 1919 the German delegation to Versailles was specifically instructed to insist that "colored troops" not be included in the army of occupation, and in June German negotiators included this statement in their protest against the treaty, seeking to make it more "difficult for our enemies . . . to bombard us and then send in their Black troops."[10]

The Black troops used in the French occupation of the Rhineland represented the first large-scale Black presence in Germany. Until the Rhineland occupation, direct contact between Germans and Blacks had for the most part been restricted to German colonial territories on the African continent and to individual Black immigrants to Germany. As Germany's first domestic encounter with a substantial Black population, the Rhineland occupation also holds symbolic importance as the first German confrontation with Blacks within its national boundaries. The total number of French occupation troops in the winter of 1919 was estimated at two hundred thousand men. This number was reduced to approximately eighty-five thousand by January 1920, when the Treaty of Versailles came into effect. The number of Black soldiers among these troops varied seasonally. In the summer of 1920, German officials estimated the number at between thirty and forty thousand, while Allied officials cited much lower figures, ranging from fourteen to twenty-five thousand.[11] These Black troops were mustered from France's colonial holdings in Algeria, Morocco, Tunisia, Madagascar, and Senegal.

The post–World War I military occupation of Germany lasted from 1919 to 1930. Exactly how long the Black troops remained is unclear. France renounced the use of colonial troops in 1923, when the occupation of the Ruhr valley began, although France had already withdrawn most of its Senegalese and Madagascan troops in 1920.[12] After the Locarno pact was signed on 1 December 1925, the number of remaining French colonial troops was significantly reduced. Approximately two thousand Black troops remained stationed in Germany in 1927, and one thousand remained as late as 1929.[13] However, they received little attention. The propaganda campaign against their presence had effectively ended in 1922, when the Ruhr conflict began to dominate international political discussions in Germany.

Black occupation troops became the focus of international attention in April 1920, when French forces occupied the German cities of Darmstadt, Hanau, Homburg, and Frankfurt following an outbreak of civil unrest in the demilitarized Ruhr territory. During the taking of Frankfurt, French Moroccan soldiers fired on civilians, causing a number of casualties. In response to these incidents, the *London Daily Herald* published an article by an English journalist, Edmund Dene Morel, "Black Scourge in Europe: Sexual Horror Let Loose by France on the Rhine," which marked the beginning of an international outcry against the alleged sexual misconduct of Black troops in Germany.[14] A prominent member of the Independent Labor Party and one of the founders of the Union for Democratic Control, Morel had been involved for many years in the fight against the exploitation of Africans in the colonies (in particular, under the regime of King Leopold in the Congo). He went on to publish other articles on this topic as well as a longer pamphlet entitled *The Horror on the Rhine.*[15]

In the chronology of the Rhineland campaign, Morel's publications effected an important change in the focus of the debates about the Black occupation troops, complicating the emphasis on race with sex and sexuality as the primary issue of contention. This new emphasis on the sexual element set off a chain reaction of outrage and exaggeration among the various international actors involved. On 23 April 1920, in response to Morel's *Daily Herald* article, six parliamentary delegates petitioned the German government for an inquiry into rapes and assaults allegedly committed by Black soldiers on civilians in the occupied territory.

Our youth in the Pfalz and the Rhineland are being disgraced, our people polluted, the dignity of Germans and the white race trampled. An English journalist calls this "a well-considered political strategy." Should our people in the Rhineland have to stomach this: the disgrace of the honor and dignity of the German people and the white race; is this fact, which was called by an Englishman the well-considered political strategy of our well-known enemies, known to the imperial government?[16]

The language of these charges links alleged rape incidents to the trampling (*zertreten*) of German national honor and dignity as well as to the purity of the white race. In this way, the initially racist objections to a Black military presence in the Rhineland were refounded on the basis of the purported sexual misconduct perpetrated by these soldiers, in addition to the most serious consequence associated with this uncontained sexual menace: miscegenation. The inextricable coupling of Black sexuality with the threat of interracial sex and miscegenation was a primary element around which the discourse of the campaign against the post–World War I Black occupation troops was structured. Nineteenth-century scientific discourses on racial mixture also played a significant role as an important vehicle for the campaign against the Black troops. Scientific conceptions of the negative genetic consequences of racial mixture had by this time won widespread acceptance and were circulating at many levels of society. Consequently, they offer an important key to understanding how anxieties stemming from German defeat came to be displaced onto Blacks and Afro-Germans in this period.

SCIENTIFIC AND COLONIAL LEGACIES: RACIALIZED REPRESENTATIONS OF AFRO-GERMANS IN PREWAR GERMANY

The images of Blacks and Africans used in this period to represent the threat posed by the Black occupation troops during the post–World War I Rhineland campaign did not originate in the Weimar Republic. In fact, they have a much longer history that considerably predates the contentious debates and inflammatory rhetoric of the postwar period. These representations were products of a scientific discourse on race that defined race as essence, locating its origins and meaning in nature and biology. As part of a long tradition of scientific thought, the notion of race as a biological human trait has been the focus of scientific research for centuries. Yet this research was never limited to the strictly "scientific" goal of understanding the biological basis of race. More often, and perhaps more importantly, this research also sought to explain the meaning of race for society as a whole and its implications for human interaction in particular.

Both in the racial discourse of the Rhineland newspaper campaign and in scientific studies of the genetic implications of race, individuals of mixed race had a special status, for the issue of racial mixture was particularly significant in this context. As a marker of difference between individuals, racial difference becomes an issue of contention only with regard to the interaction between individuals of different races. In this logic (as scientists such as Eugen Fischer and Charles Davenport attempted to prove), racial mixture was the ultimate test of racial difference, providing the context in which the consequences of racial distinctions would supposedly become apparent. For this reason, racial mixture was often constructed as a threat, as the site of the inherent conflict of difference that underlay racial distinctions. Hence, racial mixture has often functioned as a driving force (either implicit or explicit) in discussions of racial difference. As a vehicle with the potential to catalyze such discussions in volatile ways, the combination of essential conceptions of racial mixture with a discourse of racial endangerment offered a powerful tool of political mobilization, with often unpredictable results.

Racial mixture played an important role in early-twentieth-century scientific efforts to define and interpret the significance of race and racial difference. The innate or inherited differences thought to exist between the races did not in and of themselves necessarily present any problems that could not be remedied through the legislation of interracial social interaction—for example, in the form of segregation, economic disenfranchisement, demographic restrictions, or, in extreme cases, various forms of political domination. Racial mixture, on the other hand, represented the most problematic outcome of the genetic implications of racial difference, posing the questions of what racial "traits" would be passed on to children of mixed race and of what long-term implications mixed-race individuals and their offspring would have for the "future of the race." Hence, in the early twentieth century, racial mixture became an important site in scientific inquiries into race and racial difference, as the place where scientific laws of heredity (specifically, the applied and adapted theories of Mendel and Darwin, and concrete proof of the pessimistic prognoses of the racial theories of Gobineau[17]) could be put to the test. Paradoxically, people of mixed racial heritage came to be seen as absolute proof both of the untenability of racial theories of heredity and of their absolute truth.

Although racial mixture had for some time popularly been seen as a social problem, scientific studies of individuals of mixed racial heritage began in this period to formulate a somewhat different objective.[18] These investigations of racial mixture explicitly aimed to clarify how physical, psychological, and intellectual traits were transmitted genetically among humans. At the same time, these explorations were also intended as scientific investigations of "social problems," examining the social dimensions and implications of racial mixture. Almost all of these studies were conducted in the context of the European colonial territories, and each sought to determine the extent to which human social and cultural development would be influenced by the biological or genetic effects of racial mixture that were seen to necessarily accompany modern colonialism, migration, and acculturation. The assumption was that racial intermixture not only had physical effects but, more importantly, had an impact on both the intellectual capacity and psychological constitution of racial groups. In spite of the fact that these studies did not necessarily assume that racial mixture negatively affected the larger population, many of them posited the social and psychological inferiority of mixed-race people to be the result of the genetic inadequacy of racial mixture. The predominant view among early-twentieth-century geneticists was that, in the majority of cases, racial interbreeding resulted in the "pauperization" of the genetic traits of the "superior" white race.

The earliest and, by all accounts, most influential study of racial mixture was conducted in 1908 by a German scientist, Eugen Fischer, in a town called Rehobot in the German colony of Southwest Africa (currently Namibia). Fischer studied a population of mixed-race people then known as the "Rehoboth Bastards," who were the descendants of white European Boers of Dutch descent and Black women who migrated from the Cape in the late nineteenth century. Fischer

proclaimed his study a groundbreaking scientific investigation, asserting that previous anthropologists had focused primarily on the
"purest" strains of racial groups, whereas little was known about
racially mixed groups. Fischer believed, however, that science could
learn the most from mixed groups, for it was here where he claimed
that effects of the genetic transmission of racial differences appeared
most dramatically and could best be traced.[19]

Fischer's study of the Rehoboth used the then dominant methodological approach to investigating racial difference, undertaking mor-
phological analysis of a series of anthropological measurements and
categorizations of their physical attributes and reconstructing family
genealogies. His conclusions were that Mendelian rules of heredity
were in fact applicable to humans and that in this population, there
was no evidence of the dominance of one race over the other. He
rejected assertions of sterility or reduced fertility and of a higher inci-
dence of illness among this population, thus also rejecting the assertion
of "biological inferiority" of mixed-race people. Yet in a chapter on
"the psychology of the Rehoboth" (which lacked any empirical basis),
Fischer also remarked on the mental aptitude of the group. Without
relying on any scientific data, Fischer asserted that the intelligence of
many of these individuals equaled that of their white counterparts
among the Boers. Nevertheless, he made the dubious assertion that the
"cultural" psychological and intellectual aptitude of these individuals
was inferior to that of "pure whites." As a result, he declared any evidence of the equality of whites and mixed-race people based on individual cases to be irrelevant. Fisher further argued that these German
colonial "bastards," like all others, were inferior to whites and consequently needed "constant supervision."[20]

Using the body as a conceptual model for analyzing the functioning
of this discourse of racial mixture reveals a more complex picture of the
power of a conception of racial mixture as a danger to the German
national and cultural identity, particularly when this identity is articulated through the authority of a scientific discourse of race as essence.
Bodily boundaries correspond in many ways to the socially and ideo-
logically constructed boundaries of society and the national body
politic. Analogously, that which is perceived and constituted as a
threat to these boundaries (re)presents a danger in that it demonstrates
their permeability and constructedness as well as the fact that bound-

aries must continually be policed. By the same token, this national body is not neutral but is thoroughly raced and gendered. In this way, bodily fears of pollution and contamination and the desire to defend certain racialized and gendered boundaries of social interaction reflect and articulate more general fears of national and social interpenetration and mixing. In the same way that the crossing, trespassing, and violation of bodily boundaries presents a threat to the survival of an organism through pollution and contamination, the perceived threat of racial difference and mixture to the German nation/German national identity has also historically been articulated through a notion of pollution and contamination that relies on a concept of the nation and German identity as a raced and gendered body. In this formulation, the German body politic is predicated on the assumption and maintenance of certain fundamental social boundaries of racial purity whose vulnerability often becomes apparent through the female body as a vehicle, conduit, or site of entry for potential pollution/contamination.

Thus conceived, racial mixture can be seen to violate social boundaries analogous to those that threaten the core of a living organism. The notion of the body as a bounded organism retains substantial explanatory power as a theoretical tool for historical analysis. This conception of the body has been theorized most influentially by anthropologist Mary Douglas. In her seminal work, *Purity and Danger,* Douglas made her most famous and frequently cited arguments that the structure of living organisms can be read to reflect complex social formations and used as analogies to express and explain more general views of social order.[21] Her work theorizes how the perceived danger of bodily pollution and aspirations to purity and its maintenance symbolizes the relationship between parts of society and mirrors desires for hierarchy, symmetry, and homogeneity in the larger social system.

As Elizabeth Grosz emphasizes in her reading of Douglas, this idea of the body symbolizes various social and collective fantasies, anxieties, and aspirations: orifices and surfaces represent the sites of cultural marginality, places of social entry and exit, regions of confrontation or compromise. Rituals and practices designed to cleanse or purify the body serve as metaphors for processes of cultural homogeneity.[22] The concept of bodily boundaries and the real and imagined consequences of their crossing, trespassing, and violation in social terms is most significant for the study of the history of Germany's Black citizens. Particularly with respect to reading historical discourses of race and racialization and the ways in which these discourses overlap and are constituted through discourses of gender and sexuality, the stakes of these boundaries and their function in constituting concepts of nation, race, and identity demonstrate the explanatory potential of the body for understanding processes of social construction. At the same time, the body also gives us important insights into how such discourses legitimate and serve the exercise of power, enforcing forms of social order through processes of marginalization and exclusion.

Douglas outlines four primary forms of dangerous boundary crossing that reproduce certain fundamental forms of bodily endangerment:

1. danger to external boundaries (pollution or crossing from outside)
2. danger to transgressing internal lines (pollution or crossing from within)
3. danger from the margins of the lines (corruption of the borders)
4. danger from internal contradiction (corruption of the logic that sustains and upholds the borders and or the system)

Similarly, the body can also be used to explain the functioning of boundaries of community as they relate to social responses historically provoked by racial mixture. As Douglas explains, what underlies all responses to border crossings is a fundamental anxiety about bodily margins that expresses a sense of endangerment to the survival of the group. In this way, anxieties of endangerment through pollution and boundary crossing are in no way random or subjective; rather, they serve a policing function, for it is through the policing and enforcing of their boundaries that communities remain intact. The fact is, however, that communities have no real or "natural" basis; on the contrary, they are created through the boundaries they construct to distinguish and distance themselves from others. Indeed, communities are defined by their capacity to maintain these fundamental forms of distinction. By extension, the crossing of these social boundaries destabilizes the legitimacy of such distinctions and at the same time calls into question the distinctiveness of the group/organism constituted through these borders. As a result, the "boundary crosser" is conceived as both threatening and powerful. Community boundaries, therefore, (1) are not natural but thoroughly constructed, (2) are never solid, and, as a result, (3) paradoxically always constitute the condition of a community's existence as well as the inherent potential of its ultimate destruction.

Scientific and colonial discourses of racial mixture first converged on the issue of interracial marriage in the colonies. Scientific conceptions of the negative genetic consequences of racial mixture were already an element of nineteenth-century German colonial policies as articulated on the issue of *Rassenmischehe,* or racially mixed marriages between white colonial settlers and indigenous colonial peoples.[23] Only six years before the Rhineland occupation, Reichstag debates on racially mixed marriages prefigured many of the same arguments and fears voiced later in the newspaper protest campaign. Although interracial marriage was not illegal under German imperial law, colonial officials began refusing to register interracial unions in the colonies in 1890. In 1905 Governor Friedrich von Lindequist issued the first such measure in the form of a decree banning interracial marriages in German Southwest Africa. Reflecting the dominant views of the scientific community at the time, he cited what he saw as the dangerous effect of racial mixture on the purity of the white race: "Such unions do not preserve, but rather diminish the race. As a rule the offspring are physically and emotionally weak and unite in themselves the negative traits of both parents."[24] In 1907, the colonial High Court in Windhuk ruled that the marriage bans were retroactively valid, effectively nullifying mixed marriages concluded before the 1905 ban. The court's ruling stated, "Any person whose ancestry can be traced to natives either paternally or maternally must be viewed and treated as a native."[25] Consequently, many people who had been considered white Germans and who had considered themselves white Germans suddenly were counted as natives. Following Lindequist's administrative order, similar decrees were passed banning mixed marriages in the German colonies of East Africa in 1906 and Samoa in 1912. In response to this 1912 decree, protests broke out in the Reichstag, prompting delegates to debate the legality of these colonial decrees in light of their conflict with imperial law. But the objections raised in protest against the bans did not focus in any fundamental way on juridical arguments regarding the question of the precedence of imperial over colonial legislation. Rather, delegates raised explicitly moral arguments against the bans, which presented marriages between German colonialists and nonwhite colonial natives as a threat to sexual morality and existing racial hierarchies of difference.

Despite the virulence of this debate, most historians and even those involved in the debates at the time agreed that the bans could never effectively be enforced. Individuals wishing to marry in contravention to these colonial restrictions needed only to travel to any of the neighboring colonial territories or even return to Europe (including Germany): such marriages were legally binding within the German colonies. Lora Wildenthal emphasizes that these bans were unique among the European colonial regimes. More importantly, as she demonstrates, these bans marked the first attempt to introduce explicitly racial definitions into German citizenship law.[26] In point of fact, the National Socialists were the first to successfully codify race formally into law. Until that time, neither the 1913 law nor its predecessor, the Reich citizenship law of 1870, contained any explicit formulation of racial categories in their interpretation. As Wildenthal explains,

> The relevant categories of citizenship were: Reich citizen (*Reichsangehörige/r*), foreigner (*Ausländer/in*), and colonial subject (*Eingeborene/r,* lit. "native"). The colloquial designation "mixed-blood" (*Mischling*) was irrelevant to citizenship law; citizenship could not be "mixed." "Native" legally indicated that group of persons under the jurisdiction of colonial law (rather than German Reich law), not race per se. The term itself was never qualitatively defined; that task was explicitly put off to a future decree. . . . Nevertheless, colonial governors formulated working definitions of "native" in their administrative decrees that did offer racial definitions. . . . The conflict between Reich law, which refused racial definitions, and local governors' administrative actions fueled the mixed marriage debate.
>
> Jus sanguinus was not a racial principle in any simple way. That citizenship based on paternal descent was not the same as citizenship based on race was exactly what troubled those who took race seriously enough to consider the "racial" attributes of mothers. . . . The 1913 citizenship law emerged in response to

years of agitation by German nationalists who feared that jus sanguinus was failing to protect the integrity of Germandom— variously termed a "race," "culture," or "nation"—around the world. . . . Most important [the 1913 citizenship law] did not allow for the insertion of a legal category of race any more than its predecessor had. It did not change a thing as far as colonial mixed marriages were concerned. Therefore, radical nationalists and many colonialists took up their call for legal bans on mixed marriages again immediately after the 1913 law was passed.[27]

The mixed-marriage bans were not officially codified as laws sanctioned by the Reichstag but were only administrative decrees issued by colonial governors and a colonial secretary. As Wildenthal astutely argues, by restricting the rights of German men to marry and pass on the rights of German citizenship to their wives and children on racial grounds, the bans were an attempt to assert race as a legal category in defining citizenship.[28] The central issue behind the decrees banning mixed marriages clearly was that of the citizenship of both indigenous colonial spouses and, perhaps more importantly, the mixed-race children of these unions. What was thought to hang in the balance of the legality of mixed marriages was the status of Blacks as German citizens and a future Black German population with legitimate claim as German political subjects. The prospect of a racially mixed, Black German minority with equal status to a white, "racially pure" German populace was certainly a cause for concern that motivated this change in colonial policy and culminated in the Reichstag debates of 1912.

The native woman, the mixed-blood children produced by both [her and her German husband] and their offspring [become] German citizens and are thereby subject to the laws valid for the Germans here. The male mixed-bloods will be liable for military service, capable of holding public offices, and will partake of the right to vote to be established sometime in the future, as well as other rights tied to citizenship. These consequences are of a high degree of seriousness. . . . Not only is the preservation of the purity of the German race and of German civilization here very substantially impaired because of them, but also the white man's position of power is altogether endangered.[29]

This group of mixed-race Germans became a source of alarm in that their presence triggered expressions of racial endangerment that tapped into scientific discourses on the hereditary consequences of racial mixture and thus raised the question of the implications of these individuals for the future of the German (and/or white) race. The legality of racially mixed marriages and the status of their legitimate offspring was seen as a problem on multiple levels, including but not limited to the question of citizenship for these nonwhite Germans and their indigenous parents and the issue of the morality of marriages between civilized white colonials and "uncivilized" or "primitive" natives. As Helmut Walser Smith suggests, the question of mixed marriages confronted Reichstag delegates with a choice between "the ideological imperatives of modern racial theory (which proscribed miscegenation) and the sanctity of the institution of marriage."[30] Through the invocation of an imagined specter of contamination associated with the negative genetic consequences of miscegenation, racial mixture became an even more volatile issue. More than a "problem," it was seen rather as a threat both to the fragile colonial balance of power and to domestic politics within the Reich. Here, the German national body was a raced body made vulnerable through the female body as the conduit of racial pollution.

The official Reichstag discussion of colonial mixed marriages began in May 1912, when Colonial Secretary Solf was one of the first speakers in favor of parliamentary support of the colonial bans. Using the violent backlash against emancipated Blacks in the United States as a cautionary example of racial parity gone awry (American antimiscegenation laws had served as a model in the conception of the mixed-marriage bans), Solf appealed to representatives' emotions, urging them to allow themselves to be led by their "instincts." As a strategic attempt to mobilize and exploit the emotional potential of this issue, Solf repeatedly invoked the figure of a racially mixed child as a specter that threatened the purity and sanctity of the German family: "You send your sons to the colonies: Do you want them to return with woolly haired [Black] grandchildren?"[31] He continued to raise the stakes on this issue, emphasizing the particular danger racial mixture posed to white German women:

Do you want [girls sent by the Colonial Society (*deutsche Kolonialgesellschaft*)] to return with Hereros, Hottentots, and bastards? . . . Consider these facts, consider them according to your instincts as Germans and as white men! The entire German nation will thank you, if you consider nothing else than this: we are Germans, we are white, and we want to stay white. . . . Do you want our race to be bastardized?[32]

In his critical response to Solf's comments, Social Democratic delegate Georg Ledebour countered that although Solf had formally argued in favor of the marriage ban, the thrust of his arguments concerned issues of interracial sexuality and its consequences that would not be addressed by the legislation in question.[33] Representative Matthias Erzberger elaborated on this point:

Where is the logic in this? We forbid mixed marriages because we don't want to have half-castes in the colonies? . . . If we are to proceed in this way, then we must have proof that the majority of half-castes result from mixed marriages. But this is not the case—rather, exactly the opposite: 99 percent of all half-castes in the colonies result from extramarital intercourse and only 1 percent from mixed marriages.[34]

Erzberger's point was well taken. But it is also clear that the primary motivation for the Colonial Office's bans on mixed marriage was to hinder the claims of legitimate mixed-race German children in the colonies to the rights of German citizenship. If recognized as citizens, only these legitimate mixed-race individuals would gain access to the German fatherland; illegitimate mixed-race children, as Cornelia Essner explains, fell into the category of "natives" and as a result rarely left the colonies.[35]

The combination of scientific and colonial discourses of racial purity that converged on the issue of mixed marriages was also constructed around a gendered and sexualized discourse that, as Wildenthal contends, "counterposed men's rights to German racial purity."[36] Foreshadowing what would later recur in the protest campaign against the Black occupation troops, racial mixture was an imagined danger that mobilized racial and sexual fears in the form of racial parity, a specter whose power lie in the threat it posed to white men's position of power. Here gender played an integral role on both sides of the debate, with women engaged as both primary and secondary victims of this threat.[37] On the one hand, both opponents and supporters of the bans relied on gendered arguments for the protection of native women: Ledebour, for example, argued that the bans protected indigenous women from the exploitation of white male colonial settlers in search of cheap housekeepers, cooks, and concubines; on the other side of the debate, Solf also argued that because of the shortage of native women, they should be protected from white male colonists' attempts to take such women away from their men.

> The natives in Samoa will applaud this ban. Among the Samoans the female population is unfortunately significantly less than that of the men, and almost every attempt by white men to marry native women—and they prefer to marry into officers' circles—... can easily lead to awkwardness between the native clans and whites.[38]

On the other hand, opponents of the ban offered a complexly gendered argument that combined a defense of male marital and sexual privilege with a vision of the civilizing mission of a superior, white German colonist as "bearers of culture" (*Kulturträger*) among Black inferiors. For example, Representative von Richthofen, a National Liberal, emphasized that the objective of German colonial politics was to bring a "higher culture" to the natives: [in order] to educate ['civilize'] them to a higher sensibility "[um] sie zu einer höheren Lebensauffassung erziehen zu können."[39] Toward this end, both appropriate bearers of culture (*geignete Kulturträger*) and the appropriate distance between him and his "civilizing object" (*Erziehungsobjekt*) were necessary. German women thus were constructed as a necessary bulwark ensuring this distance and the maintenance of this crucial cultural (racial) boundary.

Furthermore, German women saw themselves as important protectors of the purity of the German nation/race. Their self-proclaimed mission in the colonies was based in part on a notion of white female bodies as barriers to the potential pollution of the German race via miscegenation.[40] Indeed, the availability of white female bodies offered what was seen as an important alternative to the dangerous temptations of nonwhite, indigenous female sexuality. Indigenous women's bodies were figured as vessels and conduits for transporting pollution and contamination into the German national body. The sexual lures they presented to German male colonists produced the mixed-race progeny that destabilized the equation of Germanness with whiteness and violated the imaginary boundary separating the German national body—a body constituted as pure and white—from the Others from which it attempted to distinguish itself.

Contrary to the reservations regarding and opposition to the bans on each side of the debate, the somewhat surprising result of these heated discussions was the passage of a resolution affirming the legality of colonial mixed marriages, along with a second resolution aimed at strengthening the influence of the Reichstag in colonial legislative affairs. Throughout these discussions an essential, biological notion of racial difference, superiority, and hierarchy resonates, a scientific discourse of race that pervades these debates. Though often formulated in the language of "culture" and "civilization," the discussion nevertheless belies the logic of racial purity that was used as a compelling political tool. References to "culture" and "civilization" were racialized as essential differences and immutable traits attributed according to skin color. This elision is an important tension in discourses of race and racial difference, blurring the boundaries between groups of individuals and the extent to which distinctions among them are learned or innate. Yet regardless of the attribution of such distinctions, they are nonetheless purported to matter and are seen to have extremely serious implications, particularly for those seen as trespassing the boundaries of such differentiation, as in the case of racial mixture.

In spite of the fact that the legality of mixed marriages was upheld, racial mixture continued to be viewed with ambivalence and foreboding. Indeed, when confronted in the flesh with the consequences of mixed marriages, German colonial officials responded with an equally ambivalent reaction to the threat of racial parity that these individuals were seen to embody. As Wildenthal's study shows, the cases of disputed colonial citizenship during and after this debate demonstrate that this debate was not settled with the 1912 parliamentary resolutions.[41] Rather, such instances emphasize the resilience of the gendered and sexualized threat that racial mixture was seen to pose to the German body politic, a specter that would recur shortly thereafter in an even more virulent form. The fears of racial parity articulated in these discussions did indeed return with a vengeance following the war and in many ways even came to be realized in the scenario presented by African occupation troops and their Black German children.

My father came from so-called colored Africa, as Moroccans or Algerians do. And most are, they're not Black. They . . . belong to the coloreds. Well, they weren't Aryans. . . . There was no difference in the treatment [of coloreds and Blacks]. I fell under the same laws as they did. The "Aryan Paragraph" quite clearly defined who's German or of a related race. Strictly speaking, I wasn't even allowed to join a singing club or a gymnastics club. I didn't join either. 'Cause you had to sign everywhere that you were German or a related race. . . . And the question I'm often asked is "Why didn't you marry?" At the time, I wasn't allowed to marry. I could only have chosen from one of "our girls" [the Black German children of the occupation], one of the three [girls] I knew. We would have been allowed to marry. Both of us were sterilized. That way we couldn't cause any damage to the German *Volk*.[42]

In this passage, Hans Hauck speaks to the issue of the racialization of skin color as it relates to himself and his Algerian father. He describes himself and his father as "colored [*farbig*]" rather than "Black [*schwarz*]." Hauck distinguishes North Africans and people of North African descent, like his father and himself, from Blacks on the basis of skin color. Later in this passage, Hauck points out the central irony of this issue when he emphasizes that although he makes a distinction between coloreds and Blacks, the Nazis treated him like any other non-Aryan. Here he adopts the dominant definitions of this period, which established a hierarchy between different shades of Black people according to which skin colors were associated with varying degrees of primitiveness. In the end, however, all were reduced to the same "uncivilized" status in relation to whites.

Hauck's distinction between coloreds and Blacks echoes similar tensions regarding the significance of skin color in defining racial difference and racial mixture evident in both the newspaper campaign and earlier debates of racial mixture. Although skin color significance was a subject of dispute, skin color, racial difference, and mixture were important sites for the displacement of German national anxieties in the Weimar Republic. In his reading of German responses to post–World War I Black occupation troops, Sander Gilman emphasizes that the blackness attributed to these troops was very much a relative assessment. The physical appearance of these African soldiers varied from dark-skinned Madagascans and Senegalese to fairer-skinned Asian troops from French Indochina, with soldiers from such Arab countries as Algeria and Morocco situated somewhere in between. Pointing to the different shades of individuals that comprised the French colonial force, Gilman writes, "In point of fact, there were few Blacks among the French troops." In his view, "Germans had simply perceived the otherness of the troops stationed in Germany in terms of blackness."[43]

The newspaper campaign against the Black occupation troops similarly elides Black, brown, and yellow troops with regard to danger posed to the "German race." The assertion of a set of distinctions among Madagascan, Algerian, and Moroccan, and Indochinese soldiers effectively set up a system of classification of nonwhites as uncivilized peoples, hierarchically ranked in relation to a nebulous conflation of whiteness, "culture," and racial purity. In the postwar protests, this type of differentiation is exemplified by an article, "Die Farbigenherrschaft im Rheinlande," published in the 28 May 1921 edition of the *Deutsche Zeitung:*

> Regarding the French denial of a "Black" occupation in the Rhineland, we have established the following: . . . according to absolutely reliable reports these forces are composed of the following: 9–10 regiments native Algerians, 2 regiments native Tunisians, 3 regiments native Moroccans, 1 regiment native Madagascans. Additionally there are small units of Senegalese (Negroes) and a small number of Annamites (Indochinese). . . . Thus "Negroes," in the strict sense of the word, are no longer present in separate units. But there remain the brown peoples of North Africa; the Algerians, the Tunisians and Moroccans, who are strongly mixed with Negroes, and the Madagascans, the

natives of Madagascar, who are mostly a Negro-like type. But this is no way a question of the shade of skin color. Rather it is a question of the humiliation that France is deliberately inflicting upon Germany through its use of uncivilized colored troops in the occupied zone. This alone is the object of German protest.[44]

In addition to replicating Hauck's comments quoted earlier, the article also echoes the fears expressed during earlier debates regarding the threat posed by Blacks and their mixed-race offspring. Taking up the issue of the racial/cultural hierarchies raised in these debates, this article refers to the *Demutigung,* or the humiliation Germany was seen to face through the imposition of primitives on a *Kulturvolk.* The dichotomy set up implicitly within this discourse opposed Germans as a white, civilized *Kulturvolk* to Blacks as an uncivilized or primitive *Naturvolk* characterized by savagery and unbridled passions, appetites, and instincts. The threat posed by European exposure to these primitives was that sexual interaction between the races would have long-term genetic implications. Germans would not simply "unlearn" civility and culture through this contact; rather, miscegenation would mean the pollution of their genetic stock. What was seen as being at stake in the interracial contact that transpired through the use of Black troops in the postwar occupation was the violation of the boundary that implicitly divided the *Kulturträger* from his *Erziehungsobjekt,* a boundary that formed one of the ideological cornerstones of the colonial relationship. The use of Black troops as an occupation force in Germany in this way both reversed this relation and transgressed this sacred boundary. Again, culture was naturalized as an essential attribute, access to which was mediated by race. This and numerous other articles in the campaign decried further injury inflicted on an already wounded German nation, an injury that stood at the beginning of a larger continuum. As a racial injury inflicted by the victorious powers on a vanquished German state, it was only the first element in a process of postwar victimization. As a Leipzig paper noted in a 26 May 1921 article titled, "Die farbigen Truppen im Rheinland,"

What offends European sensibility in the use of Black troops is not their blackness but rather the fact that savages are being used to oversee a cultured people. Whether these savages are totally black or dark brown or yellow makes no difference. The prestige of the European culture is in danger. That is what is at stake. And precisely those peoples, those such as England and France that are dependent upon the dominance they exercise over colored peoples, should consider that with the degradation of Germany in the eyes of the colored, they degrade the white race and with this endanger their own prestige.

Upon request, both France and the English Parliament have responded that there are no longer Black troops in Germany. In this reply, which, when one emphasizes blackness as a color designation, is formally correct, lies an evil element of sophism. In the spring of 1920, two Negro regiments remained in Germany. These were transferred to Syria in May of the same year. Today there are no longer any exclusively Negro troops in German territory, this is correct. But there are brown troops—that is, 9–10 Algerian regiments, 2 Tunisian and 3 Moroccan regiments, in addition to 1 regiment of Madagascans; in total, as the "Echo de Paris" reports, 45,000 men.

Thus the fact remains unchanged that a cultured people like the French allow another cultured European people to be overseen by savages. Whether these savages are slightly more black or brown or yellow is of no matter. They must feel themselves to be policing a people of the white race. This is what outrages the German people. At the same time, it is the dangerous thing for the white race in general. 1921.[45]

This article is one example of the accusation frequently leveled against the victorious powers of their participation in the *Schändung der weißen Rasse* ("desecration of the white race"). This charge aimed not only at compromising France and Britain's position as victorious powers but also at discrediting their status as colonial powers inasmuch as this status was predicated on the racial hierarchy that such *Rassenschande* ("racial desecration") would destroy. Discrediting these two colonial powers in turn would legitimate Germany's status through its defense of the racial hierarchy on which colonialism was based. The language of this excerpt reveals another strategic deployment of racial difference and skin color as essentialized "culture." Again, skin color is rejected as playing a role in the protests against the

Black troops, while race and racial inferiority (Blacks as a "savage" race) are emphasized as the primary danger presented by the use of these troops in the occupation. "Savagery" was constructed as a biological threat to the white race. As before, skin color was equated with culture, thus eliding racial difference with level of "civilization."

The articles in the newspaper campaign against the Black troops illustrate that Germany's defeat in World War I was not only experienced with a sense of loss and humiliation but also was articulated as a threat. As was the case less than a decade earlier during the mixed marriage debates, the threat which served as the implicit and explicit subtext of this campaign was the perceived threat of racial parity. Racial parity was the danger perceived to result from Germany's loss of the war and with which Germans were confronted in several areas, including the military and to a certain extent German society. In the military, the use of Black colonial troops by other European countries effectively set Blacks on the same level as whites. Although Germany did not use colonial troops during World War I, it had in fact considered this option. France's use of Black as well as white occupation troops presented Germany with a superficial form of racial parity that the country had never before encountered either in the colonies or in the military. As "'Die Geister, die ich rief . . .': Die Gefahr der farbigen Besatzungstruppen für Europa," which appeared in *Die Weser Zeitung* on 23 July 1921, put it,

> The main danger in the use of colored troops in the heart of Europe lies far more in the systematic awakening and cultivation of their sense of power over the white race. . . . The French have provided amply for the military training of the Blacks through the use of them in the war and as occupation forces. But, drunk with their victory, the French military still refuse to see the terrible danger. Not long ago Senegalese Negroes were exuberantly celebrated shortly before their transfer to Paris as the "Heroes of Dirmuiden, the Marne, the Dardanelles and other places where one [had to hang on] at all costs." . . . It is in this way that the feeling of power of the colored race against the whites is only strengthened by the French military.[46]

Perhaps more significantly, racial parity was also perceived as a threat to German society: a threat which again was articulated as a gendered, sexual threat. On the one hand, the white German woman was presented as the channel of this threat. Several articles portrayed her as both whore and victim and, as such, she functions as both an active and passive conduit of Black male sexuality. The Black man, in turn, was demonized as, among other things, infectious, instinctual, uncivilized, and—most notably—irresistible, insatiable, and uncontrollable. On the other hand, Blacks' access to white European women through service in the occupying forces represented another form of racial parity—that is, a sexual equality between Black and white men in relation to (or perhaps in the possession of) white women. This, in turn, was articulated in the campaign against the Black troops as a threat to the German man. "Die Schwarze Schmach," published in the *Hamburger Nachrichten* on 30 July 1921, argued,

> The white woman . . . has always had a visibly privileged position among Europeans. For this reason the Negro has also shown her, for the most part, absolute respect and submissive obedience. . . . But the white woman was also something different to him, something beyond the term *Weib*. She was something unreachable to him; something he certainly only seldom consciously desired. . . . Now the Negro, who inhabits Africa and parts of the rest of the world in countless millions and generally stands on a lower rung of the evolutionary ladder, is not only being brought to Europe, not only being used in battle in a white country; he is also systematically being trained to desire that which was formerly unreachable for him—the white woman! He is being urged and driven to besmirch defenseless women and girls with his tuberculous and syphilitic stench, wrench them into his stinking apish arms and abuse them in the most unthinkable ways! He is being taught that . . . he can do anything his animal instincts even remotely demand, without the slightest restraint, he even finds support for this from the "victors."[47]

In this excerpt, the white female body again forms the conduit of the racial pollution that endangers the German body politic. Unbridled Black male sexuality—essential in its insatiability yet socially malleable in its ability to discern between appropriate and inappropriate objects of desire—perpetrates this act of national pollution. The violation of this most fundamental of boundaries renders this sexualized form of racial parity perhaps the most intolerable threat to the German nation, one seen as a rallying point for the German people and eventually other whites. Racial parity ultimately posed the most significant danger to white German men in the threat it posed to their masculinity. This was also true of the military, where *Wehrhaftigkeit* (the ability to perform military service and protect one's country and property) has long been regarded as a primary masculine attribute. Here, racial parity threatened to emasculate the white German male. In the logic of national body politics, this masculine potency apparently could be maintained only through inequality. On 24 April 1922, the *Grenzland Korrespondent* stated in "Völker Europas...!"

> But the "Black Horror is—how long must one scream it into the ears of a deaf world"—not only a disgrace for Germany. It is much more. It represents the desecration of white culture in general. At the same time, it means the beginning of the end of the supremacy of the white man.[48]

The discourse on the Black troops in the 1919–23 newspaper campaign can also be read as an attempt to recover Germany's prewar Great Power status through the displacement and/or projection of the fears aroused by the changes occurring in postwar German society onto another surface. The Black occupation troops were one such surface, and the threat of racial parity served as a catalyst in this process. However, the ultimate result of the displacement of German national anxieties onto the Black troops was the racialization of the postwar situation: German society attempted to regain its prewar dominance or *Herrenstatus* by affirming its racial superiority to Blacks and specifically the Black troops. This was achieved through the extension or generalization of the problem of a Black presence in Germany and the exaggeration of the perceived threat of racial parity into a crisis that threatened all Europeans and the white race in general. This process of racialization was also part of a dynamic that strategically transformed the presence of a Black occupying force in Germany into the fiction of an all-encompassing racial threat to civilization. Here, the merging of fiction and reality was intended to have strategic political consequences—namely, the potential and much-desired revision of the postwar settlement along racial lines. One newspaper asked the British occupiers,

Are you not aware that through the continued increase of the French Black troops, England's current world standing is far more endangered than the life of the German nation? If we hope for particular understanding of our struggle against the French Black troops from your side, this comes not from pacifistic illusion, but from the conviction that our interests overlap, for we are threatened from the same side. Your people, who have enjoyed the wonderful mixture of Norman gentleman's pride and Anglo-Saxon justice, must finally understand that the basis of your world reputation would be shaken by the emancipation of the Black race, as France is perpetrating it. Have you no idea of . . . the dangers that the French assertion of equality of the Black race with the white race could bring? Have you no idea of the consequences that could result from the unhindered continuation of this French policy for the English colonial Negro? Consider . . . these thoughts and [you too will come to believe] that this issue is, on the contrary, a matter of the self-consciousness and self-preservation of the white race.[49]

The most dubious effect of this process was the way in which this racialized discourse presented the Black troops as a common enemy of all white nations against whom they should unite and overcome their differences. The extension of the threat posed by the Black troops to this more encompassing formulation created a point of identification between Germany and its former European adversaries via the threat to racial purity—that is, whiteness. This, in turn, led to a defensive closing of ranks among whites against an alleged threat to the white race. According to one newspaper,

Only too late will [the French] realize that they have conjured up a catastrophe for the whole of Europe through the use of colored troops in the Rhineland. All hope rests on the remaining European states and America. Hopefully the feeling of solidarity among the white race will break out in time to effectively meet the rising African threat.[50]

In addition to creating a racially inferior "Black enemy," the discourse of the propaganda campaign simultaneously constructed a position of racial superiority for the white German counterpart to this

figure, a scenario that might be described as follows: The racially inferior Black enemy poses a threat that must be controlled and contained.
The racially superior white German champions this moral campaign.
The effect is the reestablishment of the old colonial hierarchy at the
ideological level, achieved through the extension or perpetuation of the
former colonial relation of domination via the categories of a superior
Herrenrasse and an inferior *Gegenrasse,* which are made viable
through the construction of Blacks as racially primitive. Such a relation forgoes the need for external colonies, as it is tenable with regard
to all "primitive" or "inferior" peoples or all those constructed as such.
Through a racialized discourse in which the use of Black troops in the
postwar occupation is constructed as a dangerous attack on the established racial order, Germany is constituted as the victim of a racial con-
spiracy. Its defense of the racial hierarchy in the discourse of the campaign effectively makes it the last protector of the white race. In this
way, its victimization is recast as a heroic sacrifice (or martyrdom) for
the race.

The fear of interracial sex played a central role in this process of
racialization. The Afro-German children of the Black occupation
troops were the realization of the fears expressed in the propaganda
campaign, the embodiment of racial parity and postwar German
defeat and humiliation. As in the *Mischehe* debates, these children
were used provocatively as a shock tactic aimed at evoking outrage
and repulsion, creating a sense of endangerment as a result of the
deployment of Black troops in Europe. The message behind this strategy was that the use of Black troops would have long-term repercus-
sions for Germany or, more explicitly, for the "German race." In this
area, the public statements of one of the most prominent speakers
involved in the campaign, Ray Beveridge, are particularly significant.[51]

One highly publicized example of Beveridge's rhetoric was a much-
publicized speech given at a protest rally in Munich on 22 February
1921. At the rally, Beveridge presented two "little martyrs" of the occupation to the audience: an undernourished and underdeveloped white
German child said to be the victim of the Allied "hunger blockade"
and a Black German child described as "a living unfortunate witness to
the Black disgrace and white shame [*lebendigen und unglücklichen Zeu-
gen Schwarzer Schmach und weißer Schande*]."[52] Beveridge became a
much-sought-after speaker at protest rallies throughout Germany,

well known for her ability to move her audiences. Of the Munich rally, the *München-Augsburger Abendzeitung* wrote on 24 February 1921,

> Then Mrs. Beveridge stepped onto the podium. Who doesn't know it, the name of this courageous American, this selfless woman, this woman both inspiring and enthusiastic for all true humanity, this mother of all miserable and hungry German children? She is received by storms of applause, storms of applause follow almost each of her succinctly formulated sentences, which call everything by its right name. But what had an even stronger effect on the gathering was when the speaker presented two children: a 6-year-old, malnourished German child, pitiful to see, and a 9-month-old, almost as large, mixed-caste child from the occupied zone. . . . No person can speak more dramatically or grippingly than such a contrast.[53]

Beveridge's speech, which was reprinted in newspapers throughout Germany, quite literally cast these "little bastards" as symbols of German defeat and of the impending threat to the purity of the German race. As part of the deployment of the "Rhineland Bastard," the children of Black soldiers were also depicted as carriers of the infectious diseases of their fathers—in particular, sexually transmitted diseases. Sexuality played a critical role in the campaign against the Black troops, for the representation of Black soldiers as a sexual threat provoked the most vehement popular reaction. Here, racial discourses were permeated by discourses of gender and sexuality. Whenever the issue of race was raised, it was immediately and invariably posed in relation to a sexual threat—for example, essential notions of "biological difference" and stereotyped ideas of the exaggerated "sexual passions" of Blacks combined with the threat of the sexual transmission of infectious diseases. This in turn was exacerbated by the excessive "sexual appetites" of Blacks and their supposed lack of a socially developed ability to control themselves.

The Black German children of these soldiers were seen as a lasting legacy of the occupation, while their mixed racial heritage and illegitimate birth posed a moral and biological threat to the chastity and purity of the German "race." The danger these children posed surpassed that presented by the Black troops, for as German citizens whose presence in the country was in no way temporary, the children presented a more far-reaching threat. In the articles written in this period, this danger is formulated as *Mulattisierung,* or the "mulattoization" of the German race—a foreboding warning that, should this situation be allowed to continue, "one need not wonder if, in a few years, there will be more half-breeds than whites walking around; if sacred German motherhood has become a myth and the German woman a Black whore."[54]

The danger of *Mulattisierung* was best articulated in an article from the 26 April 1922 edition of the *Grenzland Korrespondent.* The author speculated from a scientific perspective on the implications for Germany of the growing progeny of Black occupation soldiers, based on a peculiar application of Mendel's theory of heredity.

In addition to the horrible poverty in which the white women of the occupied zone live, an extraordinarily great danger threatens the German people: the threat of violent interbreeding with coloreds, the threat of sexual and other types of diseases, and the offspring of the unfortunate victims of these coloreds, at least a dozen different races of which are stationed along the Rhine.

If we calculate according to the so-called Mendel Rule which holds that the human genealogical line takes 300 years to purify itself from a single mixture with alien blood, the result is that the German race will be polluted for centuries by such a multiple and many-sided mixture as the colored occupation represents. But not only the German race, the entire white race. For all the traits of both parents will be passed on. Every trait need not develop into externally recognizable characteristics in every offspring. Whole generations could be completely—[illegible]. A young couple marries from one such family, pure white "since time immemorial." They look forward to their child. But what arrives is a dreadful, mixed-breed child. Just these kinds of late-occurring bastards are usually even worse than those resulting from the initial conscious act of racial mixture. Woe to the white race should the densely populated Rhineland fall to "mulattoization" in the heart of pure white Europe!

Long after the occupation is over, the traits and skin color of these peculiar creations, loathed by the east as well as the west, will cry out for revenge against those responsible for this crime committed in the name of victory.[55]

This passage offers a vivid example of how scientific discourses on race permeated the 1919–22 newspaper campaign. The Rhineland protest campaign demonstrated a powerful convergence of scientific and colonial discourses on race and racial mixture with a postwar discourse of German victimhood. Beveridge's comments in particular synthesize some of the most important resonances between the discourse of the campaign and the earlier debates regarding racial mixture and mixed marriages: among others, the deployment of gender (via Black sexuality's threat to white women and white women's supposed role in the campaign against the use of the Black occupation troops), the deployment of race and sexuality (through the construction of Black men as uncivilized savages, infectious, and sexually depraved), and, in the case of the postwar protests, the deployment of the figure of the Rhineland Bastard as a threat to the purity of the "German race."[56]

CONCLUSION

As an echoing specter of racial mixture, the images of Blacks and Afro-Germans that emerged from the post–World War I campaign against the Black troops resonate and at the same time rearticulate both essential scientific discourses of race and racial mixture and colonial conceptions of the social and political consequences that racial mixture posed to the German nation. The concept of the nation that structured and sustained each of these discourses took the body as its model, with bodily boundaries and their defense against violation and contamination functioning as the bedrock of social order and cohesion. Using the body to read the discourses of race, nation, and identity through which Black Germans were interpellated in the first half of the twentieth century demonstrates some of the ways in which this theoretical model might enhance our understanding of how Germanness has historically been constructed as a community identity based on boundaries of belonging and exclusion that are thoroughly raced and gendered.

With respect to the specific historical contexts that came to interpellate Black Germans in German society, the raced bodies of these individuals were historically seen to have certain dire consequences for the

German nation through the threat these bodies were thought to pose to German identity and through the question of who was entitled to claim membership in the category. This chapter has examined some of the implications of the repeated early-twentieth-century instances in Germany when race was conceived as essence and German national and cultural identity were articulated as having an essential racial substance. In the discourses of race that came together in these historical contexts, both Black people and the German nation were naturalized as bodies whose substance was articulated to have very specific forms of meaning that were seen as one basis for regulating social interaction in German society. On the one hand, Germanness was equated with purity and superiority; on the other hand, racial mixture represented dangerous forms of impurity, pollution, and inferiority. The mixed-marriage debates in the colonies and the discussions of how to deal with the Black German children of the post–World War I occupation were concrete attempts to legislate and negotiate this assumed substance and the implications its meaning was assumed to have for the German nation.

An extension of the fears expressed in the 1912 Reichstag debate, the post–World War I Black occupation troops and the figure of the Rhineland Bastard represented a deeply threatening specter of racial mixture—endangerment through racial parity. Unlike in the prewar debates, in the discourse of the postwar protest campaign this specter was portrayed as a racial injury that the victorious allies had inflicted on Germany. This injury functioned as the source of Germany's victimization and at the same time elevated the country's status as such through a heroic glorification of victimhood as racial martyrdom. Like other equally compelling discursive configurations of enemies and victims in German history, the strategic dimensions of this post–World War I discourse of victimhood and the ways in which it too functioned must be recognized as what Omer Bartov has described as a "national adhesive."[57] Like the other historical occurrences of the discourse of German victimhood enumerated by Bartov, the responses to the specter of racial mixture Germans articulated through the metaphors of racial victimhood and endangerment served as a form of national adhesive that offered a source of unity and identification in this period of postwar national crisis.

CHAPTER 2 CONFRONTING RACIAL DANGER, NEUTRALIZING RACIAL POLLUTION

Afro-Germans and
the National Socialist Sterilization Program

"BLURRED VISION": THE *MISCHLING* AND NAZI RACIAL LEGISLATION

The rhetoric of the Rhineland propaganda campaign reached a peak in 1921, when protest publications were widespread and at their most intense. Shortly thereafter, public outrage regarding the use of Black troops in the occupation appears to have declined. The public campaign against the Black troops appears to have ended by 1922, when, as noted in chapter 1, the more pressing issue of the Ruhr conflict came to displace the hysteria surrounding the presence of the Black occupation troops. Yet the specter of racial danger that a Black German population presented for the German nation was a threatening trope that resurfaced long after the end of the occupation. As one of the most resilient metaphors of this specter, the continued influence of the figure of Rhineland Bastard in the Third Reich confirms the enduring power of the discourse of racial endangerment associated with the Black German population in this period. The response that was repeatedly proposed as a means of neutralizing this threat was sterilization. Calls for the sterilization of the Rhineland children were made as early as 1927, when a local official in the Pfalz, Hans Jolas, wrote to the Bavarian Minister of Health, Sperr, regarding the province's growing concern about the danger posed by the presence of these Black German children, who would soon be coming of age. Jolas asked Sperr to investi-

63

gate what measures might be taken to secure and protect the purity of
the race in the region from this emerging threat. Jolas suggested sterilization as a potential solution to this problem, though he acknowledged that such measures were illegal according to existing law. The
Bavarian ministry denied Jolas's request. Sperr's response emphasized
the fact that the ministry recognized the "serious racial danger" presented by the procreative potential of these Black German children.
Yet he affirmed that there was to date no legal basis on which to carry
out such sterilizations. Born to German mothers and thus holding German citizenship, the children could also not be deported, a possibility
also discussed by the ministry. Moreover, such an undertaking would
be hindered by the fact that few mothers would agree to it. A further
consideration was the potentially negative effects on domestic and foreign policy.[1] Yet what is most salient about these discussions is the fact
that, as was also the case earlier in the colonies and later in the Third
Reich, these discussions revolved around the protection of the purity
of the race from the dangers of "colored blood."

Beyond measures specifically directed at dealing with the threat
posed by the children of the Rhineland, National Socialist (NS) policy
toward Afro-Germans who were not part of this group was not characterized by a top-down execution of legislative power, and for the
most part, the regime's actions were neither systematic nor coherent.[2]
Rather, the actions taken toward these individuals were ambivalent,
with often-contradictory measures implemented at the local level and
usually carried out on the initiative of individual bureaucrats or community members. As a result, it is impossible to present a comprehensive account of Nazi policy toward Afro-Germans in the form of a lin-
ear narrative. For this reason, the National Socialist program to
sterilize the children of the Rhineland occupation is significant as one
of the only systematic programs directed toward Black Germans as
Blacks. This chapter examines this program's genesis as a continuation
of the trajectory of the echoing specter of racial mixture charted in
chapter 1. Unlike in the Kaiserreich and the Weimar Republic, in the
Third Reich the threat of racial endangerment formed a central part of
a political regime structured around race as the fundamental basis on
which the state was organized and functioned.

Although racial anti-Semitism was central to National Socialist ideology, this philosophy was also part of a larger biologist ideology of

racial superiority that targeted a range of individuals for elimination from society. This ideology sought to purify the German nation of racially inferior elements and eventually to expand the country's empire to include other racially superior nations, obliterating or enslaving all inferior races in service of a "master race." In this ideology, eugenic thought played an important role.[3] As Jeremy Noakes points out, National Socialism combined an ideology of racial anti-Semitism with a program of eugenics toward the end of improving German racial stock. They shared a common perspective that not only viewed humans and society in biological terms but also saw humans from a particular Social Darwinist standpoint that maintained that an individual's abilities—both mental (psychic and intellectual) and physical—were determined genetically, through heredity.[4] Put another way, the value of all individuals was determined on the basis of their essential, biological attributes—as raced subjects who were viewed only in terms of their allegedly inherited character traits. The eugenic dimensions of NS racial ideology endowed it with a program to actively control, improve, or impair certain racial qualities in the development of the race. In this ideology, not only Jews—the most explicitly targeted group—but also homosexuals, people with disabilities, alcoholics, people of African descent, individuals with emotional disorders, and the homeless were among those viewed as racially inferior. The practical implementation of such measures was possible through the positing of a logic of racially superior "master race" of individuals—Aryan Germans.

In spite of the fact that racism was and is an international phenomenon, National Socialism's innovation was the fact that it institutionalized racism at the level of the state through innumerable laws and decrees that marginalized and discriminated against those considered racially inferior.[5] To a degree perhaps unparalleled in Western history, National Socialism created a society structured around the biological poles of race and gender—what it viewed as the two paramount and immutable categories of human nature. Under the Nazi regime, these two categories came to replace class, cultural, and religious divisions as the predominant social markers.[6] For a society in the throes of the post–World War I economic crisis, humiliated by recent military defeat, and confused by the new social norms of the progressive/avant garde generation that came of age during the war, these categories pro-

vided a sense of security through the clarity of "natural" classifications
and designations of individuals and their place in society.

The specter of racial mixture figured in NS racial policy through the
complex status ascribed to the *Mischling* (individuals of mixed racial
heritage—literally, "half-caste"), most notably in the form of the Jewish *Mischling*. This threat was perhaps best articulated by the architects
of NS racial law, Wilhelm Stuckart and Hans Globke, in their commentaries to the Nuremberg Laws, where they clearly stated the dire
consequences they saw in racial mixture:

> The addition of foreign blood to one's own brings about damag-
> ing changes in the body of the race because the homogeneity, the
> instinctively certain will of the body, is thereby weakened; in its
> stead an uncertain, hesitating attitude appears in all decisive life
> situations, an overestimation of the intellect and a spiritual split-
> ting. A blood mixture does not achieve a uniform fusion of two
> races foreign to each other but leads in general to a disturbance in
> the spiritual equilibrium of the receiving part.[7]

In the deliberations that accompanied the drafting of the Reich citizenship law, the status of Jewish *Mischlinge* was a particularly thorny
issue. The law explicitly sought a reformulation of the citizenship law
to exclude Jews from the rights of full citizenship. Hitler demanded a
citizenship law broad enough to encompass racial and biologically
based anti-Jewish legislation. Members of the NS administration
debated how to categorize half-Jews, or people with two Jewish grandparents ("*Mischling* of the first degree"). Both sides agreed that three-
quarter Jews (persons with three Jewish grandparents) were to be considered Jews and that one-quarter Jews (those with one Jewish
grandparent) were *Mischlinge*. On one side of the issue, party members, particularly such radicals as Gerhard Wagner and Arthur Gütt
wanted either to include half-Jews in the category of Jews or to make
this decision the responsibility of a public agency. On the other side of
the debate, the Interior Ministry (and specialists within it such as
Stuckart and Hans Loesener) wanted to relegate these individuals to
the category of *Mischling*. The final decision was left to the Führer and
was rendered more in line with the position of the ministry than the
party. Half-Jews were classified as *Mischlinge*. Only as a result of per-

sonal choice—either by marrying a Jewish spouse or by joining the Jewish community—did they take on the status of Jews.[8] The impact of this definition became more apparent in the supplementary decrees to the citizenship law and in subsequent racial legislation (particularly in the marriage law, the Law for the Protection of German Blood and Honor). To dispel any confusion, Rudolf Hess spelled out the intent of the law in no uncertain terms in a 2 December 1935 circular sent to party agencies:

> The Jewish *Mischlinge,* that is, the quarter- and half-Jews, are treated differently in the marriage legislation. The regulations are based on the fact that the mixed race of the German-Jewish *Mischlinge* is undesirable under any circumstances—both in terms of blood and politically—and that it must disappear as soon as possible.[9]

As Saul Friedländer emphasizes, Rudolf Hess's interpretation of the law ensured that "either in the present or in the next generation, the German-Jewish *Mischlinge* would belong either to the Jewish group or to that of the German citizens."[10] In general, the policy aimed to compel half-Jews to marry only Jews and thus to become part of the Jewish group.

The ambivalent status of the Jewish *Mischling* in NS racial policy eventually came to include and ascribe an equally ambivalent status to Afro-Germans. The restrictions that the 1935 Law for the Protection of Blood and Honor imposed on mixed marriages extended these racial prohibitions beyond the Jews to Sinti and Roma (so-called gypsies) and for the first time explicitly cited "Negroes and their bastards" to be included in this legislation. Together, these laws effectively required proof of pure Aryan heritage as well as proof of the absence of a Jewish or other "alien" background as essential prerequisites to everyday life in the Third Reich. Chapters 3 and 4 will use the recollections of Afro-Germans who lived through this period to examine the racial policies directed against Black Germans and the ways in which these policies were contested at local levels of society. The memories of Afro-Germans paint an ambivalent and often contradictory picture of life in the Nazi racial state. It is clear nevertheless that the children of the Rhineland were central in Nazi formulation and codification of a racial policy toward Afro-Germans. In point of fact, the Rhineland Bastard remained the dominant, if not the sole, image of a Black German population in NS racial legislation. As such, the children of the Rhineland constituted one of the few groups of Afro-Germans that the Nazis directly targeted for persecution on explicitly racial grounds.[11]

CONFRONTING RACIAL MIXTURE: STERILIZATION AS EUGENIC POPULATION POLICY

In his classic study, *Nazi Germany and the Jews,* Saul Friedländer outlines two "different but complementary methods" used by the Nazis to achieve the exclusion of racially "dangerous" groups from the *Volksgemeinschaft:* segregation and expulsion on the one hand and sterilization on the other. The first method was applied primarily to Jews, homosexuals, and Sinti and Roma; the second was applied to carriers of so-called hereditary diseases and those "racially contaminated individuals" who could not be expelled or interned in camps.[12] With regard to the Black children of the Rhineland, the Nazi response was somewhat more complex and in some ways highlights the ways in which such categories blurred and overlapped. In spite of the efforts of those responsible for the administration and execution of racial policy within the Reich, Black German children exceeded these categories. For a variety of reasons, the NS administration was unable to fully incorporate these children under the terms of the carefully crafted existing racial policy, despite the flexible terms in which this legislation and these policies were drafted and despite the fact that this flexibility was intended to cover just such cases.[13]

The Nazi response to the Black children of the Rhineland took essentially two forms: a concrete attempt to neutralize the threat of pollution of "Aryan racial stock" through compulsory sterilization and the more indirect attempts to use legislation to limit and regulate social interaction between Aryans and non-Aryans. The first of these approaches was a strategic policy of persecution directed against the only group of Black Germans popularly acknowledged to exist in Germany. Yet although the sterilization law specifically restricted its application to certain categories of individuals deemed to suffer from hereditary diseases or defects, the threat of sterilization was perceived to be far more general and, in certain circumstances, came to be used beyond the boundaries outlined by the sterilization law.[14] The second approach was a less coherent policy of social management that was thoroughly ambivalent in its attempt to regulate and define particular forms of contact between Aryan and non-Aryan members of Nazi society. Chapter 4 will focus on the implications of this second approach to dealing with Afro-Germans in the Third Reich. This chapter examines the first approach, the concrete persecution of Afro-Germans—specifically, the NS sterilization of the Black children of the Rhineland.

The NS sterilization program must be understood as part of the Nazis' larger goal of achieving a racially pure Aryan state by means of both positive and negative eugenic measures. The NS regime pursued a positive eugenic agenda through a pro-natalist policy of encouraging procreation using a combination of propaganda and incentive programs aimed at compelling women to bear as many children as possible. At the same time, the regime embarked on a negative eugenic program by enforcing an antinatalist program of birth prevention in which millions of men and women were discouraged or physically prevented from having children. This program's goals were accomplished primarily through the compulsory sterilization program, enacted six months after Hitler came to power in July 1933 as the first in a series of racial legislation.

The sterilization law was the culmination of an international eugenic and racial hygiene movement that institutionalized what had previously been largely restricted to ideology and scientific research. Yet the use of sterilization (both voluntary and compulsory) as a means of achieving a variety of social ends was in no way an innovation of National Socialism. As a central element of eugenic thought, sterilization had long been part of public and scientific discourses both in Germany and abroad. This was particularly true of the United States, which had eugenic policies regarding criminals and the mentally ill that served as models for eugenicists and racial hygienists from the 1920s until the implementation of the more far-reaching measures of the NS eugenic program. In fact, the United States had established some of the first laws legalizing eugenic sterilization for patients in mental institutions. California in particular was seen as a leader in this context, legalizing sterilizations as early as 1909.[15] By 1928, California's status at the forefront of these measures caused such leading physicians and supporters of eugenic sterilization as Robert Latou Dickinson to praise officials for the state's widespread use of the practice. Dickinson's research on eugenic sterilization in California's state mental institutions formed the basis of his successful lobbying campaign to gain the American Medical Association's endorsement of sterilization as a legitimate and ethical procedure to prevent procreation.

During the Weimar Republic, eugenic thought gained new legitimacy through a combination of factors. The tremendous number of war casualties coupled with the much-publicized declining birthrate led widespread popular articulation of trepidation with regard to the perception of a growing imbalance in post–World War I demographics that seemed to offer strong evidence of unrestrained growth among the lower classes. Thus, the fear that breathed new life into the postwar eugenic movement was first and foremost an issue of class that came to be articulated in racial terms. The anxieties regarding the rapid growth of the lower classes were expressed through dichotomies that relied on powerful metaphors of inferiority and superiority, purity and pollution. At issue was not only the quantity of births but also their quality. This concern prompted a renewed Weimar Republic interest in positive eugenics but even more in negative eugenics. Positive measures aimed at encouraging procreation among eugenically favorable segments of the population. Negative eugenics discouraged those considered eugenically inferior, dysfunctional, or defective from procreation through such measures as marriage restrictions, confinement, and sterilization.

Despite the model character of early-twentieth-century U.S. sterilization policies, the advent of National Socialism gave sterilization as well as other eugenic measures a long-awaited legal, institutional, political, and perhaps even moral backing, allowing for their implementation on a widespread basis. Here it is important to note that sterilization was portrayed less as a negative measure than as a positive and beneficial form of prevention. By omitting any explicit reference to sterilization in the measure's title, NS legal experts hoped to avoid a hostile response from the Catholic Church and other religious or diplomatic circles by effectively packaging sterilization as a "truly beneficial deed for the hereditarily sick family."[16]

Between 1934 and 1945, between three and four hundred thousand individuals were sterilized by the National Socialist regime under the 1933 Law to Prevent Hereditarily Sick Offspring (*Gesetz zur Verhütung erbkranken Nachwuchses*). These forced sterilizations were undertaken for the purpose of "uplifting the Aryan race" by eradicating "inferior hereditary traits" and preventing "racially unfit" people from having children. As the Ministry of Propaganda put it, "The goal is not 'children at any cost' but 'racially worthy, physically and mentally unaffected children of German families.'"[17] The sterilization program was an integral component of NS racism. Racism in the Third Reich involved not only discrimination against "alien" races or peoples but also the "regeneration" of its own peoples, for the "master race" not only had to be maintained but also selectively (re)produced. As one member of the Reich Ministry of the Interior put it, the "degenerative effects on the racial body may arise not only from outside, from members of alien races, but also from inside, through unrestricted procreation of inferior hereditary material."[18] Nazi experts stressed that from a racial standpoint, childbearing was not in and of itself necessarily a merit. Instead, the point was whether the "biological basis"—that is, a particular hereditary value—was present. This alone would determine a child's value for the race. According to this logic, not just a small minority but about 20 percent of the German population was considered undesirable for procreation.[19]

The unifying logic of National Socialist racism was the definition and treatment of each individual according to what was assessed as her or his differing "biological value." Nazi racism attempted to resolve what it conceived as social and cultural problems through biological means—that is, by intervening in the body and private life. This biological conception of social relations justified the state's authority to legislate the affairs of the body and private life in the service of social order. The sterilization law was the first manifestation of this policy. When enacted, the law was officially declared to embody the "primacy of the state over the sphere of life, marriage, and family."[20] Through this policy of birth prevention, the private sphere came to be subordinated to and ruled by the political sphere. The sterilization program was thus an expression of a state policy under which the private was political and under which any decision regarding the dividing line between private and political was the terrain of politics and the state.

NEUTRALIZING RACIAL MIXTURE: IMPLEMENTING
EUGENIC STERILIZATION

The sterilization law legalized voluntary and compulsory sterilizations for individuals diagnosed as suffering from genetic disorders (*Erbkrankheiten*), including "hereditary feeblemindedness [*angeborener Schwachsinn*]," schizophrenia, manic depression, epilepsy, Huntington's chorea, hereditary blindness, hereditary deafness, severe physical handicaps, and severe alcoholism. Most of the sterilizations were carried out in 1934 and 1935, and the vast majority of the affected individuals were diagnosed as either hereditarily feebleminded (54 percent in 1934 and 60 percent in 1935) or schizophrenic (24.4 percent in 1934 and 20 percent in 1935).[21] The exact number of sterilizations carried out under the 1933 law is difficult to determine because Hitler outlawed publication of information about the sterilization program in 1936, in response to the increasingly negative public reaction both in Germany and abroad. Gisela Bock estimates, however, that roughly 1 percent of the German population between the ages of sixteen and fifty was sterilized. In spite of this statistical uncertainty, the NS sterilization program remains a well-researched area of German historiography. Less well known, though, are the dimensions of the Nazis' illegal sterilizations, carried out in contravention of the 1933 law.

> I began my apprenticeship with the railroad at fifteen. It had to be approved by the child welfare department. . . . I experienced hardly any discrimination on the job. I knew, though, for example, that I could never become a civil servant . . . because of my heritage. I was a non-Aryan. . . . That's what they told me. . . . Of course, I always wanted to be [Aryan]. I always wanted blue eyes and blond hair. As a child I even straightened my hair with sugar water, because . . . it was kinky. . . . But that didn't work. . . . [When I got older and was clearer] about my heritage, about my existence . . . it was too late by then. Hitler was already in power and during my apprenticeship, in 1936, I was sterilized. I was called up by the police with my grandmother. And I was sentenced in a pseudo-court proceeding and sterilized. I was an orphan. Had my mother remarried . . . then the children were no longer registered with the child welfare department. Through this

registration it was really easy to find out. There were five others sterilized with me. . . . After the judgment they immediately loaded us up and took us to hospital. There we were operated on, and in ten days I was released. And there I stood, back on the job. They had been informed at the railroad. And they informed me, too. I wasn't allowed to marry—I could marry no German girl. That was clear. It was part of the Nuremberg Laws.[22]

The figures quoted above on the number of sterilizations conducted during the NS Regime *exclude* countless illegal sterilizations carried out in secret on the basis of racial rather than "hereditary" or "biological" grounds. This *Nacht und Nebel Aktion,* which went well beyond the legal boundaries of the sterilization law, was directed at "alien" races (*Fremdrassige*) and asocials, including homosexuals, Sinti and Roma, a small number of Jews, and several hundred Black German children of the Rhineland occupation. Of the estimated 600–800 children in this group, approximately 385 were sterilized.[23] Hans Hauck, quoted here, was one of them. Hauck stated that he was sterilized in 1936, a year after most of the legal sterilizations were carried out; however, the timing of the sterilization of the Rhineland children was only one respect in which it differed from the other legal and illegal sterilization programs carried out under the Nazi regime.

Calls for the sterilization of the children of the Rhineland were revived with the Nazi ascent to power. In a 1933 publication entitled *Rasseprobleme im Dritten Reich,* Dr. Hans Macco demanded that strong measures be taken to mitigate the danger posed by these children's continued presence in the Reich:

Another essential reason for our racial deterioration is mixture with alien races. In this regard there remains a residual of the Black shame on the Rhine that must be eliminated. These mulatto children are either the products of violence or their mothers were whores. In both cases, we haven't the slightest moral obligation to this progeny of an alien race. Approximately 14 years have passed; those of the mulattos who remain are now coming of reproductive age; thus, there is little time for long explanations. Let France and other nations deal with their racial problems as they like; for us there is only one possibility: the eradication of all aliens, particularly those born of the damage wrought by this brutal violence and immorality. As a Rhinelander I demand the sterilization of all the mulattos left to us by the Black Shame on the Rhine. These measures must be taken within the next two years or else it will be too late, and this racial deterioration will be felt for another century. Nothing can be achieved through the legal prohibition of marriage with alien races, for what is not possible through legal channels happens illegitimately.[24]

Macco's comments demonstrate both the perceived threat these children posed and the way in which these anxieties echoed Kaiserreich and Weimar Republic discourses on the specter of racial mixture. Yet despite the uncanny resonances of his demands with both earlier proposals and later concrete policies, Macco could not have anticipated the extent to which these demands would be implemented in the flesh within a year of the publication of his comments.

Between 1933 and 1937, various state agencies undertook painstaking research to establish the racial background and whereabouts of the Black children born during the French occupation. On 13 April 1933, Hermann Göring, the Prussian minister of the interior, requested that police authorities in Düsseldorf, Cologne, Koblenz, and Aachen register all "Rhineland Bastards" with state health officials. In many cases, similar concerns had already led local governmental agencies to collect this information through surveys conducted during the Weimar Republic (in Wiesbaden, for example, where such statistics were collected in 1924), with an eye toward possible sterilization even then. Yet neither the statistical findings alone nor the mere presence of this population offered sufficient grounds to justify the compulsory sterilization of these children, for there still existed no proof of inferiority based on hereditary illness or racial danger to the German *Volk,* the two key criteria that formed the basis of the 1933 law. As mentioned earlier, postwar Weimar Republic requests for the sterilization of these children had been rejected on the grounds that such measures were illegal under existing law, and such remained the case even in the Third Reich. Citing as an example the lists submitted by the Regierungsbezirk Wiesbaden, Reiner Pommerin writes,

All of these lists prove that the Interior Ministry's interpretation [of the sterilization law] could not be satisfied. It had hoped to be able to sterilize most of the mixed-race children of Moroccan heritage by means of the "Law to Prevent Hereditarily Sick Offspring" on grounds of alleged mental inferiority. . . . But since averting the danger to Germany through mixture with such "alien blood" remained the primary goal, an alternative solution for the sterilization of the mixed-race children had to be found.[25]

To provide moral justification for the sterilization of these children, the Nazis enlisted the authority of science, a discourse that had both set the terms for and catalyzed discussions of race and racial mixture in Germany in previous decades. Upon its completion, the results of the survey were forwarded to Dr. Wolfgang Abel, at that time a researcher at the Kaiser Wilhelm Institute for Anthropology, Human Genetics, and Eugenics and an assistant to the renowned geneticist Eugen Fischer, whose groundbreaking writings on racial mixture had had a profound effect on the study of racially mixed populations. Abel was commissioned to undertake a racial-anthropological evaluation of the Black children of the Rhineland to establish the effects of racial mixture on their physical and intellectual constitution. His findings were used to assess the broader social implications of this racially mixed population for the German population at large. Abel's study, conducted in late July 1933, found that his subjects demonstrated various degrees of deficiency in intellectual ability and behavior.[26] The study provided the NS regime with a scientific rationale that supported (at least in principle, though not according to the letter of the law) its claims for the necessity of sterilization. The Prussian Ministry of the Interior used Abel's findings to show the dire consequences if this population were allowed to procreate with the German population and offered these arguments as justification for a procedure for which the ministry had been able to find no other legitimate basis.

On 28 March 1934, the Interior Ministry presented the results of Abel's study to the Foreign Office. In addition to emphasizing Abel's scientific findings regarding the "inferior intellectual and emotional predisposition [*minderwertige geistige und seelische Veranlagung*]" of the *Mischlinge,* the ministry's arguments in support of sterilization focused on the threat posed by the protean nature of these *Mischlinge,* who could not easily be distinguished from the rest of the German community.

> For obvious reasons, many mothers hide the alien racial heritage of their children. . . . and for these and other reasons, a more accurate assessment is not possible, because in addition, in our experience the *Mischlinge* often appear to be an almost pure European type and therefore cannot easily be distinguished from the German population even by racial experts. This is particularly the case for *Mischlinge* fathered by white Frenchmen who are themselves of African blood and already have mixed with the French population in substantial numbers.[27]

The letter also emphasizes a cautionary example from France to demonstrate why the children should not be allowed to procreate and to illustrate the danger of unchecked intermarriage between *Mischlinge* and the white population.

> In France today there are already half a million coloreds. With the low birthrate of the French people, in four to five generations the *Mischlinge* may already make up half the population. Thus there exists the obvious danger that through the increasing number of Moroccan offspring, the racial differences in the Franco-German border zone will in time become increasingly more diffuse and that the current protective boundary between the races will be leveled.[28]

The specter of racial mixture reappears as a threat of mulattoization that was familiar from earlier discourses on Black Germans. Again, a fear of the dissolution of the distinction between whites and Blacks or "colored people" fuels eugenic arguments for controlling the procreation of inferior human mixtures and cultivating the production of pure racial stock. The response to such a threat is again all too familiar:

> This danger can, without a doubt, be confronted with every hope of success through the use of a conscientious population policy . . . since this appears to be the only measure available to us at this

time. Even if it is recommended by various sides that *Mischlinge* in the older age groups who are about to become capable of reproducing be sterilized, it must be said that according to the stipulations of the Law for the Protection of Hereditarily Ill Offspring, only those *Mischlinge* who are hereditarily ill in the sense of the law can be sterilized.

Nevertheless, it can be assumed on the basis of the results of previous studies that of the *Mischlinge* named of Moroccan heritage a large number are genetically inferior, and the law of 14 July 1933 could be applied to these individuals. If the responsible agencies would be instructed to pay particular attention to these *Mischlinge* in their execution of the law, we could expect that not an insignificant number of these unwanted seeds could be prevented from reproducing on the basis of the already existing law.[29]

The anxieties expressed in this memo were taken very seriously by the NS regime. As this excerpt shows, the ministry was also attuned to the complexity of negotiating the stipulations of the law as it applied to using sterilization to confront this perceived threat to racial purity. The regime would take up more directly precisely these issues in response to concerns voiced about the future of this population. On 11 March 1935 the Expert Committee on Population and Racial Policy (Sachverständigenbeirat für Bevölkerungs-und Rassenpolitik, or SBR), Work Group II for Racial Hygiene and Racial Politics discussed the question of how best to deal with the so-called *Bastardfrage*.[30] From the outset of the committee's deliberations, members acknowledged that this case went beyond the boundaries of the existing law. The discussion centered on a presentation by the head of the Office for Racial Politics of the Nazi party (NSDAP), Walter Gross. Gross's presentation outlined a number of different options that might be pursued with regard to the Black children of the occupation.

Gross proposed to the committee three primary means to accomplish the sterilization of the Rhineland children.[31] The first proposal called for sterilization by means of an unspoken agreement among regional doctors, the health department, and medical evaluation committees "in an awareness of the greater good, that ran contrary to moral objections (*im Bewußtsein des höheren Zweckes wider besseren*

Wissens)." The necessary legal infrastructure for sterilization thus could be constructed through "collusion."[32] However, the SBR saw this proposal as far too dependent on the cooperation of individual doctors to be effectively implemented on a large scale. A second proposal involved the creation of a new law specifically legalizing sterilization for the Black German children of postwar French occupation troops. Committee members believed that this proposal was impractical, since the current sterilization law had already provoked negative reactions abroad as well as among the German population. Nevertheless, participants in the debate argued that the 1933 law remained tenable inasmuch as it supposedly affected only those individuals diagnosed with "genetic illnesses" and as such was arguably not racially motivated. The third proposal advocated illegal sterilization by means of secret authorization, with a precedent in the abortions carried out during this period on eugenic grounds through a special directive from the Führer. Although an additional suggestion to deport the children was also briefly considered, the third proposal was eventually agreed upon as the most feasible: "Sterilization should be carried out either voluntarily or by compulsion based on the law from 14 July 1933, or illegally on a voluntary basis."[33] In his remarks, Gross took pains to emphasize the central difficulty of the task at hand.

It is regrettable that even today, Germany does not yet have at its disposal a discreet and reliable apparatus for dealing with such special cases—an apparatus for the silent and unnoticed commission of breaches of the law out of a *völkisch* sense of responsibility.[34]

It is unclear on what authority the sterilizations of Black German children of the Rhineland occupation were carried out. The sterilizations began soon after the SBR deliberations based on what seems to have been administrative initiative. The sterilizations of Afro-German children were still technically illegal when, in the spring of 1937, Sonderkommission III was established at the Gestapo Headquarters in Berlin and charged with the task of accomplishing "the discrete sterilization of the Rhineland bastards."[35] Similar to the procedure followed in the case of eugenic abortions, medical evaluations from regional health officials were required for the sterilization of the Rhineland children, giving the procedure the appearance of legal sanction. To further maintain the appearance of legality, parental permission was also required for each sterilization. These measures gave superficial legitimacy to the procedure in spite of the program's illegality.[36] Moreover, secrecy was key to this action. The requirement that the initiative be kept covert was necessary not only because it was technically illegal but also because of the desire to avoid potentially negative effects on foreign policy and trade negotiations—an issue discussed at length several times during the SBR's deliberations. As we have seen, party officials and Nazi administrators were already concerned about foreign as well as domestic responses to their actions in this area and, given the growing dissent over the current law, were unwilling to risk any further bad publicity. In instituting its eugenic policies, the NSDAP consistently strove to maintain at least the semblance of legality. However, in the end, the NS program to sterilize the Rhineland children was carried out "illegally on a voluntary basis [*illegal auf freiwilligem Wege*]."[37]

CONCLUSION

The sterilization of the Afro-German children of the Rhineland occupation represents a curious anomaly in the NS eugenic sterilization program. These children constituted a special group for whom a special procedure was required. Although the exact details of its evolution from idea to reality remain unclear, these sterilizations were carried out illegally, in spite of the fact that extensive forethought and discussion had been devoted to considering ways of circumventing legal complications, and in secret. One question raised by these events is why the sterilization of this small population was regarded as sufficiently important to warrant such complicated measures rather than, for example, the amendment of the original July 1933 law to include explicitly racial provisions.[38] On one level, the use of explicitly racial language in the law seems not to have been deemed necessary, as the sterilizations appear to obviously have been racially motivated. Although the sterilization of the Rhineland children had been discussed at least five years prior to the 1933 law, even under the Third Reich no such sterilizations could be authorized without a genetic basis for doing so. For this reason, the NS initiative against the Rhineland children was instituted on neither a legal nor a genetic basis but by means of an "administrative initiative" that apparently did not require official authorization. The assumption of the legitimacy of racially motivated sterilization seems to have been enough.

However, on another level, like the disproportionate amount of concern and alarm that the presence of a Black German population provoked in both the immediate post–World War I period and in the Kaiserreich during the debates on racially mixed marriages, the symbolic threat that these children were seen to pose to the German nation was interpreted as greatly exceeding their small numbers. As a specter seen to have long-term consequences for the future of the German race, nation, and culture, a domestic Black population repeatedly gave rise to exaggerated responses of dire and impending threat that rarely bore any relation either to the size of this population or to the actual circumstances of their existence. On the contrary, these responses must be read as important historical articulations at moments when Germany was forced to confront the limits of its reliance on concepts of purity as a constituent element of German national identity. Faced with nonwhite Germans in the flesh, such responses in each of these contexts demonstrate Germany's attempts to negate, contain, or control this population's claims to the category of Germanness while securing this category for those seen as entitled to the status of German by virtue of dubious claims to purity.

PART II MEMORY
NARRATIVES/MEMORY
TECHNOLOGIES

Race, Gendering, and the

Politics of Memory Work

As we have seen in the preceding chapters, during the first half of the twentieth century, German public discourse regarding Afro-Germans was structured around the threat they were perceived to pose to the purity of the white race and the German nation. This population's mixed racial heritage was articulated as a looming specter in need of containment. The public discourse on racial endangerment that emerged in the mixed-marriages debates, the Rhineland propaganda campaign, and later in the Nazi sterilization of the children of the Rhineland was fueled by a conception of the German nation as a bodily organism—a national body that could be maintained only through the defense of its purity. Its primary vulnerability was figured as the threat of pollution posed by racial mixture. This public discourse of racial endangerment must also be read as a type of national and/or historical memory technology that anchors the dominant historiographical interpretive paradigms of the prewar generation of Afro-Germans. These paradigms assume a teleology of Afro-German history in which all Black Germans living in the Third Reich are perceived as *Besatzungskinder* (war babies) born of the Rhineland occupation, at the same time predicting and inscribing these individuals' eventual demise as innocent and passive victims of Nazi persecution. As illegitimate racial subjects, Black Germans are presumed not to have survived the racial regime of the Third Reich, thus fulfilling early prophesies of their demise as the embodiment of the specter of racial endangerment.

Yet we must ask what explanatory power these paradigms hold for the history of this population. Are they accurate or appropriate representations of this history? What about individuals whose life histories do not correspond to this model? And for those whose biographies do correspond to this model, how significant were these experiences? Finally, what if any insights do such interpretations offer into the effects of National Socialist racial politics on the racial and gendered subject formation of German Blacks living in this regime?

The chapters in this section set out to deconstruct the dominant narrative of German collective memory of Black Germans examined in chapters 1 and 2 through a critical reading of the private memories of individual members of this group. In these chapters, I seek to show how an examination of the memories of Afro-Germans highlights the workings of memory as a technology that produces not only dominant accounts of history but also the potential for alternative forms of knowledge production and meaning making. The chapters in this second section shift the focus away from German responses to what they saw as the harrowing consequences of the presence of a Black German population in their midst, exploring the concrete implications of these historical discourses of racial endangerment for Germans of African descent in the period directly preceding and during World War II. The following chapters theorize the effects of racial discourses and processes of gendering on Afro-Germans in the Nazi regime, focusing on the imbrication of private memories and social processes of subject formation for Black Germans in the Third Reich.

The readings presented in chapters 3 and 4 perform a kind of memory work that engages memory as a technology in two senses. First, memory work serves as a mode of transforming these individuals' oral recollections into historical texts of memory (that is, historical "sources"). Second, these readings engage memory as a process of knowledge production or, in other words, "meaning making." The narratives of memory that my Afro-German interview partners construct in their accounts demonstrate the ways in which these individuals came to contend with the meanings imposed on them as raced and gendered subjects in the racial state of Nazi Germany. Perhaps more important, their narratives also reveal alternative forms of meaning they produced in their efforts to constitute their own understandings of their subjectivities as German Blacks. In this way, their memory narratives offer new sources of knowledge, both on the effects of racial politics in the Third Reich and on processes of subject formation more generally. One important dimension of the technology of memory is its capacity to transmit and reproduce existing conceptions of the nation and national identity while revealing fissures and gaps in these conceptions, most notably through the ways in which the processes of inclusion and exclusion constitutive of nationhood and nationality are engaged and contested in creative ways by individual social actors.

In "Space, Time, and the Politics of Memory," Jonathan Boyarin eloquently makes this link between the politics of memory and discourses of the nation and the body, in a manner that is particularly instructive in the German context. Arguing against the prevalent tendency to construct an absolute distinction between the technological and the organic, Boyarin asserts that technology can never be outside or separate from the body. In the case of memory, the body is also always crucially linked to memory and its technologies. Warning against a notion of memory as superorganic, he emphasizes that on the most material level, the "place" of memory remains the brain. Boyarin makes clear that memory is always at once intersubjective, technical, and physical (that is, bodily/organic).[1] This crucial point underlies the links among memory, the body, and the discourse of the nation for, as he asserts, the nation also "works through the body" via memory on a number of different levels, enlisting the rallying power of both collective memory and identity in strategic ways.

> [The nation] generates loyalty analogous to that owed to parents. It rallies allegiance to its sovereign power through dramatizing the threat to its integrity from alien "bodies," to preserve its organic identity: "for the nation to be itself—for it to be strong dominant, for it to save itself and resist its enemies—it must be racially and/or culturally pure" (Balibar 1990: 284). Like a "body," the nation must grow or decay; and hence expansionary adventures are made to seem vital necessities. Like organisms, popularly and scientifically understood until quite recently to be controlled by a master logic, the nation must be hierarchically organized in order to maintain systemic functioning (Haraway

1991). Furthermore, if nations are bodies, then they inevitably grow from childhood to maturity. Hence the paternalistic domination of certain "Other" nations (e.g., Native Americans, Koreans, Palestinians) can be rationalized by rhetorically casting them as being in their "infancy," not ready for self-determination.[2]

Boyarin emphasizes that focusing on the relations among memory, the body, and the nation—in the sense of what he refers to as "embodied memories"—reveals some of the less obvious ways in which "state ideologies appeal to organic experiences and common sense dimensionality to legitimize themselves." He further asserts, "Those who elaborate and maintain such ideologies pretend, quite often with great success, to dictate both the contents of appropriate 'memory' and the proper spatial borders of the collective."[3] Yet Boyarin is careful to point out the most important implication of this complex imbrication of memory, the body, and the nation. As he rightly contends, memory can be neither solely individual (in that it is symbolic and thus intersubjective) nor thoroughly collective (since it is, on some fundamental level, embodied rather than superorganic). Boyarin concludes that what is most important for understanding this conundrum is the recognition that the aim of an inquiry into this complex configuration is not an explanation of a relation between body and group via culture. On the contrary,

> What we are faced with—what we are living—is the constitution of both group "membership" and individual "identity" out of a dynamically chosen selection of memories, and the constant reshaping, reinvention, and reinforcement of those memories as members contest and create the boundaries and links among themselves.[4]

We can learn much from Boyarin's astute reading of the politics of memory, nation, and the body, and much of his argument resonates in the German context. A similarly constructed German national discourse of racial endangerment and national body politics also functioned to define the terms of membership and exclusion from the national body for Black Germans and, in the case of the Third Reich, often had substantial material effects on those deemed unfit for membership. The negotiation of these processes of inclusion and exclusion was by no means unproblematic but rather was rife with paradoxes and contradictions.

The memory narratives of Afro-Germans recount dynamic processes of negotiation, reinvention, and reinforcement of individual identity and group membership as well as the ways in which these processes are characterized by complex forms of resistance, contestation, and creativity. The accounts of two individuals serve as case studies for the analysis in this section. Here I must acknowledge the fact that basing my analysis on only two cases raises certain obvious methodological questions about what kinds of conclusions can be drawn from such a narrowly focused study. Indeed, a more direct formulation of this question might do more justice to the important issues that underlie it. Plainly put, why only two cases, and why these two cases in particular? The most straightforward response to this question is that the two accounts presented here are in many ways the most complex of the larger corpus of oral histories collected for this project. The contradictions and contestations they detail make them rich and revealing sites of analysis. Yet the broader problem raised by the use of these two accounts is the status of the local and the quotidian for scholarly analysis. Specifically, what can the minutiae of the lives of two individuals tell us about the monumental processes of social administration and subject formation in the Third Reich? In other words, what can we learn from looking at two individual cases?

At the heart of these questions lie fundamental issues about how the narratives of these two individuals will be used as sites of scholarly inquiry into the racial politics of the National Socialist state. These questions point to the fact that as the premier historical case of a racial state, the Third Reich occupies monumental historical stature as the exemplar of an authoritarian racial regime and its ultimate consequences for humanity. Seen in this context, using the memories of only two people to unpack even a small piece of this complex system would seem at the very least a questionable undertaking, woefully insufficient to its goal. Yet I would argue that such a project can in fact be extremely fruitful, and I will take precisely this approach in analyzing these individuals' memory texts. My intention is not to use these accounts either as representative of the history of an entire population or as privileged sites of personal experience. As stated in the introduction, my approach to reading these accounts of memory explicitly attempts to avoid the trap of using oral historical accounts as one-dimensional documents of experience or as an irrefutable form of truth, fact, or evidence. It is important to view the testimony of each of my interview partners as a retrospective evaluation of the narrator's past screened through the prism of memory.

But how exactly do we connect the workings of this monumental racial state to the minutiae of the lives of Afro-Germans? I make this important link through memory or what I call historical memory work. One of the most important sites of such memory work is oral histories. Yet in many ways, our popular perception of memory is also one of our most prevalent prejudices against it as the object of histori-cal study. We think of memory as individual, subjective, and specific. We consider it always partial, inherently flawed, and ultimately intrin-sically unreliable in that it can give us only a single individual's percep-tion of the past, colored by that individual's very subjective interpreta-tion of events or experiences. But although memory is in fact all of these things, it is also far more than just an individual cognitive process. Memory is also a deeply social process through which individ-uals construct and articulate their relationship to the world and the events transpiring around them, both now and then.

Memory (both recollection and remembering) involves the subjec-tive reconstruction of past events and experiences from the speaker's standpoint in the present. Years ago, the Popular Memory Group described memory as the process through which an individual's sense of the past is produced.[5] Their point was that memory is never solely an individual, subjective process. Memory is neither a question of storage nor of recall; rather, memory is about the continual process of attribut-ing meaning to events of the past in the present. In this way, memory is most certainly a social process or, to repeat Maurice Halbwachs's oft-cited observation, it is individuals who remember yet they remember as members of groups—that is, through common points of reference, contexts, and associations.[6] Memory is about individuals making the past meaningful, not so much for what it was but for how it is of use to us today. Similarly, my interview partners' accounts must be read not as records of immediate experience but as selective reconstructions of their life histories produced through the configurations of memories from which they strategically construct a narrative of their past (and, by implication, of the self). Their conceptions of memory narratives emphasize that we are dealing with highly mediated representations of the past.[7]

It is important in this regard to stress that the objective of the memory work in which I will be engaged, as well as the analysis of memory more generally, is not to ascertain "how it really was" or even to record "actual" perceptions from the past, for such narratives neither represent actual experience nor can ever be an absolute index of the accuracy of a speaker's account of "back then." It is impossible to capture or assess "immediate" or "authentic" experience, because "real" or "pure experience" is inaccessible to any type of scholarly evaluation. Indeed, to state a truism, all historical evaluation is in fact mediated by the lens of memory and, therefore, to some extent, is both selectively and subjectively reconstructed. Nevertheless, as James Young asserts, such mediated representations of the past offer rich sites for interpreting and understanding the ways in which individuals made sense of their lives and their historical contexts as well as what they viewed as the possibilities for action and agency available to them in a given historical context.[8] In this way, memory work is a valuable historical tool: precisely because these narratives are already filtered through the screen of memory, they offer important perspectives on the past as seen through eyes of the present.[9]

The three chapters in this section offer readings of race and gender in the stories and memories of ordinary Germans—ordinary people who happened to be black. Yet the emphasis is on their stories and memories of "little" things. My aim is a nuanced and sophisticated reading of the details that constitute the fascinating memory narratives of individual Black Germans. This focus on the little is an attempt to emphasize questions that we frequently overlook or that often get obscured in our desire to explain the larger overarching social and political systems. Blackness was a big little detail in the lives of my informants: lives which were lived in complicated and contradictory ways in the Third Reich. Blackness was recognized and misrecognized, scrutinized and overlooked—it was the single most important and insignificant fact of their lives as Germans in this regime.

The memory narratives of my informants offer a complex rendering of racialized and gendered social topographies of Nazi Germany. At the same time, these stories narrate the ways in which these social land-

scapes became differentially visible and invisible, internalized and contested by Black Germans. In this way, these complicated narratives of
memory present highly textured representations of the past that allow
us to read racial and gender formation in the Nazi regime through a
finely tuned historical lens. The minute details of these memory narratives allow these individuals to articulate and explain the local politics
of race and gender in the Third Reich and help us to better understand
the monumental impact of Nazi ideology as it was deployed both
nationally and symbolically. In this way, the importance of remembering "little" things begins with shifting our sense of the status of the little to conceive of it not as necessarily small or insignificant but on the
contrary as a window on what we tend to think of as larger "more
important" things.

This connection between the local and the national or the monumental and the minute is one of the most revealing dimensions of the
memory narratives of Black Germans in the Third Reich. The Nazi
regime clearly was a monumental social, historical, and political phenomenon that affected the lives of countless millions of individuals and
that continues to ripple throughout our society in its implications for
how we think of questions of evil, justice, human rights, responsibility,
complicity, and forgiveness. The Nazi era has also had a major impact
on how we understand such fundamental concepts as race, racism, and
anti-Semitism. Yet the monumentality of this system is rooted in the
fact that it had such a pervasive effect on individual lives and in the fact
that that effect took the form of shaping life at the local level. In this
way, the monumental is rooted in minute questions of the local—in the
"little" details of the everyday, or what I will call the monumental
minutia of individual lives. For this reason, the history of this population is particularly significant.

My readings of the memory narratives of these two Afro-German
informants insist on an ongoing recognition of the deep connection
between the monumental and the minute—the monumental phenomena of National Socialism and the Holocaust and the minutiae of the
lives and memories of two individuals. This connection highlights the
fact that we are often able to apprehend larger monumental social,
political, and discursive systems of organization only through an
examination of the minutia of the everyday and the local. In point of
fact, the minutiae of everyday lives can provide a greater appreciation

of the monumentality of National Socialism. The memory work of the chapters that follow uses the narratives of two individuals to unpack the intricate functioning of processes of racialization, gendering, and subject formation and thus shifts our basic understanding of the functioning of the Nazi racial state.

My selection of these particular individuals' narratives is not made on the basis of an understanding of them as representative exemplars of the experiences of all Afro-Germans or Blacks in Germany during this period. By the same token, I have also not chosen to use them to demonstrate their status as exceptional illustrations of the most extreme consequences of race for Blacks in this regime. My aim is in fact both far more complex and far simpler. The significance of the lives and memories of these individuals lies in the fact that they are less representative than exemplary—not of all Black Germans but of the dynamics of race and gender in the Third Reich and the complex and contradictory ways in which it produced particular forms of legitimate and illegitimate German subjecthood in the service of sustaining this regime. Memory work serves as a self-conscious attempt to acquire mediated access to the processes of subject constitution these individuals recount, access that makes explicit the connection between the monumental and the minute. As we will see in the pages that follow, examining the dynamics of the production of racialized and gendered subjects through these individuals' memories of the politics of the local has a significant impact in shifting and reshaping how we understand the workings of race in the Third Reich.

Historical memory work offers a crucial tool for examining the monumental minutiae of the lives of Black Germans in the Third Reich. A critical reading of memory reveals the richness inherent in the lives of each of these individuals and allows us to see the ways in which their lives were in fact monumental. Thus, in response to the questions posed earlier regarding what the memories of two individuals can teach us about the functioning of such monumental social systems, this section will seek to emphasize the extent to which understanding the minutiae of the lives and memories of my Afro-German interview partners allows us to understand the workings of race and gender in the Third Reich not only more generally but also more minutely.

CHAPTER 3 CONVERSATIONS WITH THE "OTHER WITHIN"

Memories of a Black German Coming of Age in the Third Reich

In the National Socialist (NS) state, race served as the primary signifier of difference through which specific groups of Germans were produced as subjects in particular ways. The memory narratives of Afro-Germans offer a unique view from within this regime—one that focuses our attention on the everyday politics of race. Their testimony reveals some of the very local processes of subject formation in this regime that produced individuals as differentially valued legitimate and illegitimate racialized and gendered subjects. Yet before exploring the testimony of these individuals, it seems important to dwell momentarily on what might seem an obvious point—that race is neither an essence nor a scientific fact of biology. Individuals are not born "raced" but rather become raced subjects through complex social processes of constructing meaning. As I argued in chapter 1, defining race as essence or as a "natural" biological trait that differentiates individuals has never been either objective or restricted to a separate province of science or biology. Defining and establishing racial difference has always been a political project with concrete social consequences. As we saw in both the colonial mixed-marriages debates and during the Rhineland campaign, in spite of the fact that the power of a scientific discourse of race lies in the authority of its claim that race is an objective term of human classification, this has never been the case. There is no "essence" of race (biological or otherwise), only the social and political consequences that arise from social definitions of race that impute certain meanings to what are seen as racial differences. Race is nothing more and at the same time nothing less than a mode of differentiation between individuals in society, yet race is such a mode with particularly powerful material and symbolic effects.

In this study, both race and gender are conceived as powerful modes of social differentiation that produce and inscribe meaningful forms of subjectivity. With respect to defining each of these categories, I adopt Judith Butler's concept of "materialization" as way of describing the social and discursive processes through which not only gender and sex but also the raced body come to take on meaning in society. Materialization is particularly useful concept that at once connotes both the ways in which gender and/or race are produced as meaningful (that is, how they come to matter [verb]) and the equally social processes through which we come to think of the sexed, gendered, or raced body as "real" or material substance (that is, as matter [noun]) in ways that erase and obscure the processes of their production as such. Butler argues that both sex and gender come to matter and are produced as material through the forcible reiteration and citation of regulatory social norms. Her notion of materialization is particularly helpful with regard to the functioning of race, allowing us to conceive of social construction as more than simply a linguistic process and accounting in important ways for the historical accumulation of meaning of the category of race as substance and its often quite material effect on the lives of individuals in society.[1]

Thus, specifically with regard to defining the concept of race, rather than speaking of racial essences or experiences, we must think of racialization as a process through which particular meanings of social differences are produced and come to be attributed to, synonymous with, and identified as the differences we refer to as *race*. In this way race is both a representation of social difference and, at the same time, the social process of representation through difference produced as meaningful. Beyond a notion of social construction that focuses primarily on language and discourse, the meaning of race is also the product of histories and bodies whose meaning has evolved from historical and material groundings (that is, from concrete situational and ideological contexts that have evolved over time). Indeed, at the most basic of levels, the "raced bodies" of Africans and Afro-Germans and their presumed racial difference from whites have historically come to take on diverse forms of social meaning in German society. The situation of Afro-Germans exemplifies this process.

As a potentially important marker of identity, it is tempting to say that the raced bodies of these individuals have historically been the decisive factor in the constitution of their subjectivities. One could certainly argue that the basis or "substance" of identity is intrinsically linked to the "experience of race" and living the material consequences of this raced body. On one level, this is an obvious and verifiable conclusion. Yet it is an issue that provokes me to recall the comments of one of my Afro-German interview partners, Fasia Jansen, whose testimony will be explored in depth in chapter 4. At one point in our conversation, Jansen remarked that she never "felt" Black. When I asked whether this was really the case, Jansen turned the tables on me by asking whether I had in fact felt this myself. When I replied that I did in fact feel my blackness, she responded with a second unanswerable question: exactly when was this the case? Jansen's insightful challenge led me to recognize at that moment that I never actually felt my blackness—in other words, I could not say that I experienced either the substance of race or race as substance.

As this example demonstrates, it is necessary to conceive of experience in terms that are just as complex as those of race, gender, and identity. Experience is not simply something that people have or that which happens to people. As my interview partner emphasized, both of us had often had to contend with what was not so much the "experience" of race as events that "happened to us" but rather with situations in which we were made to feel "raced"—moments when we became different from others, when our skin color, our bodies, became Black and when that category was seen to carry particular forms of social meaning. At the same time, we in turn constructed our own often very different interpretations of the meaning of these situations. Here both race and experience have little or nothing to do with any underlying substance.

The effects and consequences of the meanings attributed to race interpellate us as individuals and make our presence as Black people (our physical bodies) come to mean in specific ways. Thus, it is difficult to speak either of any substance of race as "essence," of the "experience" of race as a substantive defining moment of identity (that is, the "formative experience" of the raced body in the world), or, for that matter, of the "construction" of race as purely a discursive effect. The way in which the raced body comes to matter as a meaningful social object is a process that exceeds each of these concepts and shapes and concretely affects the interactions of human bodies in the world. As I will show in the following pages, the memory narratives of Afro-Germans in the Third Reich both affirm the apparent truth of the link between race, body, and subjectivity and point to a far more complex and often contradictory interpretation of this relation.

THE "MARKED" EXCEPTION: AN AFRO-GERMAN IN THE HITLER YOUTH

In his memory narrative, my first interview partner, Hans Hauck, repeatedly refers to his experiences of racialization in terms of his "heritage." As mentioned earlier, Hauck was one of the Afro-German children born of the Rhineland occupation. He was born in Frankfurt in 1920 and at the time of our interview resided in Dudweiler-Saarbrucken, where he had grown up and lived for many years. "Heritage," as we have seen, was a primary element of German responses to the Afro-German children of the Rhineland, specifically their blackness and mixed racial heritage, their illegitimacy, and their connection to German defeat and the country's subsequent occupation. In chapter 1, I quoted a brief statement from Hauck's narrative in which he addresses the issue of his heritage in relation to his father and his experiences growing up in post–World War I Germany as the son of a former enemy. His heritage, he explains, was an issue of which others made him aware. On closer examination, however, the role of heritage in Hauck's narrated biography becomes far more complex. In this connection, it is instructive to look at a longer version of the interview.

EXCERPT A

TC: What are your memories of your first eight years with your mother?

HH: That I was always happy, that I cuddled a lot with my mother. Of course. You see, I saw her so seldom. I wasn't with her all day. Otherwise, it was a childhood like anybody else's. I forgot about the rejection just as fast as it happened. I just kept being reminded of it. But it's no special case. There are other children who — where for example the father is in prison or where the children are in a similar situation. Just for me it was because of my heritage, or my father's heritage.

TC: Did you ever talk about this in your family?

HH: I — not in my presence, never. That was taboo. It was a subject that wasn't talked about. Although when I was small I often heard them talking about it—even when I was older and in school. But when I came around the conversation ended.

TC: What kind of an impression did that make on you? That they always spoke about it but not in your presence?

HH: Well, I became aware of what it means when something is different than the rest. But I couldn't say that this was any different from other illegitimate children.

TC: But the issue of your heritage, that wasn't —

HH: That wasn't an issue. That was taboo. You can be sure of it.

TC: Who did you grow up with? Your mother and your grandmother?

HH: My grandmother. And an aunt was also there. Sometimes my uncle came by—my mother's siblings. They didn't live here, or at least not all the time. She had married and he worked out of town. But when they were there, the whole family was together. The photos prove it.

TC: And did you have the feeling that you were accepted in your family?

HH: Yes. You can't say that I wasn't accepted. I myself — because I always heard things, but nothing *real,* I was also sensitized to or more sensitive than other kids, quite early in my life. Even then, I was already very perceptive. It's something that came in handy in school. But it made a lot of things in my life more difficult, not easier.

TC: How would you describe this? For example?

HH: When one gets over things easily or is less motivated or less sensitive, one doesn't take as much in. People who are less — some people are just narrow-minded. And life is much easier for them. They don't think as much about things. Right or wrong, that's another question. I thought about my heritage and such things quite early on. But I was too young to talk to my mother about it.

TC: And what kinds of thoughts did you have about your heritage? How did you understand or name it? Did you talk to anyone about it?

HH: I was told about it. I knew that my father was Algerian. But we never talked about it. It was just sort of mentioned in conversation: "You can't deny your heritage"—which was not at all meant to be mean. They always said that to me when I yelled or acted silly.

TC: How did you respond to that?

HH: I couldn't imagine that Algerians were different. I didn't even know what that meant. I came to understand it much later. But my mother was dead by then. I couldn't talk to her about it.

TC: How old were you when you began to understand this?

HH: I was eight and a half years old when she died—eight and a quarter.

TC: And when you started to understand [what it means to be Black]. . . .

HH: The neighbors' kids taught me that soon enough.

TC: How?

HH: It's hard to understand. I was insulted and verbally abused about my father's heritage. That was just after the war. The fathers of all the other kids were German soldiers. And mine was the enemy.

TC: That was after the war?

HH: That was after the war. The war ended in 1918, and he was here as an occupation soldier. He fought in the war and was here later as an occupation soldier.

TC: And how did you respond to these insults?

HH: At first I always defended myself, and later it was always my fault. It was something in my life that worked to my disadvantage. Without even questioning, it was my fault. Back then, people were really, really backward. It's something I've often noticed about other occupation children after World War II.

TC: Did you know other occupation children — ?

HH: Twenty-five years later, sure I did. I knew a lot after World War II.

TC: Did you know any from World War I?

HH: I got to know them when I was sterilized.

TC: When were you sterilized?

HH: 1935. Actually the trouble started when I left school.

TC: How old were you then?

HH: I was fourteen when I left school. And then at thirteen— that was when Hitler came—I was in the Hitler Youth.

TC: You had no problems getting in?

HH: No problems!

TC: Even though it was well known that your father —

HH: Even though it was well known—no problem. And that was something new for me, no — At thirteen you don't think about politics. But the whole thing, the games and the marching and playing soldier, that was fun. But —

TC: And that's why you joined?

HH: That's why I joined. In the Catholic Youth I had more problems.[2]

In this extended excerpt, we see that Hauck's statements discussed earlier are embedded in a discussion of his memories of his family situation and his childhood environment. Directly following the sequence describing his father, Hauck recalls his reaction to the negative responses to his Black heritage he encountered in his youth. He compares his experiences with Germans in the post–World War I period to the situation of children of occupation troops following World War II. When asked if he also knew children like himself from the post–World War I occupation, he replies that he first met such individuals when he was sterilized. This first mention of his sterilization occurs relatively early in Hauck's narrative (page 5 of the interview transcript). Remarkably, when asked to describe this childhood experience, Hauck does so by first speaking of a period in his life that in my reading of his narrative becomes at least as significant as his sterilization: the two years directly preceding his sterilization that he spent as a member of the Hitler Youth. The connection Hauck makes between these two experiences in his narrative—sterilization and membership in the Hitler Youth—seems an implicit attempt to resist an interpretation of his life defined solely by persecution or victimization, for he effectively qualifies his experience of sterilization (marginalization) by mentioning his membership in the Hitler Youth (integration), almost in the same breath.

Hauck begins telling the story of his forced sterilization by placing it in direct relation to his memories of an experience that can be seen as its exact inverse: membership in the Hitler Youth, arguably the ultimate symbol of assimilation within National Socialism. However, in the context of Hauck's life history (as well as the experience of Afro-Germans more generally), assimilation is a highly problematic concept, as it not only connotes an adaptation to norms or values that are not one's own but also implies a distancing from, rejection of, or displacement of some supposedly "authentic" set of sociocultural values (or, in this case, a community) to which one "belongs." To describe Hauck as having been "assimilated" into German society would assume that he did not originally belong to it as well as presume the existence of and his implicit rejection of another community in favor of acceptance in German society.

Hauck mentions his participation in the Hitler Youth in such a way that it seems more or less unremarkable. It is almost as if the story of his Hitler Youth experience, in many ways an almost ironic example of "normality" and conformity to the norms of this period, is meant to counterbalance the implied "abnormality" or exceptional status associated with sterilization. The experience of social rejection that Hauck indirectly cites through his reference to his sterilization is in this way destabilized when placed in the context of his equally significant experience of integration in the Hitler Youth—in effect, the two events appear to be irreconcilable. Yet although his membership in the Hitler Youth seems highly improbable, Hauck seems not to have perceived it as unusual: he was simply doing the same as the other German boys of his generation. After all, Hauck was not only a child of African heritage but also a German boy who, contrary to the dominant perceptions of his society regarding the Afro-German children of Black occupation troops, aspired to many of the same things as other "Aryan" German youths. Thus, he was probably attracted to the Hitler Youth for some of the same reasons as the more than 3.5 million other boys who voluntarily joined the organization between 1932 and 1934.

The Hitler-Jugend (HJ), including the Bund Deutscher Mädel

(BDM), was the largest youth organization in Western Europe up to that time. By 1939, 8.7 million of the 8.87 million Germans between the ages of ten and eighteen were members of either the HJ or the BDM.[3] Many of these youths had political as well as what might be described as more "trivial" motivations for joining, including those Hauck mentions: "play" or, more specifically, "the games and the marching and playing soldier [*das Spiel und das Antreten und Soldatenspiel*]." The question remains, however, whether the Hitler Youth served the same function in Hauck's life as it did in the lives of the white German children of his generation. What role did "play" serve for Hauck within the Hitler Youth? As we shall see, in Hauck's narrative play will come to take on several different meanings with regard to the HJ and military contexts in general, including a gendering function, a protective function, survival, and finally an identificatory function that produces him as a legitimate German subject by virtue of group membership.

Hauck joined the Hitler Youth in 1933, the year the Nazis' seized power, at a time when membership was voluntary (after 1936, membership in the Hitler Youth became compulsory under the provisions of the *Jugenddienstpflicht*). Furthermore, the fact that the Saarland was first integrated into the German Reich in 1935 makes even more significant Hauck's early membership in the HJ. On the one hand, joining allied him with the NS regime before the Saarland's official entry into the Reich, in this way setting him apart from the French sympathies also present in the Saarland. On the other hand, Hauck's acceptance into the Hitler Youth so soon after its official government sanction and despite public knowledge of his Black heritage attests to the fact that he was at least to some extent accepted by his community and, by extension, integrated at this local level into German society.[4] This observation directly challenges the dominant interpretation of the history of Afro-Germans in the Third Reich. Rather than portraying himself in a manner consistent with such historical readings—namely, as a marginalized victim of Nazi persecution—Hauck's memories of his membership in the Hitler Youth highlight experiences of integration into the social fabric of his community in ways that complicate and contest both the images of fear, loathing, and endangerment portrayed in earlier public discourses on Black Germans and the forms of marginality posited by the paradigm of victimhood that dominates contemporary historical representations of Black Germans in this period.

Perhaps most significantly, although Hauck's narrative does not discount other equally valid Afro-German accounts of persecution (including his own sterilization), his memories of his experiences of integration within the Hitler Youth demonstrate that this was not always necessarily the case at the local level. The insights revealed by exploring the contrast between his recollections of local enactments of racial ideologies and those operative at higher levels of state and institutional discourse and policy are some of the most important products of memory work, adding another layer of complexity to our understanding of the differential effects of the Nazi racial state.

In Hauck's narrative, the counterpositioning of the seemingly contradictory experiences of sterilization and membership in the HJ is neither superficial nor coincidental. Rather than being an attempt to defend his membership in the HJ from criticism, these dichotomous tendencies in his life history—integration versus marginalization, typicality versus particularity, his status as an "insider" (German) versus "outsider" (Other) and, perhaps most provocatively, victim versus participant—reflect the tenuous and complex position that Hauck occupied in his society. Throughout his narrative, Hauck emphasizes the tensions arising out of such oppositions, which, I believe directly reflect the process through which he came to be constituted as the raced German subject now referred to as Black German.

As an individual situated squarely between the binaries that structured the construction of German subjecthood at the time—binaries of legitimate and illegitimate racial, national, and political subjecthood—Hauck's account suggests the extent to which these categories are both inextricably intertwined and always already incommensurate with the complexity of the experiences and subject positions of any given individual. In this way, Hauck's narrative reflects how the categories intended to produce legitimate German subjecthood in the Third Reich were thwarted because of their inherently flawed and unstable status as the basis of a system of racialized state politics. Here it is most instructive to read Hauck's account through the ways in which it undoes the stability of the categories constructed as most stable and unquestioned in the Third Reich as well as for our understanding of who constituted its "victims." Moreover, what is perhaps most compelling about his account is how it undoes this not from the outside but from within—through the system's foundational logic. In other words, the power of Hauck's narrative lies less in its portrayal of an individual struggle against a system of racial oppression than in how it reveals the inherent instability of a system based on oppositions of inside and outside, self and other, purity and pollution, integration and marginalization. Because of their intrinsically contradictory nature, these oppositions served ironically as the most available site of contestation for some Black Germans, whose lives were situated both precisely and precariously on the lines of these distinctions.

Hauck's narrative of his life is structured around a selection of memories that are often contradictory in the picture they paint. The tensions of the association he makes between his sterilization and being a member of the HJ exemplifies this. But precisely through these contradictory memories Hauck necessarily articulates his subjectivity as a Black German because of the fact that for Hauck, neither blackness nor Germanness is in any way a self-evident or self-explanatory term. It is necessary to read below the surface of his memory text and engage the tensions of his recollections as illustrations of the complicated texture of his life and his understanding of himself as a German of African descent. This texture is expressed both thematically, through the events he recounts in his memory narrative, and more subtly at the discursive level, through the narrative strategies he uses to render these memories. One example of this is a strategy I have termed indirect negation or "relativization," which occurs repeatedly in Hauck's narration.

A first example of indirect negation occurs at the beginning of excerpt A. In this passage, Hauck describes his memories of his mother. Although he saw very little of her, he describes their relationship as close. He then immediately qualifies this statement by remarking that his childhood was more or less typical and unremarkable: "Otherwise, it was a childhood like anybody else's [*Ansonsten war es eine Kindheit wie alle anderen auch*]." This statement serves as a preface to his next remark, which, like his later statements regarding his sterilization and the Hitler Youth, calls into question his claim to typicality by asserting that he quickly forgot the discrimination he experienced (though he also remarks that others often reminded him of it). In this case, he relativizes his memories of the discrimination he suffered as the son of a Black occupation soldier by likening it to that which the child of a prison inmate might experience. He does so again a few lines later, remembering how he was made to feel different from others because of his heritage, when he likens this memory to the experiences of other illegitimate children.[5]

Hauck's use of indirect negation in his narration emphasizes the tensions in his life arising from being totally integrated into his society (an insider) yet at the same time being made to feel like a complete outsider within this same environment. The tension of being marginalized at the center rather than the peripheries of German society is a central element in Hauck's life history. Indeed, for Hauck, marginalization involved neither being relegated to the margins of society nor being expelled from it. Contrary to the image of the marginalized passive victim of Nazi racial politics that pervades many accounts of Afro-German history during this period, Hauck's memory narrative shows a more complex positioning in which his status as a subject was constructed in relation to simultaneous processes of inclusion and exclusion, recognition and misrecognition, belonging and not belonging. The process of positioning exemplified both by Hauck's involvement in the HJ and by the narrative strategies of memory and storytelling he uses to render them are central elements of the Afro-German experience in the Third Reich to which I refer as "Other within." I use this term to articulate the paradox of being internal to and to some extent an acknowledged member of this society yet also thoroughly marginalized by and within it.

The notion of the Other within which I have developed in relation to the accounts of my Afro-German interview partners stands in direct contrast to Patricia Hill Collins's notion of an "outsider within." Collins's formulation relates to the contradictory social positioning of African-American women in the United States. She asserts that, on the one hand, through their role in the political economy (in particular, their ghettoization in domestic work), African-American women have a unique insider perspective on the dominant group and thereby the opportunity to see white power demystified. On the other hand, they can never belong to this group and thus remain outsiders. The result is an outsider within status in which Black women have "a distinct view of the contradictions between the dominant group's actions and ideologies."[6]

The difference between our two concepts hinges on the role of a Black community among African-Americans versus the lack of any such community for my Afro-German interview partners. Implicit in Collins's notion of Black women's positioning in American society is a conception of a discrete separation between inside and outside that presumes the existence of two distinct racial communities, Black and white. Beyond the fact that such a description of the experience of Blacks in the United States is rather simplistic and, as such, severely limited, this conception of inside and outside is quite problematic (if not untenable) with regard to Hauck's experiences as well as those of much of the Afro-German community. For although Hauck experienced marginalization and discrimination and thus was made to feel like an outsider, as with the issue of assimilation, there exists no real outside for Hauck—either actual or imagined—because once again, there is no alternative community to which he can return.

Michelle Maria Wright offers a compelling alternative conception of the Other within in the Afro-German context. Focusing on a very different object of analysis than my own, Wright engages the counter-discourse of the Black German subject constructed in the work of contemporary Afro-German writers. In her analysis of the poetry of May Ayim, Wright reads the Black German subject as paradoxically both an "Other-from-Within" and an "Other-from-Without," or as she terms this in the title of her essay, "Others-from-Within from Without."

Whereas African Americans function in white American racist discourse as the Other-from-Within (i.e., they are recognized as having been born and raised in the U.S., even if racists believe they do not belong there), white Germans insistently and consistently misrecognize Afro-Germans as *Africans,* or Others-from-Without, even though they obviously share the same language and culture. In other words, unlike African Americans, Afro-Germans must confront a racist discourse directed at Africans, rather than Afro-Germans. Technically speaking, there is no such thing as an *anti-Afro-German* discourse, only an *anti-African* discourse, raising the question of how one, as an Other-from-Within, should respond to a discourse that posits one as an Other-from-Within, should respond to a discourse that posits one as an Other-from-Without.[7]

Although I agree with the paradox that Wright highlights in this passage, the differences in our respective uses of the trope of the Other within as a model for analyzing Black German subject formation can be attributed to the very different historical contexts in which our respective Black German subjects are situated. In the case of the Black German children of the Rhineland occupation, this population was construed as a threat to the German national body politic not on the basis of a conception of them as external to the nation (although the stereotypes on which this construction was based were drawn from an exteriorized colonial imaginary); rather, the threat they were seen to pose was the potential to pollute the national body from within (in other words, the threat of "invisible blackness"). This was particularly the case in the NS racial state, where the sterilization of Black German children was a direct attempt to interrupt what was portrayed as the insidious interiority of the Black in the German national body by means of a scientific solution that terminated the reproductive capacity of a population assumed to exist as an internal national pollutant.

Wright's insightful points notwithstanding, in the context of the Third Reich the concept of the Other within remains a useful interpretative model for explaining the seemingly contradictory configurations of memory that comprise Hauck's narrative and the complex positions he occupied in the Nazi regime. This concept illustrates how, although "marked" by race as an exception to his society's norms and made to feel this difference through discrimination, he nevertheless also was well integrated into this society as a German. Hauck's membership in the Hitler Youth is a striking example of this fact.

"BEING A MAN/PLAYING SOLDIER"—THE HITLER YOUTH UNIFORM AS SOCIALIZATION, (DIS)GUISE, OR SURVIVAL

Despite the explanatory potential of the concept of the Other within for interpreting his life history, Hauck's membership in the Hitler Youth provokes a number of questions about the specific nature of his involvement in this organization. From its inception, the Hitler Youth was intended as the primary socializing sphere or educational force for the youth of the Third Reich. Its central task was that of racial indoctrination, or, in Hitler's words, instilling "both a rational and instinctive sense of race in the hearts and minds of the youth entrusted to it."[8]

Thus, the Hitler Youth explicitly sought to produce specific forms of racialized subjectivity among its members that were consistent with the aims of racial purity and productivity at the core of the NS regime. In this way the HJ was intended as an institution concerned primarily with the production of legitimate racial subjects.

The stark contrast between the intended function of the Hitler Youth and Hauck's account of his participation in it as a non-Aryan of African descent begs the question as to what function the Hitler Youth served for him and whether the socializing role of this NS institution had its intended effect. Perhaps more significantly, how did this process function when the object of this process was not its intended object? Hauck's comments beg the question of whether and to what extent his difference from other "Aryan-German" Hitler Youth was "visible" or apparent to him or others at the time. As we will see, the "*un*-remarkableness" or self-evidence that characterizes his account of this period of his life reflects in interesting ways his understanding of the nature of his social interactions at the time and as such, offers one indication of how Hauck engaged and negotiated the processes of racialization and gendering that played out in this regime. In a later passage in the interview, Hauck addresses some of these questions and the issue of his complicated position in German society when he comments more extensively on his experiences in the Hitler Youth.

EXCERPT B

TC: How long were you in the Hitler Youth?

HH: At thirteen, fourteen, and fifteen years old. And after that, I always had the right to wear the uniform. You can't forget that I worked for the railroad. And I can thank him for that, the SS officer I mentioned earlier. . . .

TC: And what exactly did he do for you?

HH: I was never denounced. Even when I was no longer in the Hitler Youth. No one even asked after that. No one pressed me anymore, and that was worth a lot.

TC: Compared to the time before you were in the Hitler Youth?

HH: Compared to others, to German boys who couldn't get away with that.

TC: And during this time, did you try to understand for yourself what the difference was, being inside of these organizations, in the Hitler Youth or the Wehrmacht, as you say, "being accepted," as opposed to had you not been in them, having had "problems"?

HH: Of course after my sterilization, it was clear that it was over for me with the Hitler Youth, with the whole spirit of it, which I more or less understood at fifteen or sixteen, in contrast to the thirteen-year-old.

TC: I don't quite understand what you mean.

HH: In contrast to the thirteen-year-old who enjoyed the whole Hitler Youth game, the fifteen-year-old didn't anymore. He was able to think more about it, but he had to go along.

TC: "Had to"?

HH: Well, what should I have done? No one forced me. But the circumstances forced me. I had to. I was an apprentice with the railroad. Without being in the Hitler Youth, I wouldn't have been allowed to do that. We appeared at all sorts of different occasions in uniform, in Hitler Youth uniform.

TC: Did that make a difference in how you were treated? When you wore this uniform?

HH: Yes. No one saw anymore that I didn't really belong.

TC: No one?

HH: No, no one. And those who did know said nothing. It wasn't at all like that. There were many who knew. [But] as far as I can remember it never caused me any problems.

TC: With the uniform?

HH: With the uniform.[9]

Here, Hauck recalls an important dimension of his involvement in the HJ to which he had also referred earlier in our interview, the issue of "play." In this passage, play (the "Hitler Youth game") involves taking on a military guise—in this case, playing soldier. His description of his experience in the Hitler Youth focuses primarily on the aspect of appearance through the element of disguise. In this passage, Hauck recalls how, in the Hitler Youth, "play" on military appearance (the uniform) functioned in his case as a disguise ("No one saw anymore that I didn't really belong [*(Es) hat ja niemand mir angesehen, daß ich eigentlich gar nicht dazugehörte*]"). The uniform simultaneously marked him as German and masked his difference from other Germans. As a form of disguise, the uniform seems not only to have masked his difference but also to have supplanted it with masculinity. In this way, Hauck's participation in the Hitler Youth can be seen less as a question of socialization than as a process of subject formation through a curious form of camouflage. Indeed, according to Hauck, his membership in the Hitler Youth was in many ways responsible for the silent acceptance he encountered in his social interactions, most often in relation to his uniform. As he describes it, the uniform silenced opposition and doubt through its symbolic presentation of belonging to the NS regime (and indirectly Germanness) and in this way provided not only a form of privilege but also a means of protection. Moreover, the uniform may even have offset Hauck's racial Otherness with an alternate form of belonging or identification that strengthened a different aspect of his identity, his masculinity. This, of course, would later be symbolically robbed of him through sterilization, when Hauck's body became the racialized object of both scientific and political intervention. In Hauck's life history, sterilization can be seen as a form of emasculation that occurred during puberty, almost simultaneously with the end of his involvement in the HJ.

As this reading of Hauck's memory narrative demonstrates, Hauck's association of his forced sterilization with his membership in the HJ not only underscores the gendering function of the HJ but also indirectly makes that of his sterilization more apparent. Reading these two sets of memories in relation to one another foregrounds the fact that both had a substantial gendering impact on his status as a German subject. If, on the one hand, the Hitler Youth represents a masculine ideal via the uniform and "play" on military disguise, sterilization, on the other hand, has equally significant implications for gender in a negative sense, representing an extreme form of emasculation and a direct attack on male sexual and procreative potential. Sterilization was not only an antinatalist strategy of racial hygiene intended to accomplish racial purity by preventing the procreation of and racial mixture with "inferior races" but also an explicit attempt at emasculation—in this case, of Black German sexuality and the desexualization of this threat to the purity of the Aryan race. The tension that arises from the counterpositioning of these two events in Hauck's narrative can in this way also be seen as the gendered tension of masculinity versus emasculation. Hauck's reference to the Hitler Youth when asked about his sterilization indirectly compensates for his symbolic emasculation through reference to a form of adolescent masculinity, membership in the HJ.

The Hitler Youth uniform is the central point of reference in Hauck's memory of the Hitler Youth and its function in his life. The uniform was a symbol not only of membership but also of belonging in general, expressing a relation to this institution that went beyond official ties. Specifically, the HJ uniform established a relation of "belonging to" by way of appearance. "Belonging to" is perhaps more appropriate than simply belonging in this case, for it goes beyond a subjective feeling of inclusion in that belonging is materially expressed by the institution or group of which he is a part. Hauck's "belonging to" the HJ and by implication, the NS regime, is both confirmed and documented through the uniform, an external form of marking that signifies his affiliation to these institutions and its members. His emphasis on the HJ uniform affirms this fact and underlines the importance of the visible signification of his belonging to this group. The uniform not only confirms this internal tie but also offsets the visible markings of race (deracing him and effectively erasing race). Indeed, for Afro-Germans in the Third Reich, the markings of race implicitly signified precisely the opposite: not belonging, or otherness.

Ironically, in his account of his experiences in the Hitler Youth, Hauck narrates that which was most visible about him—his skin color—through that which mitigated this visibility at the time—the uniform. Yet what is particularly noteworthy about Hauck's narrative is how his memories of these experiences background race and gender in ways that indirectly make their effects more visible almost by virtue of their absence. Similarly, Hauck's memory narrative presents an interesting mapping of the social topography of race and gender in the Third Reich—one in which some of the details that shaped social interactions most profoundly (like race and gender) are also remembered in ways that make them seem differentially visible or totally unremarkable, while this visibility or invisibility makes their negotiation much more profoundly present.

Sociologist Karen Fields provides a useful vocabulary for understanding such indirect modes of articulating the differential visibility of racial and gendered social relations reflected in individual narratives of memory. In her analysis of the oral account of her grandmother,

Mamie Garvin Fields, Fields introduces the term "inward invisible topography" to describe how complex processes of racialization are recorded, internalized, and articulated in and through individual accounts of memory. Fields uses this concept to explain and account for how her grandmother represents the subtle intricacies of Southern racial order in her recollections of local social interactions during her youth in Charleston, South Carolina. Fields explains:

> Such features are often not the main subject of the story, from Gram's point of view. . . . These did not command Gram's front-burner attention as they do mine. They are there in the way Mt. Kilimanjaro is there in Africa. For many intents and purposes, it is *merely* there . . . it is hardly to be missed yet hardly to be noticed, at once native and alien to the life around it. Tourists are the ones who preoccupy themselves with looking at it. I am saying this to give warning that, as Gram's interlocutor, I was a tourist to her life with a tourist's habit of gawking. . . . The Kilimanjaro I gaze at . . . often comes into view in the form of unintended or unintendable memory. The inner horizon of the South's racial order is not the aspect we generally tend to think of first. It is easier to think of the South's Jim Crow regime in its outward and visible signs—its laws, its segregated spaces, its economic arrangements, its intermittent physical atrocities. . . . But one learns through the testimony of inhabitants that it can at the same time be mapped out as an inward and invisible topography. It has objects analogous to mountains, rivers, and the like, which must be climbed, crossed, circumambulated, avoided, or otherwise taken into account. At the same time that these are not visible to the naked eye, and not immediately obvious to aliens on the scene, to insiders, much of the time, they are not specifically noteworthy. They remain, in the phrase of Harold Garfinkle, "seen but unnoticed" features of social life. As such they enter human memory. They often emerge in oral testimony as unintended memory. In actual life they emerge above all as social order.[10]

In his memory narrative, Hauck articulates the "seen, but unnoticed" dimensions of his racial and gender formation through the subtle *lack* of emphasis he initially places on his membership in the Hitler Youth. What his narrative highlights is less his membership than the seemingly insignificant detail of the uniform. The Hitler Youth was part of Hauck's life in Nazi Germany that he seems almost to have taken for granted as a normal part of the childhood of a German boy of his generation. It is a naturalized part of his social landscape—one that he narrates as an almost unremarkable detail in his memory. To use Fields's terminology, as part of the familiar topography of his everyday life in the Third Reich, he navigates it blindly; its unremark- ability rendering it essentially invisible. It is I, his interlocutor, who stumble upon it as a huge obstacle in the landscape of his life that can- not be overlooked. In response, Hauck explains that through the uni- form, the Hitler Youth was in fact not only remarkable but instrumen- tal in his survival within this regime. Hauck's subtle narration of these memories offers one example of a kind of backgrounding or minimiz- ing of race and gender that characterizes his narrative. Yet his articula- tion of the significance of these events in his life through side comments on such details illustrates one of the ways in which processes of race and gender come to matter and materialize, and thus produce individual subjects socially. However, while these processes come to produce indi- viduals as raced and gendered subjects, they also necessarily and simul- taneously produce modes of navigating these differentially visible and invisible social topographies. For what Hauck also recounts are the ways that his production as a Black German subject within this regime paradoxically worked against the grain and to his advantage. In fact, Hauck's account of his experiences in the Hitler Youth suggests that this organization did not necessarily serve the function intended for it by the Nazis as one of its primary socializing institutions, designed to instill a sense of racial pride and superiority in German youth as the future of the so-called Aryan race. On the contrary, through the uni- form and his ability to "play" an Aryan German Hitler Youth, Hauck was able to lay claim to a form of legitimate subjecthood as a German— one to which he would otherwise not have had access.

Hauck's emphasis on the significance of the uniform makes clear the extent to which the Hitler Youth did indeed function to construct him as a particular type of German subject—one visibly associated, allied, and identified with the Nazi regime. One significant reference to this in excerpt B occurs when Hauck links his memories of the HJ uniform to the element of "military play"—specifically, military presentation ("We appeared at all sorts of different occasions in uniform, in Hitler Youth uniform"). The military presentation of the Hitler Youth and the legitimacy of its affiliation with the NS regime, symbolically represented by the uniform, enabled Hauck to gain access to other forms of acceptance or respectability in German society—in his case, access to professional training.[11] But again, the HJ uniform symbolized a legitimacy and acceptance that were not only National Socialist but more specifically a privileged form of masculinity. In this way, the uniform and his membership in the Hitler Youth gender Hauck as they engender in him a sense of belonging as a German, at the same time marking this Germanness as masculine.

Hauck's account of his memories of the Hitler Youth reveals that the organization functioned not only to produce legitimately indoctrinated racial subjects but also that these subjects were necessarily gendered. As a central institution for the production of legitimate forms of German masculinity among youth, the HJ served a gendering function as a masculine point of identification that in some ways counterbalanced the rejection Hauck experienced on the basis of his ethnic heritage. His memory narrative reveals that, at least initially, the Hitler Youth produced him as a subject recognized as German and male yet did so in ways that occluded the fact that he was also of "illegitimate" racial heritage and had been "branded" as such through sterilization. In this way, Hauck's narrative shows us how racialization is a process that necessarily begins with bodies and the assumed meaning of their substance as such but is also a process of constituting meanings for those bodies that often has little to do with their physical attributes. The function of the uniform in Hauck's narrative is key to understanding this process.

Recognizing the significance of such a "little" detail like the uniform in Hauck's story is the key to understanding this process. Similarly, engaging the status and function of what Hauck describes as play allows us to see how it reflects the simultaneity and mutual constitution of processes of gendering and racialization in his life. In Hauck's narrative, play enacted a form of masking that effectively "deraced" Hauck's blackness in ways that seem superficially to have mitigated some of the effects of race for him in this regime. At the same time, it also indirectly raced Hauck as a German subject through its gendering of him as a masculine Aryan male. The masculinity ascribed to him through the military presentation of the uniform was necessarily and simultaneously a form of masculinity achieved through his ability to play an Aryan-German Hitler Youth. Indeed, for German males in the Third Reich, masculinity was constitutive of Aryanness, and Aryanness was attainable only through privileged forms of masculinity such as the military.

The masking of racial difference that Hauck describes in his account of his experiences in the HJ also mirrors a kind of discursive masking effected through his seemingly unreflective association between the two sets of memories. In his narrative, this takes the form of a rapid and almost too easy shift from the topic of his sterilization to what ironically seems the less volatile issue of his participation in the HJ. But this masking in no way accomplishes an erasure or complete silencing of this more deeply embedded story. Hauck does indeed tell the story of the effects of his sterilization—the gendered effects of an attempted racial emasculation. Yet he tells this story indirectly and between the lines. Hauck's comments on the gendering effects of the uniform and the HJ directly expose those of his sterilization.

Hauck's sterilization is the loud silence in his narrative, present both chronologically, as it occurs in the midst of his tenure in the HJ, and discursively, as the implicit reference that frames and introduces the story of the HJ. Hauck's cryptic allusion to his sterilization when intimating that this action initiated an inarticulable shift in his relation to the HJ marks the sterilization as a very visible gap, an event whose effects are undeniable yet are never explicitly described in the interview. In fact, Hauck mentions the sterilization only once in detail, and then only in the form of a sequential recounting of the events leading up to his sterilization. This silence is in no way an absence but is rather a presence representable only indirectly through the telling of this other related story. This tension vividly recalls Jean-François Lyotard's conception of silence as a sign of "something that remains to be phrased which is not, something which is not determined."[12] This tension is at the same time inherent to the process of memory and storytelling, where the telling of one story always involves the masking—though not erasure—of another.

Although he makes no direct statement to this effect, the end of Hauck's "active" participation in the Hitler Youth at age fifteen seems chronologically to have coincided with his sterilization. Hauck comments indirectly on the connection between these two incidents in his somewhat cryptic remarks in excerpt B—in particular, the statement that, "In contrast to the thirteen-year-old who enjoyed the whole Hitler Youth game, the fifteen-year-old didn't anymore. He was able to think more about it, but he had to go along."

Hauck's statements in this passage express a change in his perception of the Hitler Youth and perhaps in the implications of National Socialism in his life more generally. Although the element of military play in the Hitler Youth functioned to Hauck's advantage as a form of disguise prior to his sterilization, it appears that up until this point he was not necessarily conscious of this fact. At age thirteen, Hauck probably did not originally regard joining the Hitler Youth as a strategic move. It is important to underline the fact that Hauck was compulsorily sterilized between the ages of fifteen and sixteen (at a time when he was at the peak of puberty and in full consciousness of his sexuality), whereas his experiences in the Hitler Youth preceded this, occurring at the beginning of puberty. That Hauck suffered such a violation of his sexuality at this important stage in his psychosexual development must necessarily have affected his recollections of this experience and explains in part the distinction he makes between the impressions of a thirteen-year-old and a fifteen-year-old. Thus, Hauck's sterilization can be seen to have initiated a process of retrospective reinterpretation of this experience as well as a reevaluation of the strategic value of his membership in the Hitler Youth. At this point, the play = appearance = disguise equation became a conscious strategy for Hauck. He describes this in his subsequent statements, in which play in the Hitler Youth is rearticulated as strategy and consequently takes on the aspect of survival: "Well, what should I have done? No one forced me. But the circumstances forced me. I had to. I was an apprentice with the railroad. Without being in the Hitler Youth, I wouldn't have been allowed to do that."

In excerpts A and B, the strategic value of Hauck's membership in the Hitler Youth is primarily that of protection by means of disguise. The protective function of the Hitler Youth in Hauck's life is closely linked to and supplemented by his embeddedness in a supportive local community. As we shall see in the next section, these two elements also play a central role in the events of his later life.

As my reading of these excerpts from Hauck's memory narrative shows, it is important to be as attentive to the forms of meaning and articulation displaced in and through silence as it is to engage the content of more direct utterances and articulations. The silences in Hauck's narrative offer compelling expressions of the effects of race and gender in his life. Hauck's account urges us to think of race and gender as complicated processes of differentiation where neither race nor gender is something that people either are or have but is that which they acquire to be socially recognizable or intelligible to others. None of my interview partners were either "Black" (that is, raced) or gendered prior to their social interactions in a public sphere that made it necessary for others to discern a place for these individuals in society. Both race and gender were attributed to them, but because the category of "Black German" was more or less unthinkable, the concrete way in which this category was lived in relation to the racial politics of the Third Reich was highly paradoxical.

The Hitler Youth served a different function for Hauck than the Nazis intended. Beyond and in addition to its role as an institution intended to produce legitimate German subjects for the Nazi regime, the Hitler Youth provided Hauck with a chance for survival and, paradoxically, an opportunity to elude Nazi scrutiny at least temporarily. Through the uniform, Hauck came to benefit from the privileges of being identified as a legitimate German subject. At the same time, the military dimension of the Hitler Youth strengthened the gendering function of the HJ, thus fulfilling its original objective as a primary instrument of Nazi German subject formation. In fact, military institutions can be seen to have served a gendering function more generally in Hauck's life history that continued, if not intensified, later in his life. Masculinity was subsequently symbolically restored to him through his membership in another military institution that also affirmed in him a sense of belonging in ways that again ran completely counter to Nazi racial ideology and that compel us view this regime in even more complex terms.

Hauck was inducted into the German Wehrmacht in 1942. He served three years of active duty on the Russian front until being interned as a prisoner of war in the Soviet Union from 1945 to 1949. The experiences that Hauck describes in the interview (membership in the Hitler Youth, sterilization, military service in the Wehrmacht, and internment by the Soviet army) complicate and provocatively challenge a perception of Afro-German children of the Rhineland occupation as thoroughly marginalized in German society. We will engage these issues more directly in the final sections of this chapter.

THE GERMAN WEHRMACHT:
THE MILITARY AS A "CHANCE"

Before proceeding to a more extensive discussion of the implications of race, military institutions, and processes of gendering, it is helpful to begin this section with a summary of the chronology of Hauck's life discussed thus far in this section. Hauck voluntarily joined the Hitler Youth at the age of thirteen and was a member of this organization for approximately two years (1933–35). In 1935, at the age of fifteen, he began his training as an apprentice with the railroad. Between the ages of fifteen and sixteen Hauck was compulsorily sterilized by the Nazis.[13] A gap exists in Hauck's narrative of his life between the ages of sixteen and nineteen, a time about which he provides no information. Hauck then refers to events that occurred between 1939 and 1942, when he was inducted into the German Wehrmacht. He served three years of active duty on the Russian front until being interned as a prisoner of war in the Soviet Union from 1945 to 1949. However, his induction into the army was far from a seamless process.

EXCERPT C

Perhaps I've been more desperate than others in desperate situations. I was once. I attempted suicide. . . . I shot myself, and my friend's father came to my rescue. Later, I was in the hospital, and it was covered up by a police officer. . . . I was twenty-one. They wanted to take me to premilitary training, and I was always afraid of that. The premilitary training was conducted by the SA. I never had anything to do with them. *Here, in the Hitler Youth, everyone knew me.* No one would have — I can't put it any other way, would have wanted to do me any harm. Some even good. But there, where we were evacuated to during the war, no one could guarantee anything. Saarbrücken was empty because of the war. . . . The border was three kilometers away, and the French artillery was shooting in here. There was no one here. And our department of the railroad was moved into central Germany . . . to different places. I myself was with a few other colleagues in Paderborn and afterwards in Schneidemuhl and then in Opladen. And in Opladen I attempted suicide, because I couldn't get away from it any more, from the notices to report to premilitary training with the SA. And I didn't want to go there under any circumstances. That would have led to complications that I was afraid of. . . . Proof of Aryan ancestry and that whole mess. *They didn't know me there.* And I couldn't possibly prove Aryan ancestry— where would I get that from? . . . Here I was supported. I already said before that I had people here who helped me. . . . *Out there, no one knew me.* And there's no doubt that there I was really up against something. I wanted to avoid that. Because at the time we were already at war with Russia and you could already tell that they were going to call us up as soldiers. In the meantime there were already lots and lots who had become soldiers who didn't have to become soldiers before. And that's how it was with me too. I was asked if I wanted to become a soldier. I said yes. I now had a chance, the normal—I explained it before—the normal chance, 50–50. Either I make it through or not. And I made it.[14]

Hauck entered the army in 1942, following a failed suicide attempt at age twenty-one that occurred out of desperation regarding being drafted into the army. After being evacuated from the Saarland, Hauck was ordered to appear for premilitary training. He recalls that at the time, premilitary training (*vormilitärische Ausbildung*) was conducted by the SA, adding, "I had nothing to do with them [*Mit der hatte ich nie was zu tun*]." Here, the local—in the form of local community ties—plays a central role in his memories of this period, to which he refers on three occasions in this excerpt (see statements highlighted in excerpt C). Unlike in the story of his experience in the Hitler Youth, the important detail in his story of his induction into the army is his description of space—specifically, the way in which Hauck narrates his memories of his interactions in different locations. Hauck tells the story of how he came to be accepted into the army, yet he tells this story through the local spaces of community that made it possible for him to do so without incurring substantial harm to himself.

Local space plays a critical role in Hauck's memories of his life in this period, and he refers to these spaces on three occasions in the passage. In the first instance, Hauck contrasts the SA with the Hitler Youth. After being evacuated from the Saarland, Hauck was ordered to appear for premilitary training. He recalls that premilitary training was conducted by the SA and emphasizes that he "had nothing to do with them." In his memory, the SA represents the threatening unknown, while, ironically, the HJ is portrayed as familiar and protective. The HJ, on the one hand, is presented as part of Hauck's small-town milieu, taking on the related attributes of support, community, and perhaps even "home." On the other hand, the SA is set in the context of Hauck's evacuation from the Saarland—that is, his displacement to a "foreign" environment outside the boundaries of his community and beyond the reach of familiarity. In these sequences of his narrative, the Hitler Youth continues to be remembered as serving a protective function in Hauck's life. Again, this function is embedded in the broader context of the local as community and personal ties.

The second instance where Hauck mentions the importance of the local as a protective space occurs in relation to his Black heritage. Here, he implies that proof of Aryan heritage would not have been an issue in his local community, which played a crucial role in his life as a protective buffer. Following his evacuation, however, Hauck refers to himself as being "out there," in the realm beyond the boundaries of his local community, remembering this space as his greatest threat. These comments provide Hauck's third reference to the importance of the local: "Here I was supported. I already said before that I had people here who helped me. . . . Out there, no one knew me. And there's no doubt that there I was really up against something. I wanted to avoid that."

Although the protective buffers in Hauck's life did not always protect him from harm (as his sterilization and failed suicide attempt indicate), in many cases these buffers were instrumental in providing important alternatives for him in disadvantageous situations. That the father of Hauck's friend from the Hitler Youth intervenes in his suicide attempt dramatically illustrates this point. Hauck explains at length later in the interview that the friend's father was the former leader of Hauck's Hitler Youth group. He rescued Hauck by arranging his induction without the need for proof of Aryan heritage—a relatively easy task at this point because of the army's need for manpower at this point in the war. Hauck's memory narrative demonstrates that although in the Third Reich race and racial difference served as the state's mode of defining membership in the larger German collective, this was contested in important ways at local levels of society, where community ties often functioned in oppositional ways to create and enable the recognition and inclusion of subjects deemed unworthy of membership in other social contexts.

Returning to excerpt C, the fear of the conscription process that Hauck describes in his memory narrative can be attributed to one primary factor, *Fremdsein* (Otherness)—specifically, the situation of finding himself outside of his home community. Surprisingly, this was not the first time that Hauck had been called up for military duty.

EXCERPT D

HH: I was conscripted at nineteen, like everyone else.

TC: Conscripted? What is conscripted?

HH: Conscripted. That means for the army, drafted into the army. It's called conscription.

TC: That was at nineteen. That was two years after you were sterilized?

HH: That was two years, yeah, after I was. . . . I wasn't quite seventeen, I was sixteen when I was sterilized. And at conscription, 1939—it's called conscription into military service—I was unworthy for service.

TC: "Unworthy"?

HH: Yes. I was allowed to work, but back then I wasn't allowed to become a soldier. Only in the course of the war, in 1941 they got looser. And in 1942, I was called up with my own permission. It depended, I could have then said, "You didn't want me, and now I don't want you." But then I wouldn't be sitting here today. It's that simple. We've got examples of that.

TC: But back then you had to do it, you had to join the Wehrmacht. Or?

HH: Yes, maybe I could have refused. But then I wouldn't be able to talk about it now. I know about one such case. A

mate that I was sterilized with, he never came back. He got
sent to a camp. And I went because I saw it as a chance. It
was the first time that I was treated the same as others.
Because the other "Aryan" German boys, my mates, my
schoolmates, they were called up, too. And I wanted that,
and then I was called up. And then I was quite conscious of
my fate, that I had a chance, 50–50. Either I survive it, or I
don't. And I survived.[15]

Hauck explains that he underwent his first military review at the age
of nineteen, sometime around 1939. Hauck presents this fact with a
similar sense of self-evidence as that with which he describes his membership in the HJ, remarking once again that he was reviewed for military service "like everyone else [*wie alle anderen auch*]." This is yet
another example of the narrative strategy of relativization discussed
earlier. With this phrase, Hauck again emphasizes his perception of
himself as representative of the norm in this period. Yet the norm in
relation to which Hauck seems pressed to identify is a gendered and
racialized one—the masculine, racially pure norm of military induction,
to which he refers in excerpt C, is established by the young Aryan-German men who met the requirements of racial purity that defined their
status as legitimate representatives of the Nazi state. Again, Hauck
emphasizes normality and integration through masculinity and the
institution of the military. His emphasis on his own typicality again
seems to minimize or relativize the exceptional dimensions of his situation—that it was in fact quite unusual that a non-Aryan who only a
few years before had been compulsorily sterilized by the Nazis was not
only called up for duty in the Wehrmacht but also eventually accepted
for service.[16]

Hauck's memories of his induction portray it as a relatively uncom-
plicated process over which he exercised a certain amount of control,
yet he qualifies this impression by explaining that although he consented to join the Wehrmacht, this was in no way a question of free
choice. Instead, joining the Wehrmacht was a matter of compulsion
and/or survival. In many ways, the Wehrmacht played a role in
Hauck's life similar to that of the Hitler Youth. In the preceding passage, Hauck describes the Wehrmacht as a "chance" in two respects:
first, it offered 50–50 odds of surviving the war, and second, it offered

a chance to be treated as an equal to Aryan Germans. It is significant that he saw another military institution as presenting this chance, for in his memory narrative Hauck presents his experience in the Wehrmacht as the first time that he was treated as an equal, not only to the Aryan soldiers but also in the more general context of Nazi Germany, through the privileged status ascribed to soldiers as protectors of the Fatherland. Contrary to his statements, however, the Hitler Youth appears in fact to have been Hauck's first experience with equal status. The treatment he received as a soldier and as a member of the Hitler Youth can be attributed largely to the role of the military uniform in each of these organizations. Hauck's Wehrmacht uniform can be seen to have functioned as *Verkleidung* (a disguise) in the same way that the Hitler Youth uniform did in his adolescence. The structures and the uniform of the Wehrmacht would probably have functioned in a similar way.

Furthermore, in Hauck's narrative, equal status is represented not simply as equal status as a German but specifically as equal status as a German male. In excerpt D, for example, he states, "It was the first time that I was treated the same as others. Because the other 'Aryan' German boys, my mates, my schoolmates, they were called up, too. And I wanted that [*Das war das erste Mal, wo ich mit anderen gleich gesetzt wurde. Denn die anderen 'arischen' deutschen Jungen, meine Kameraden, meine Schulkameraden, die wurden auch eingezogen. Und das wollte ich*]." Hauck's comments illustrate how the gendering function of military institutions through the vehicle of masculinized masquerade/disguise (the uniform) gave him access to a form of German subjecthood that had previously been denied to him. Hauck's membership in the German *Männerbund* of the Wehrmacht can be seen to have compensated symbolically for that which Hauck lost sexually through sterilization. As with the Hitler Youth, masculine gender identification (male German subjecthood) at least temporarily supplanted or displaced ethnic heritage and racial difference.

What becomes increasingly apparent in Hauck's memory narrative is that his status as a German subject and the elements central to it— his sense of belonging and parity with other Germans—are most clearly articulated in relation to his experiences in military settings. The gendering function of both the Wehrmacht and the Hitler Youth played a crucial role in defining the military as a site for the articulation of Hauck's German subjecthood. Military organizations appear in Hauck's memory narrative as environments in which he was either able or forced to reflect more critically on his status as a German, which, in turn, seems to evoke clearer and more complex formulations of his conception of his German identity. This is true not only with respect to his experience in the Wehrmacht and the Hitler Youth but also in a third military episode in Hauck's biography, his experience as a prisoner of war in the Soviet Union.

LIFE AS A SOLDIER: "GERMANNESS," BELONGING, AND MILITARY SETTINGS

EXCERPT E

HH: I was drafted and became a soldier, and in 1945, I was taken prisoner. I was wounded five times. I was home twice, on leave and when I was wounded. And in '45, in January, I was taken prisoner by the Russians.

TC: How long were you a prisoner?

HH: Until 23 April 1949. . . . I can't really describe what it was like being a prisoner. Imprisonment isn't easy—everyone knew that — But I was treated more humanely by the Russians than I ever was by my own countrymen. .

TC: In what way?

HH: In what way? Because no one made a big deal about my heritage there.

TC: And the other German soldiers, did they notice this? That you were treated differently?

HH: I wasn't treated differently.

TC: Just more humanely?

HH: I was treated just like the other Germans. Just they didn't make any distinctions. My own Fatherland didn't do that. It discriminated against me. Only as a soldier did it treat me as an equal.

TC: And did you have the feeling during your time as a soldier that you were really accepted?

HH: In the army, you didn't notice any difference.

TC: In spite of your —

HH: I made private first class after the first five months—that
    means I was promoted. You didn't notice any discrimina-
    tion in the army. There were many army officers who didn't
    agree with the system and didn't say anything. But you
    noticed that. In the army they didn't discriminate against
    me.[17]

Hans was taken prisoner by the Soviet army in January 1945 while
in Polish territory, just south of Warsaw. He was interned for just over
four years in a Soviet prison camp in or near Minsk until his release in
April 1949. In his narrative, Hauck comments, "I can't really describe
what it was like being in prison. Imprisonment isn't easy—everyone
knew that." But this silence in his testimony is again not one of absence
but selective presence. At precisely the moment when Hauck emphasizes that he cannot describe his experience of internment, he in fact
begins to tell a different story of this same experience. As in his narration of his sterilization, Hauck shifts the topic slightly, focusing instead
on his perception of having been treated better by his Russian captors
than by his German comrades. When asked to explain this statement,
he replies that unlike the Germans, the Russians did not make an issue
of his Black heritage. In the exchange that follows, I misinterpret two
remarks, "I was treated more humanely by the Russians than I ever
was by my own countrymen [*Ich bin von den Russen mehr als Mensch
behandelt worden, als wie vorher von meinen eigenen Landsleuten*]" and
"Because no one made a big deal about my heritage there [*Weil dort
wegen meiner Herkunft niemand ein Trara gemacht hat*]," to mean that
Hauck received special treatment from the Russians and hence ask,
"And the other German soldiers, did they notice this? That you were
treated differently? [*Und die anderen deutschen Soldaten, haben sie das
auch mitgekriegt? Daß du anders behandelt wurdest?*]" Hauck corrects
my misinterpretation of his statements by clarifying that he did not
receive special treatment. Yet the events of Hauck's internment are left
unsaid. However, Hauck's description of this related experience outlines what was inarticulable, allowing it to speak through its salience
for his identification as a German. What Hauck found remarkable
about the treatment he received from the Russians was that they made
no distinction between him and the other German prisoners, effectively
giving Hauck equal status by acknowledging him as a legitimate Ger-

man subject: "I was treated just like the other Germans. Just they didn't make any distinctions. My own Fatherland didn't do that. It discriminated against me. Only as a soldier did it treat me as an equal."

In the comparison that Hauck makes in this sequence, it is significant not only that he differentiates between his treatment by the Russians and Germans but also that he distinguishes between how he remembers being treated as a civilian by his "Fatherland" and how this treatment changed when he became a soldier. In German society (*das Vaterland*), Hauck recalls being discriminated against (*benachteiligt*), whereas in the Wehrmacht (*als Soldat*), he was treated equally (*gleich behandelt*). Hauck emphasizes the equal status and treatment that he enjoyed as a member of the Wehrmacht no fewer than three times in this excerpt.

Equal status provides one possible answer to the question of why Hauck articulates Germanness in relation to military contexts. Military settings were sites where Hauck enjoyed unquestioned status as a legitimate German subject. This is certainly one effect of the military as an institution in which processes of group identification play a significant role. At the same time, these particular military contexts were more than symbolically representative of Germanness: the Hitler Youth and the Wehrmacht were institutions that not only personified Aryan masculinity but also were intended to produce privileged forms of male subjectivity. In all the military settings in which he found himself, Hauck's status as a German was reinforced by the fact that he enjoyed this status as a member of a group of men (or boys) in uniform. In this way, the play in which Hauck participated, not only in the HJ but also in the Wehrmacht, must also be read as the pleasure of playing an Aryan man or, in another formulation, playing masculinity as a soldier. Yet the central paradox of Hauck's participation in both the Hitler Youth and the Wehrmacht is that the specific form of German subjecthood (the pure Aryan male) produced, constructed, and conveyed through these institutions should have excluded Hauck as a person of African heritage. Like the Hitler Youth, the Wehrmacht may have also served its intended role of subject formation (that is, producing legitimate and recognized forms of subjectivity) in spite of the fact that the object of this process was not its intended recipient.

When Hauck distinguishes his treatment in German society from that of the military, he identifies the army as the vehicle of change:

"Only as a soldier did it treat me as an equal [*Erst als Soldat hat es mich gleich behandelt*]." In this sequence, the structure of Hauck's statement marks this distinction in his memory. *Das Vaterland* is the agent of the grammatical structure, executing the action as the subject of the final three sentences of this passage. In his recollection, the army initiates and enables the transformation of the actions of Hauck's Fatherland, for Hauck effectively acquired equal status in German society as an adult through the army. A still more provocative example of the association of Germanness and the military in Hauck's memory appears in the following excerpt.

EXCERPT F

TC: Did you ever experience any aversion because of your heritage in other countries?

HH: Nah. Because of my heritage, no. Because of being German.

TC: It was because of your being German and not — ?

HH: Yes! I mean — I didn't travel around with or I didn't posture with the fact that I . . . that [I was] "inferior" under the Nazis — In the Russian camp, I could have gone home much earlier, being from the Saarland.

TC: Why?

HH: If I had [gone along with] the other Saarlanders–who I'm not saying were wrong—they said they were French and marched around like that, even though they could barely speak a word of French. They got home sooner. It's understandable from a human point of view. But I didn't have such a standpoint. I needed a position for myself. Not for the Russians—to get home. I needed it for myself, personally—"Who/What am I?" I never listened to [the soldiers]. I'm German and was so, contrary to what Hitler thought, or the Nazis. I'm German, even [in Russia]. I didn't want anything more. . . . I'm not saying that those comrades who did it were wrong. They were right. They got home sooner. But they had never experienced that inner conflict like I had. And that's the difference. That's why I couldn't be abroad and somehow make out — I've never been an opportunist, never in my life. I would have had it much easier. I was in the Hitler Youth, but not for opportunistic reasons.[18]

In excerpt F, I begin our exchange by asking whether Hauck encountered negative responses to his Black heritage outside of Germany. During this time, he spent several years working on building and reconstruction projects in various European countries. Hauck responds by stating that, on the contrary, the negative responses he remembers were related to his being German rather than to his Black heritage. He alludes to the fact that he did not draw attention to or speak openly about his experiences as a German of color under the Nazis: "I didn't travel around with, or I didn't posture with the fact that I [was] 'inferior' under the Nazis [*Ich bin ja nicht damit gereist oder ich habe ja nicht damit posiert, daß ich es . . . unter den Nazis minderwertig*]." His comments seem intended to contrast his memories of his negative experiences as a German abroad with those of the negative treatment he suffered as a German of color by "Aryan" Germans under National Socialism. His recollections emphasize the irony of the fact that following the war, he was identified as a German and associated with Nazi Germany, whereas in the Third Reich, his status as a German was officially rejected.

The account Hauck offers in excerpt F is characterized by a series of shifts in his memory. Taken together, they form a memory technology that structures Hauck's articulations of himself as a German subject in the Third Reich. Each shift expresses important associations among Hauck's conception of himself as a German, the military as the site of his articulation of this subjectivity, and the NS discourses of German subjecthood that influenced this articulation. Hauck's statement in the second line marks the first of five memory shifts in this excerpt. This initial shift is structural rather than thematic. Here he reinterprets the topic that I set out in my question (his negative experiences related to his Black heritage) to assert almost its inverse. Hauck indirectly questions my assumptions that his blackness rather than his Germanness was the primary source of his negative experiences. Curiously, almost as soon as he introduces this subject, he seems to foreclose it as the topic of discussion, initiating a second shift in the narrative just a few lines later. Rather than elaborating on this topic, he introduces a different, seemingly unrelated one—his memory of his experiences as a German and, in particular, as a Saarlander during internment. Indeed, Hauck's abrupt transition from one memory to the next prompts the question of whether one has anything to do with the other or whether these could be explained as more random elements in a "stream of consciousness" structure of memory. Consistent with the fact that memory is rarely if ever a random process, the statements that follow clarify the connection between these two memories. Their relationship is predicated on the fact that both are examples of situations in which it would have been to Hauck's advantage to have distanced himself from being German. In each of these situations, Hauck faced the choice either of playing down or denying his Germanness or of acknowledging it and accepting the less favorable consequences.

Hauck recounts that during his internment, other German soldiers from the Saarland falsely claimed to be French to obtain early release. His remarks in this sequence are prefaced with an open-ended supposition: "If I had gone along with the other Saarlanders . . . [*Wenn ich mit den anderen Saarländern . . .*]." Introducing his memories of these events with this phrase positions Hauck in a particular relation to the other Saar-German prisoners. The supposition that connects these episodes in his narrative emphasizes his participation in and status as a potential member of this group—as a Saarlander himself, Hauck fulfilled the constitutive criterion of this group and in this way could have made the same claim to being French to forgo internment. When recalling his memories of this episode in his life, Hauck expresses understanding for the actions of his fellow Saarlanders but makes a distinction between their ability to assert this claim and his own inability to do so. As we will see in the following section, the distinction that Hauck makes between himself and the other Saar-German prisoners of war is particularly important for understanding his conception of himself as a German.

"STANDPUNKT BEZIEHEN": POSITIONALITY AND CONSTRUCTING AN IDENTITY AS A BLACK GERMAN IN THE THIRD REICH

Central to Hauck's account of his memories of his internment as a Russian POW is what he refers to as his "standpoint" (*Standpunkt*). The notion of standpoint he articulates is perhaps Hauck's most direct expression of his subjectivity as a German of African descent. The concept of positionality, which has been most extensively developed in the field of feminist theory, offers substantial insight into the subjectivity Hauck articulates in his narrative.[19] Synthesizing and elaborating on the work of leading feminist theorists, Leslie Adelson defines positionality:

> Positionality does not demarcate a *place* nor does it consist of choice alone (although it does entail a standpoint). Rather, it characterizes a set of specific social and discursive relations in a given historical moment. These relations concern and also produce gender, race, class, sexuality, ethnicity, and other practices through which power is constructed, exercised and resisted or challenged. . . . Positionality can serve as an analytical as well as a strategic tool with which to explore women's roles as both subjects and objects of construction.[20]

Feminist theorists have used positionality primarily to theorize "the fundamentally relational nature of identity."[21] In her critique of Linda Alcoff's interpretation of positionality, Adelson cautions against a conflation of the notion of standpoint with positionality that would reduce positionality to a "place" located "*outside* of an allegedly monolithic center of power, on the *margins* of power, or subsequently in an *alternative* center of power."[22] Adelson asserts that the notion of positionality as place renders agency problematic by always setting its subject in relation to a totalizing source of power. Alternatively, Adelson argues that positionality is not merely about places but also about movement, drawing on Teresa de Lauretis's notion of

> a movement between the (represented) discursive space of the positions made available by hegemonic discourses and the space-off, the elsewhere of those discourses: those other spaces both discursive and social that exist, since feminist practices have (re)constructed them, in the margins (or "between the lines," or "against the grain") of hegemonic discourses and in the interstices of institutions, in counter-practices and new forms of community. These two kinds of space are neither in opposition to one another nor strung along a chain of signification. The movement between them, therefore, is not that of a dialectic, of integration, of a combinatory, or of *différance,* but is the tension of contradiction, multiplicity, and heteronomy.[23]

The significance of de Lauretis's formulation of movement across social and discursive spaces lies in her emphasis on being both within and without representation. Movement is central to the sense of agency inherent in the concept of positionality, for it is the movement between these spaces of representation (rather than outside of them) that enables a form of agency in one's own construction. De Lauretis's emphasis on movement between and across discursive spaces of representation offers a compelling framework for reading Hauck's narrative of his experiences in internment in fascinating ways.

As discussed earlier, Hauck's memory narrative in excerpt F is marked by a series of shifts where his memories of these experiences link what seem to be unrelated experiences. "Standpoint" gives the passage its organizing structure both as a narrative and temporally, with respect to how he links experiences from different periods of his life. At the same time, this narrative sequence is based on this memory association: "If I had [gone along with] the other Saarlanders–who I'm not saying were wrong—they said they were French and marched around like that, even though they could barely speak a word of French. They got home sooner. It's understandable from a human point of view. But I didn't have such a standpoint. I needed a position for myself."

In the preceding sequence, Hauck explains that the actions of the other Saarlanders are understandable *von Menschenstandpunkt*—that is, from a human perspective or standpoint. But he emphasizes that he personally lacked such a self-evident standpoint or position. The process of *Standpunktbestimmung* (finding his own place) was more complicated for Hauck than for the other Saar-German soldiers because his position as an Afro-German was much less clear. Hauck's reference to his lack of a self-evident standpoint is in fact an indirect reference to his racial difference from the other German soldiers. This difference ruptures the male solidarity and group identification of the Wehrmacht, the element that until this point had made such military contexts protective spaces of acceptance for Hauck. However, in his account of his memories of this period, the white German Saarlanders betray this bond of solidarity, and the actions he describes and simultaneously excuses in his recounting are told in such a way that they ironically render his own difference more substantial. What Hauck portrays as these men's choice to "pass" as French without jeopardizing either the security of race/whiteness or the privileges of this identification underscores the very different stakes of his own decision not to do so. Hauck's articulation of this decision is ambivalent. This ambivalence draws attention to the fact because of his African descent, his own status as a Saar-German soldier of the Nazi Wehrmacht might itself be seen as a form of passing—yet a form that undermines his German status in a qualitatively different way.

In his memories of this episode, Hauck differentiates himself from the other Saar-German POWs through standpoint, or a recognized and acknowledged position as a legitimate German subject. For it is precisely his lack of a self-evident position made it necessary for Hauck to define one for himself: "I needed a position for myself. Not for the Russians—to get home. I needed it for myself, personally—'Who/ What am I?'"

In this sequence, Hauck's memory narrative shifts once again, setting his struggle with positionality in internment in relation to other contexts in which he experienced this same struggle. In this way, his memories of internment come to represent the role of positionality in his life more generally, in ways that relate it directly to Hauck's status as an Other within. To borrow from de Lauretis, Hauck's position as an Afro-German as an Other within constructs him as both "within and without representation."[24] As a German he shares the language, cultural values, and socialization of this society and in this way is fully a part of it. Hauck's membership in the HJ and the Wehrmacht are evidence of this paradoxical interiority, and in his memory narrative, he uses these aspects of his biography to represent himself most strongly as a German. Yet his status as a *Black* German contests this representation, in many ways undermining the basis of the dominant construction of Germanness to which he refers in his narrative. Hauck is forced to engage and confront these boundaries when he recalls these memories of his experiences as an Afro-German in each of these contexts.

The patterns of memory Hauck uses to articulate his standpoints in the context of each of the episodes he recounts reflect a form of subjectivity as a German that is characterized by a relational process of positionality. The standpoint on being German that Hauck constructs in and through his memory narrative of internment can be read as part of an ongoing struggle to develop and articulate his German identity. However, this struggle should not be mischaracterized as an individu-

alistic process of continual self-invention. Positionality is not solely a
question of situational contingency. As we have seen thus far in his
narrative, for Afro-Germans such as Hauck, positionality is a complex
social process through which individuals are constituted as raced, gendered, and often sexualized subjects in relation to larger discourses of
nation and national identity.

What is perhaps most important to the concept of positionality is
the notion of continuity that I would argue distinguishes my understanding of positionality from those cited previously. Hauck's memory
narrative of his experiences as a POW is one example of such an articulation of himself as a German of African descent. His account of these
experiences emphasizes his ability to develop and maintain a sense of
continuity within this process. This emphasis on continuity can be seen
in a third shift contained in the following sequence of his memory narrative: "I needed a position for myself. Not for the Russians—to get
home. I needed it for myself, personally—'Who/What am I?' I never
listened to [the soldiers]. I'm German and was so, contrary to what
Hitler thought, or the Nazis. I'm German, even [in Russia]. I didn't
want anything more."

In this sequence, Hauck makes a seamless transition from describing his struggle for a standpoint as a Saar-German POW in relation to
the Russians to describing his standpoint as a German in relation to
Nazi discourses on German subjecthood in the Third Reich. This third
memory shift is characterized more by a transition than by a break in
Hauck's narrative. This shift emphasizes continuity between these two
contexts, for Hauck is challenged on the issue of his German identity in
both of the situations to which he refers. In the Third Reich, the discourse of Aryan purity posed the primary challenge for Hauck. In the
POW camp, not his Soviet captors but rather the Saar-German prisoners challenged him. Setting his memories of each of these contexts in
relation to one another, the story Hauck recounts of the Saar-German
prisoners' actions foregrounds the issue of his relation to his subjectivity as a German—or as he states the question, "Who/What am I now?
[*Was bin ich jetzt?*]" On first reading, this challenge appears to cast
doubt on the sense of belonging that Hauck associates with the military and the equal status he feels he has by now achieved. At the same
time, this challenge reinscribes him as an Other within this institution.
Here, acceptance and belonging through masquerade and male gender

identification are displaced by a sense of Otherness that returns as a challenge from his past. However, Hauck's response to this challenge is self-affirming. The provocation his narrative asserts serves to reactivate the reflective process of *Standpunktbestimmung* (positionality) that Hauck describes in memories of his youth in response to NS discourses on Germanness. In this third memory shift, Hauck establishes this link between these formative moments of subject formation in his remembered past. His response to the question/challenge regarding his identity is the affirmation, "I'm German," rendered through a form of cross-temporal intertextuality, explicitly redirecting it backward in time to address the other German and Saar-German prisoners and the Nazi racial ideology that excluded Hauck during his youth in the Third Reich. In this way, his narrative reflects the larger structure of memory, which is always inherently dialogical and intertextual. Always cross-temporal, memory is that which links the present and the past, making the past meaningful for today and allowing both the past to speak to the present and the present to speak to the past.

Despite the fact that these challenges and Hauck's resulting struggle concerning his German identity recur in different contexts and under different circumstances, a continuity exists in his positioning(s) vis-à-vis Germanness in each of the contexts he cites. An important difference between the Russian POW camp and the Third Reich, however, is that whereas in Germany, the status of being German was advantageous, in the POW camp his affirmation of Germanness disadvantaged him. Yet this distinction does not seem to make a difference to Hauck. But why not? Hauck's response is found in the fourth shift in his memory narrative: "I'm not saying that those comrades who did it were wrong. They were right. They got home sooner. But they had never experienced that inner conflict like I had. And that's the difference."

In this sequence, Hauck shifts the context of his narrative from describing his memories of the position he came to develop as a German of African descent in the Third Reich back to his standpoint in the Russian prison camp. After explaining the relationship he sees between the two, Hauck returns to discuss the actions of other Saar-German POWs that served as the initial point of departure for this memory narrative. He begins by directly comparing his actions with those of his comrades and by comparing their respective standpoints. He explicitly refuses to pass judgment on their actions, opting rather to acknowledge them on the basis of what he sees as their legitimate motivations from what he referred to previously as *Menschenstandpunkt.* However, Hauck's acceptance hinges on the fact that despite the potential similarities of their position as Saarlanders, he views them as being in a very different situation than himself—they were constituted as white and therefore were legitimate German subjects, whereas he was a Black and thus illegitimate German subject. At this point, what began as a comparison in Hauck's narrative becomes, through the invocation of race, a direct contrast. This contrast revolves around the experience of *innerer Widerstreit* (inner conflict) regarding his German subjecthood, which serves as the central motivating force in this situation. Hauck's inner conflict on the issue of his status as a German subject had been an ongoing struggle for him long before the POW camp; it shaped and defined his relation to Germanness in this particular situation and is presented by him as the decisive factor in his narrative.

To return to the earlier question of why Hauck chose to affirm his position as a German even when it was disadvantageous for him to do so, his narrative demonstrates that although his position as a POW was comparable to that of his Saar-German comrades, his past and continuing struggle for recognition of his status as a German made it impossible for him to behave like the others. In fact, this recurrent struggle for affirmation led him to develop a standpoint on his identity that made it extremely difficult for him to renounce or distance his Germanness, even under such potentially advantageous circumstances. Relinquishing or repudiating this hard-won and conflicted status would in effect have meant conceding to those who had sought all along to deny his status as German.[25]

In the concluding lines of this passage, Hauck's explicit reference to the Hitler Youth provides the most important context for understanding the final shift: "That's why I couldn't be abroad and somehow make out. . . . I've never been an opportunist, never in my life. I would have had it much easier. I was in the Hitler Youth, but not out of opportunistic reasons."

This last memory shift is again a temporal one, moving from Hauck's more recent past to his internment as a prisoner of war and finally to his experience in the Hitler Youth. In spite of these temporal transitions, Hauck maintains a thematic continuity within this narrative sequence. What links his earlier comments on his and other Saarlanders' motivations for either affirming or distancing themselves from being German to his remarks on his participation in the HJ is the issue of opportunism.

In this concluding sequence, Hauck's transition begins once again with a sentence fragment that relates his comments back to the question posed at the beginning of the excerpt, which initially evoked this particular configuration of memory associations. He continues by linking his previous description of the inner conflict he experienced early in his life with the issue of opportunism. Hauck's reference to opportunism certainly needs unpacking. In one sense, Hauck's remark is negative, as he rejects an opportunistic interpretation of his actions. Here he implicitly refers to the other Saar-German prisoners. His statement, "Opportunist war ich noch nie," is an almost defensive gesture of demarcation, seeming to make explicit what went unspoken in the rest of the excerpt—that the true opportunists were the Saarlanders who pretended to be French. In this way, Hauck's remark indirectly places him in opposition to these "real opportunists."

The issue of opportunism (his own and that of others) seems a preoccupation that Hauck articulates only late in this excerpt. Opportunism appears as a double-edged form of critique that Hauck directs not only at the Saarland POWs but also, and more importantly, at himself. This issue goes beyond the context of his experiences in internment, a subtext or submerged self-critical discourse querying his memories of his struggle for legitimate status as a German. Hauck seems to respond to this criticism, defensively emphasizing his point three times in this sequence. In another sense, though, Hauck's reference to opportunism must be read in relation to the issue of passing. Despite the problems that accompany Hauck's situation in these terms, it seems clear that in this sequence of his memory narrative he responds to a potential interpretation of his actions as taking advantage of his situation by passing—pretending to be something or someone he is not. It is nevertheless somewhat ironic that Hauck feels it necessary to make such a defensive statement at this point in his narrative rather than earlier, when describing his memories of the Hitler Youth, a context in which such an accusation would in some ways appear more likely. Yet precisely this link between these sets of memories (the Hitler Youth, the Wehrmacht, and internment) in the final lines of this passage helps to explain their significance in Hauck's memory and their role in his subject formation.

Hauck's reference to the Hitler Youth underscores it as another episode in his life that might also be interpreted as opportunistic. He speaks to the issue raised at the beginning of this chapter regarding the function of his membership in the Hitler Youth. The association he makes by linking his memories of the Hitler Youth to those of internment underscores the fact that opportunism is also an underlying self-critique with regard to Hauck's membership in the HJ, for his references to both situations appear as attempts to justify strategic situations in which he came to assert himself as a German. In each of these situations, Hauck's assertion of his status as a German was supported by or orchestrated through his membership in a uniformed male institution that represented the German nation and in this way both directly and unintentionally sanctioned his status as a masculine German subject in spite of his official status as an inappropriate racial subject.

In the final analysis, the comparison/contrast Hauck makes between himself and the other Saar-German prisoners revolves around their respective status as German subjects. In excerpt F, Hauck articulates his status as a German as a dynamic process of positioning where the decisive factors are what he refers to as *innerer Widerstreit* (inner struggle) and *Standpunkt* (standpoint). Both are active processes through which he enacts a form of German subjecthood that he was repeatedly denied (though unevenly and often in contradictory ways) on the basis of his racial heritage. In Hauck's memory narrative, this process is enacted as a continual negotiation and renegotiation of positions in relation to changing contexts, situations, and circumstances, yet he does so without relinquishing a sense of continuity.

In the end, the notion of identity as positionality directly addresses the aspiration toward equal status with other Germans that Hauck expresses in various ways through his memories of his youth in the Third Reich, particularly in relation to military settings. The positionings that Hauck constructs in his narrative allow him to constitute himself as a legitimate subject in his memories of the past. At the same time, these positionings indicate some of the ways in which Nazi institutions like the HJ and the Wehrmacht had a crucial impact on the formation of Hauck's subjectivity in ways that, in fact, worked very much against the grain of their intended function.

What is most remarkable about Hauck's account is how it vividly testifies to the fact that, in some ways, race proved too slippery even for National Socialism. This is, of course, in no way intended to dispute the effectiveness of the Nazi state as a monstrously successful system of racialized genocide. Yet although race was this regime's primary organizing principle for both participation in the state and recognition and inclusion in the social collective, because race is a signifier with no fundamental basis, the Nazi regime was unable to harness race completely to either one fixed meaning or even the plethora of negative associations with which the National Socialists sought to justify their policies of racial hygiene and eugenics. Hauck's narrative attests to the fact that even the most extensive attempts to reduce some racial Others to their essence and to exclude them from society were unable to account for the central paradox of race: its simultaneous excess and lack of meaning. Paradoxically, this conundrum in the end worked to Hauck's distinct advantage.

CHAPTER 4 IDENTIFYING
AS THE "OTHER WITHIN"

National Socialist Racial Politics and

an Afro-German Childhood in the Third Reich

Hans Hauck's memory narrative demonstrated how the processes of racial differentiation and signification that formed the core of Nazi racial politics came to produce him as a complex German subject in ways that appear to contradict the regime's fundamental goals. The emphasis placed on reading subjecthood and the productive effects of National Socialist racial politics in his narrative are in no way intended to minimize the fact that Afro-Germans also suffered greatly from the persecution and discrimination many of them endured within this regime, even when their experiences were ambivalent and contradictory, as in Hauck's case. As I argue in the preceding chapter, such tensions both exemplify the politics of race in the Third Reich and reflect the specific situation of Afro-Germans, whose status was thoroughly ambivalent at numerous levels.

In this chapter I once again seek not to assess the extent of these individuals' victimization by this regime but rather to examine the effects of a state-sponsored system of racialization and the processes through which, both in spite and because of the role of race therein, Black Germans came to constitute themselves as particular kinds of German subjects when, paradoxically, exactly the opposite was the regime's goal. Individuals like Hauck and my next informant, Fasia Jansen, articulate complicated forms of belonging and subjectivity as Germans that are precisely what the racial policies of the Third Reich sought to extinguish. In Hauck's memories of his life in this regime, military institutions serve as sites through which he articulates this subjectivity and thus reflect the critical role these institutions played in constructing him as a legitimate German subject. At the same time, local spaces also play a key role in his narrative. In Jansen's narrative, the racialization of space takes a more central role. It is crucial to read the processes of subject formation she recounts through the complex social topography she constructs in her memory narrative of her life in this period.

When reading narratives of memory and oral history, it is important to pay attention to how individuals describe and narrate their memories of the places and spaces of their past. Closely examining these descriptions is necessary because, particularly with respect to issues of race and gender, social interactions occur not just on a verbal level but also and quite profoundly on a physical level through the ways in which we physically encounter one another and the barriers often erected (materially, politically, socially, and symbolically) to hinder such contact and interaction. The ways in which individuals describe the landscapes of their social interaction can offer a vivid reflection of their societies' larger social and political organization.

This is particularly the case for Nazi Germany, a regime that worked not only through terror, coercion, ideology, and propaganda but perhaps most importantly through physically "placing" people, relegating them to particular sites and spaces inside and around the center and periphery of society based on the different value placed on human lives. The National Socialist (NS) government attempted to regulate all contact (both public and private) between those it deemed legitimate and illegitimate members of this society. In ways even more pronounced than Hauck, Jansen's memory narrative is structured around compelling descriptions of the places and spaces that served as formative sites of social interaction in her life in the Third Reich. Both accounts map an intricate social geography of subjecthood where race and gender came to signify and interpellate her in ways that reveal important tensions and contradictions in Nazi attempts to "rule by race" in the Third Reich.

As I argued in chapter 2, National Socialism's most explicit response to its Afro-German population focused primarily on policies directed against the Black children of the Rhineland occupation. This project aimed first to neutralize the threat of racial pollution through compulsory sterilization, with a supplemental politics of containment that attempted to prevent interracial contact between Aryan and non-Aryan Germans (including people of Black racial heritage) through racial legislation that policed and prohibited social interaction. Both policies explicitly aimed to protect the purity of the Aryan race and formed part of the larger NS program of social administration that aimed at comprehensive regulation of the social sphere by subordinating private life to the rule of the state. This chapter is concerned with the application of this second approach to managing the perceived threat a Black German population might pose. In Jansen's memory narrative, Nazi intervention in her life took the form of its efforts to remove her as an illegitimate racial Other from public and private interaction with the privileged, legitimate subjects of this regime.

As we shall see in the pages that follow, Jansen's memory narrative demonstrates that in her case, rather than accomplishing the erasure of a racial Other from German society by relegating her to a place outside or at the margins of social contact, these processes unintentionally produced a contestatory and resistant subject, even in the context of the overly regulated spaces of marginality to which she was often assigned. Moreover, reading Jansen's narrative in relation to Hauck's articulations of the effects of the processes of racialization and gendering gives us an even more concrete sense of the extent to which these processes are neither separate nor overlapping but rather simultaneous and mutually constitutive. The significance of this distinction helps us to understand the power of National Socialism as productive, producing subjects to be regulated on numerous levels and subjects with equally multiple avenues of resistance within these same complex subjectivities. Although my two interview partners' narratives differ substantially with regard to the picture they paint of their local encounters with the Nazi regime's racial politics, they nevertheless offer compelling accounts of the ways in which Afro-Germans came to be signified as raced and gendered subjects and document in profound ways complex processes of subject formation in the Third Reich.

AMBIVALENCE AND AMBIGUITY IN THE NAZI PERSECUTION OF AFRO-GERMANS

Unlike Hauck, Fasia Jansen's life history is completely unrelated to the Rhineland occupation. Jansen was born in 1929 in Hamburg; her father was a Liberian consul general living in Hamburg, her mother an employee at the Liberian consulate. Her parents never married, and Jansen never met her father.[1] In her narrative, Jansen does not describe the nature of the relationship between her mother and her biological father (her mother married another man in 1936), nor does she say how long they were in contact or the circumstances under which their contact ended. She does, however, describe several later interactions with her Liberian half-siblings—Jansen's father was married to a Liberian woman at the time of his involvement with Jansen's mother.[2] In addition, she describes having a very close relationship to her stepfather, a communist who was later denounced to the Nazis and eventually interned in a work camp because of his political convictions.

One of the most striking aspects of Jansen's memory narrative is her unequivocal articulation of herself as a German. Yet the affirmation of Germanness expressed in her narrative is most often articulated through her memories of the discrimination and persecution she faced through the Nazi regime's attempts to constitute her as precisely the opposite—specifically, NS practices of racialization aimed at negating her status as a German subject and member of the racial collective of Nazi Germany.

EXCERPT G

TC: And with your [step]father, did you talk to him about racism, about the racism you might have experienced because of your skin color?

FJ: Well, my family loved me particularly intensely, perhaps because of that.

TC: Do you think?

FJ: I always wanted to be a dancer, and my father was crazy about Josephine Baker.

TC: Aha.

FJ: She was a tap dancer, and I absolutely wanted to be a dancer. Then I got accepted to train as dancer. So I started when I was a little over eleven years old. And at thirteen I had to leave the school, because the director of the dance school said, "She can't become a dancer," and "I'll get in trouble with the Reich Culture Office, the Reich Chamber of

Culture," and "You have to imagine, when the curtain goes up and there's a Black girl standing there. I'll get in trouble if I keep Fasia in school here." So I had to leave the dance school and that was awful for me.[3]

In 1940 Jansen began training as a dancer at a dance academy in Hamburg, despite the Law against the Overcrowding of German Schools and Universities (Gesetz gegen die Überfüllung deutscher Schulen und Hochschulen) passed on 25 April 1933, which restricted the number of "non-Aryans" attending German schools and universities to no more than 1.5 percent.[4] A later measure, the Directive on the Admission of Foreigners and Foreign Non-Aryans to German Schools and Universities (Runderlaß zur Zulassung von Ausländern bzw. ausländischen Nichtariern zu den deutschen Schulen und Hochschulen) of 3 May 1933, recommended that to avoid diplomatic difficulties, foreigners and non-German citizens should not be informed of the reason for their exclusion from German universities and schools.[5] More significant than these general regulations was a 22 March 1941 directive from the Ministry of Science, Child Development, and Education (Wissenschaft, Erziehung und Volksbildung) regarding "the admission of Gypsies and people of mixed Black and white blood to public schools [*Zulassung von Zigeunern und Negermischlingen zum Besuch öffentlicher Volksschulen*]," which established the following guidelines:

The admission of Gypsy children who do not hold German citizenship and therefore are not required to attend school is fundamentally rejected. Inasmuch as the fact that these children do not attend school poses a danger to public order or safety, it will be the responsibility of the police department to take the appropriate steps against these elements, if necessary through deportation.

For Gypsy children who hold German citizenship and thus are required to attend school, the fundamental rejection of their admission to public schools will not be feasible. Since the number of Gypsy children is, as a rule, insufficient, it will not be possible to establish special schools. Insofar as these children present a moral or other danger to their German-blooded schoolmates, they may be removed. In such cases, the notification of the police department is recommended.

For the treatment of Negro mixed-blood children, the same principles are to be observed. This directive is not to be published.[6]

This measure provided the precarious legal basis for Jansen's removal from the dance academy, though the wording of the directive ("they may be removed [*können sie jedoch von der Schule verwiesen werden*]" left its implementation open to the discretion of local authorities.[7] In spite of these regulations, however, Jansen was admitted to the dance academy and allowed to complete two years of training before being forced to leave. On the basis of her expulsion from the dance school, Jansen applied for compensation after the war.

EXCERPT H

FJ: I applied for compensation.

TC: Did you get it? Did you . . .

FJ: No, it was rejected umpteen times. First of all, they couldn't establish that Negroes fell under the racial laws, and then, of course, there were contradictory statements made about the wrong done to me when I was a small child, at eight, nine, and ten years old. And then my relatives had to testify, you know, about when [things happened], was that then and then, or was it like this. . . . Well, these kinds of complications came up in between, you know. But for example, it was established without a doubt that I was forced to leave dance school—I wanted to become a dancer—I had to leave on racial grounds. The dance school also confirmed this even after the war, that they had to get rid of me because they would have gotten into trouble, and it was for racial reasons that they had to get rid of me. But sometimes I ask myself how I actually withstood all that. I sometimes ask myself, was I trying to be German? Which is what I am. I come from Hamburg, I speak this Hamburg dialect, which always shocks people from Hamburg, and which also gives you a bit of a plus, when you speak Hamburger Platt.[8]

Jansen directly relates her experience of marginalization to her subjectivity as a German. Here, her memories of the difference she was made to feel under National Socialism are articulated through reference to her sense of herself as a German. After explaining the reasons for the rejection of her claim for compensation, her narration becomes more reflective. At this point, Jansen's memory narrative recalls Hauck's use of the narrative technique of relativization. Shifting the focus of her narration in this passage, Jansen poses the rhetorical question of why and how she withstood this treatment. Her response is a second question: Was it because she was trying to be German? But she in fact already is German. She affirms the undeniable fact of her Germanness in her reference to herself as a Hamburg native and through her identification with this very specific sense of Germanness through her regional dialect, Hamburger Platt. Yet Jansen's Hamburger Platt—the ultimate measure of her Germanness—stands in direct contrast to her color. Moreover, this reference seems structurally intended to contrast the memory of marginalization Jansen recounts only moments earlier. Yet her shift when she moves from the topic of the rejection of her claim to compensation to her identification as a German should, once again, not be read as coincidental. Rather than an interruption of the flow of her narration, this shift establishes an important associative link within her memory narrative. As we will see, Jansen's claim to compensation is intimately linked to her sense of herself as a German.

In excerpt H, Jansen states that her entitlement to compensation was rejected because the authorities disputed her claim to have been the victim of racial discrimination. The definition of racial persecution established in the Law for the Compensation of Victims of Nazi Persecution (Bundesentschädigungsgesetz zur Entschädigung für Opfer der nationalsozialistischen Verfolgung, or BEG) took as its legal basis the NS definition of race and the individual groups that the Nuremberg Laws explicitly targeted for persecution. Thus, the issue of Jansen's status as a victim of racial persecution is intimately tied up with the thorny question of the more general legal status of Germans of African descent in the Third Reich. In this way, the link in Jansen's memory narrative between compensation for Nazi crimes and her status as a German foregrounds this issue as exemplary of the troubled forms of recognition and misrecognition of legitimate and illegitimate subjects experienced by Afro-Germans like Jansen as well as Hauck both in the Third Reich and thereafter, most notably in the postwar prosecution of the regime's crimes.

Although the primary focus of NS racial persecution was the Jewish population, Michael Burleigh and Wolfgang Wippermann maintain that it is impossible to separate Nazi anti-Semitic policies from the regime's racial hygienic measures: "the two are indivisible parts of a whole" because Nazi racial legislation aimed at the racial hygienic improvement of the body of the German nation.[9] These laws were directed not only at Jews but at all individuals of alien blood (*artfremdes Blut*) and alien races (*Fremdrassigen*) as well as "racially less valuable" members of the German population. For Afro-Germans, the definition of the categories of "non-Aryan" and *artfremdes Blut* are most relevant, particularly in Jansen's case.

The First Decree to the Law for the Restoration of the Professional Civil Service (Erste Verordnung zur Durchführung des Gesetzes zur Wiederherstellung des Berufsbeamtentum), promulgated on 11 April 1933, defined a non-Aryan as "an individual descended from non-Aryan (in particular Jewish parents or grandparents), where at least one non-Aryan parent or grandparent was present. This is particularly the case when one parent or grandparent belonged to the Jewish religion."[10] Thus the legal definition of a non-Aryan was based on the two preceding generations, when the decisive issue of confessional membership in the Jewish religion was not a factor. Marianne Sigg contends that one of the major contributions of the Nuremberg Laws was the refinement given to the category of "non-Aryan," a result of the legal profession's growing and insistent demands for clarity regarding the definition of key terms in NS racial legislation, in particular *non-Aryan* and *Jew*.[11]

The Nuremberg Laws further refined the distinction between "Aryan" and "non-Aryan" by replacing the category "non-Aryan" with "Jew" and the category "Aryan" with "persons of German or related blood" (*Deutsche oder artverwandtes Blut*). Directly opposed to this last classification was the more flexible category of *artfremdes Blut*.

> The following stipulations are to be observed in determining which racial requirements must be fulfilled in order to obtain the rights of a Reich citizen:

a) In principle, only German citizens or those of related blood shall have the rights of Reich citizens. The German *Volk* is composed of members of different races and their mixtures. The blood resulting from these mixtures and present in the German *Volk* is *German blood* [*deutsches Blut*].

Blood *related to* [*artverwandt*] German blood is the blood of those peoples whose racial composition is related to that of German blood. This is without exception the case for those peoples wholly settled in Europe and their offspring in other parts of the earth outside of Europe that have maintained the purity of their blood.

The term "German or of related blood" [*deutsches oder artverwandtes Blut*], replaces the until now traditional term of "Aryan descent." Individuals of German or related blood shall be referred to with the term "German-blooded" (compare Ordinance from 26.11.1935, MbliB.S.1429) paragraph 2f, 151 ff.

b) *Alien blood* [*artfremdes Blut*] is all blood that is not German blood, nor related to German blood. Alien blood in Europe is, as a rule, only the Jew (see below comment c) and gypsy. Persons of alien blood cannot obtain the rights of a Reich citizen.

c) *Jewish* [*Juden*] citizens, in particular, cannot become Reich citizens. The group of persons who are prohibited from employment as Jews is determined according to paragraph 5 of the Blood Protection Law. According hereto, a Jew by blood is he who is descended from at least three full-Jewish grandparents; furthermore, by virtue of the law, a Jew is also any citizen of Jewish mixed-blood in the first degree who belongs to the Jewish religious community, or who through marriage to a Jew converted to Judaism, or belongs to this religion because of the decision of his parents; this is assumed to be the case when a half-caste is born of a marriage—legal or illegal (see note 6 to paragraph 1 of the Blood Protection Law)—to a Jew that occurred after the Blood Protection Law came into effect, or when the individual was born of extramarital relations with a Jew after 31 July 1936. For specific cases, see notes to paragraph 5 of the First Reich Citizenship Law. Half-castes of the second degree or German-blooded individuals are not considered Jews when they do not belong to the Jewish religious community. An exception to this rule is only with regard to the racial classification of the grandchildren. Here paragraph 2, line 2, and paragraph 5, line 1 of the Second Reich Citizenship Law stipulates that a grandparent is without question a full Jew if he belonged to the Jewish religious community. See notes to paragraphs 2 and 5 of the First Reich Citizenship Law.

d) Aside from persons of alien blood, *half-castes* [*Mischlinge*] born of relations between persons of German blood and those of alien-blood are neither German-blooded nor of related blood. These half castes can also not be considered people of alien blood. The half-caste has both German and alien hereditary factors. The legal treatment of half-castes is based on the recognition that they are the same neither as those of German nor as those of alien blood. The status of half-castes is explicitly specified only for persons of Jewish blood. According to this, the Jewish half-caste is an individual who is descended from one or two full-Jewish grandparents; an individual with more than two full-Jewish grandparents is a Jew; an individual with no full-Jewish grandparents will be treated as German-blooded and will no longer be counted as a half-caste, even should he prove to have a slight influence of Jewish blood. The same principles for the racial classification as a Jewish half-caste will serve as the basis for the classification of other types of alien blood. Even if, according to paragraph 2, the half-caste is not entitled to the rights of a Reich citizen, as this is limited to citizens of German or related blood, paragraph 2 of the First Reich's Citizenship Law bears out the biological fact that the half-caste possesses at least one-half German genetic makeup, taking this into account in that the Jewish half-caste citizen is also provisionally awarded the rights of a Reich citizen.

e) Which race a person belongs to can never be judged simply through their membership in a particular group of people. Rather, it can only be determined by their personal, racial-biological characteristics.[12]

Although this explication of the category *artfremdes Blut* explicitly defines only the status of Jews and Gypsies, it was nevertheless intended to serve a model function for all others of *artfremdes Blut und deren Mischlinge.* For Afro-Germans, the decisive legal stipulations were made in the supplementary decrees to the Law for the Protection of German Blood and Honor and the Marriage Protection Law. In their official commentary to these laws, Wilhelm Stuckart and Hans Globke on three occasions explicitly refer to the application of the laws to "Negro half-castes [*Negermischlinge*]." The most important of these references concerns paragraph 6 of the First Supplementary Decree to the Blood Protection Law of 14 November 1935 which forbade marriages "if their offspring were likely pose a danger to the purity of German blood."[13] Stuckart and Globke provide the following explication:

Whether grounds for preventing a marriage according to paragraph 6 exist will usually be established through the certificates of proof of ancestry required of the engaged couple before the marriage, according to the ordinance of 26 November 1935 . . . (birth certificate, marriage certificate of parents, in cases of doubt, other certificates). Yet there are also cases where the certificates provided do not allow a decision to be made with ample certainty. One might imagine, for example, the situation that an intended husband shows the obvious influence of alien blood—for example, Negro blood—without any indication in his certificates of where this influence comes from. In these cases, as a rule, illegitimate birth would play a role, where the progenitor of these illegitimate children could not be established. In this context, one is reminded of the Negro bastards of the Rhineland occupation, where the establishment of the progenitor was greatly hindered by French law.[14]

These commentaries again show that the specific point of reference for a German population of African descent is the figure of the Rhineland Bastard. Despite the fact that Stuckart and Globke's other references to "Negroes and their bastards [*Neger und ihre Bastarde*]," contain no specific mentions of the Rhineland children, this initial reference is implicitly cited.[15] It becomes apparent that although Afro-Germans are not explicitly mentioned in the laws, the authors did in fact incorporate Black Germans in this way, making subsequent, more specific, racial legislation unnecessary. The status of Black Germans in the Third Reich affirms the protean nature of Nazi racial legislation through the versatility and mutability of its categories. As Burleigh and Wippermann explain, Nazi racial legislation was formulated so elastically that it could be expanded to include and incorporate further groups of people into the regime's categories of racialized social administration without necessitating the introduction of new laws.[16] Thus, rather than emphasizing the creation of these categories as monolithic sites of power, the situation of Afro-Germans within this regime directs our attention to their flexibility as dynamic conduits through which power was exercised and configured in complex and differential ways. At the same time, this discussion of NS legal theory also illustrates the undeniable persistence of the figure of the Rhineland Bastard as the dominant image of an Afro-German population in this period.[17] These important points notwithstanding, what is arguably most important for understanding Jansen's account of the rejection of her postwar claim for *Wiedergutmachung* or compensation is the definition of the categories of persecution on which such claims were based. BEG paragraphs 1 and 3 defined the relevant categories as follows:

(1) Those entitled to compensation according to this law are individuals who, in the period from 30 January 1933 to 8 May 1945 (period of persecution), because of their political convictions against National Socialism, for reasons of race, religious beliefs, or philosophy of life (reasons for persecution), were persecuted through the violent measures of National Socialism, and for this reason, suffered injury to life, body, health, freedom, property, or wealth or suffered in professional or financial advancement (victim of persecution). . . .

(3) The violent measures of National Socialism are those measures that, on the orders or approval of an agency, functionary of the nation or state, or any other body, institution, or foundation of public law or the NSDAP or its organizations or affiliated associations were executed for reasons of persecution on the persecuted. It is presumed that such measures were directed against the persecuted if this individual belonged to a group of persons that the government or NSDAP intended through such members to exclude in its entirety from Germany's cultural and economic life.[18]

The commentaries to the BEG specify further that in their references to victims of racial persecution, the use of the wording "for reasons of race [*aus Gründen der Rasse*]" was intended to be more expansive than the formulation persecution "because of one's race [*wegen seiner Rasse*)]" in that the former would include those who suffered discrimination based on their relationship to individuals belonging to racial groups specifically targeted by the Nazis ("eine vom NS bekämpfte angebliche Rasse").[19] What is most salient for assessing both Jansen's narrative and the status of Black Germans who suffered persecution in the Third Reich is, as she explains, the fact that individuals of African descent were not recognized as a group targeted for racial persecution under NS law. This was the case in spite of the aforementioned explicit references to individuals of "mixed Black and white blood [*Negermischlinge*]" in the commentaries to the Nuremberg Laws. Because of the absence of an explicit and precisely defined category for Afro-Germans beyond the paradigm of the Rhineland children (some of whom, including Hauck, received some forms of compensation) both within the Reich and in the postwar period, Jansen was deemed ineligible for compensation under BEG paragraph 5l. This specific clause addresses the issue of *Ausbildungsschäden* (compensation for damages to an individual's career through the forced disruption of or exclusion from professional training).[20] Despite the obvious applicability of these stipulations to Jansen's expulsion from the dance academy, she nevertheless did not fulfill the criteria set out in BEG Paragraphs 1 and 2 for entitlement to compensation under this clause and all others in the law—specifically, loss of life or damage to body, health, property, or wealth through persecution on the basis of race, political, or philosophical conviction, or religion.[21]

In his 1986 study of the Nazi persecution of Sinti and Roma, Wippermann argues that the polycratic nature of the NS state made the implementation of both racial ideology and racial legislation a complicated process in which numerous individual and state actors played a part in facilitating or hindering the goals of Nazi racial purity within the Reich.[22] Wippermann's arguments offer an important point of reference for explaining the complex positioning of Afro-Germans in the National Socialist state, particularly when viewed in relation to the insights of Zygmunt Bauman regarding the significance of the bureaucratic nature of the NS state and the centrality of the act of definition within this regime. The issue of a Nazi policy toward Afro-Germans hinges on the questions of how and to what extent these individuals were *erfaßt* (registered) or defined within this system. These issues move us beyond the juridical definition of Aryan and non-Aryan subjects to the more pragmatic level of the bureaucracy—that is, the bureaucratic interpretation and implementation of the racial ideology set out in laws and directives within the Reich. Because Germans of African descent were not seen as a racial group specifically targeted by the Nazis, Jansen's claim to compensation for being forced to give up her training as a dancer was also rejected. Yet, as both Hauck and Jansen's narratives attest, although the active implementation of a consistent policy of persecution for Black Germans beyond the Rhineland paradigm is difficult to document, Afro-Germans were indeed objects of racial persecution, and the image that motivated this effort was that of the Rhineland Bastard. The enduring power of this image within Nazi racial policy was its ability to fuel the fantasy of and desire for the purity of the German body politic by justifying its defense when threatened.

LIFE BETWEEN PERIPHERY AND CENTER: LOCAL POLITICS OF RACIALIZED GENDER AND GENDERED RACIALIZATION

Jansen's memories of her life in the National Socialist state paint a complex and uneven landscape of social interactions for individuals living in this regime, a picture that provokes a deeper engagement with the local and the local effects of Nazi racial politics. Indeed, the contours of local space(s) play a particularly important role in Jansen's narrative, which is marked by the striking way in which she describes a series of very local sites of racialized social interactions. Jansen narrates these sites in richly textured and sedimented ways that reveal their deep analytical significance for reading the dynamics of race in Nazi Germany. The most important of these sites relates to events that followed her expulsion from dance school.

After leaving the dance academy, Jansen was required to labor as a cook for the female inmates of the Neuengamme concentration camp. In her narrative, she describes this in relation to the required year of service to the Reich, officially known as *Dienstverpflichtung.* Unlike the so-called Aryan girls she emphasizes that it was "out of the question" for her to work in homes doing domestic service like other girls she knew. For her year of service, she was required to work for the camp.[23] What is most remarkable about her memories of this experience is the fact that Jansen was not interned in the camp itself; rather, she describes working in a kitchen barracks, located in a suburb of Hamburg called Rothenburgsort, where women inmates labored in an *Außenlager* of the Neuengamme camp. An ambivalent and contradictory recognition of Jansen as a German is implicit in Jansen's obligation to work for the camp. What distinguishes her treatment from the more prevalent forms of persecution and marginalization deployed by the NS state to remove or disenfranchise those individuals deemed unacceptable for membership in the (Aryan) German collective is the fact that, despite being forced to labor under appalling conditions in close proximity to the regime's abject, Jansen was nevertheless allowed to retain a form of subject status as a German, maintaining her status as a German citizen and not being deported. At the same time, she was not interned in the same way as, for example, German Jews, Sinti and Roma, or other groups of individuals (political prisoners or homosexuals, for example) seen as unfit for the mainstream of German society. Jansen's narrative brings into clearer focus some of the ways race worked not only through bodies but also and quite profoundly through location and space by "placing" its subjects in particular social locations that inscribed differential meanings and, in equally substantial ways, often a lack of social value.

EXCERPT I

TC: What did you do after you couldn't go [to dance school] any more?

FJ: That was really awful for me. I had to do service under the Nazis. There was a year of service, where all German girls had to do a year of service at the age of fourteen. That meant, before they were sent to work in families somewhere, to help out in families and do housework. For me that was out of the question. I ended up in a barracks in Hamburg, in a part of the city where there was almost nothing left standing, in Rothenburgsort, an area where they had put Jewish women from Poland.

TC: Where? In what part of town was that, again?

FJ: Rothenburgsort. I was required to work in the barracks kitchen. It was this little thing with a big stove, and I still don't quite grasp it even today, that four or five or six people had to sit in there. I was among war prisoners, French ones—well, prisoners. . . . I was among Ukrainians, among forced laborers from the east.

TC: Ukrainians.

FJ: Ukrainians and an Italian POW, a POW—I'll tell you about him later. So [I was] among all these men. And we, I was supposed to peel potatoes, but there was this stinking broth of stinking, rotten cabbage that came, that you could only throw a few leaves of cabbage into. The broth stank, and I had to take it to the women, the Jewish women, in buckets with a Ukrainian boy. They, it's interesting, these, these— but you want to hear about me and not about the Polish-Jewish women.

TC: No, I'd like to hear your impressions.

FJ: Well, I'll make it real short. I saw horrible things: women with their hair all cut off. I experienced how, in a few months, people can be turned into animals when you scarcely give them anything to eat. And when you then come by with some broth, how people go after one another just to get a little something in their stomachs. These Polish-Jewish women were all exterminated. None of them lived.

TC: Which camp was this?

FJ: Neuengamme.

TC: Neuengamme?

FJ: Yes, but the kitchen, the camp kitchen, the barracks, it was in Rothenburgsort. There where they had to work.

TC: And did you have to stay there?

FJ: I can, could go home. I could go home.

TC: Ah, you could.

FJ: I could go home.

TC: It was sort of like a job, you could say, but horribly enough, it wasn't that at all.

FJ: No, no. At the time, I was under the control of the women's supervisor, Frau Kappeler, from Rothenburgsort, NS women's supervisor. And she was in charge of me, she

checked whether I was there, how I worked, and more
threatening things like, I would have to be sterilized soon. I
got my period, you see. I got it, and of course they were
afraid, because our Führer wants a white race and for God's
sake, I was now at the age when boys would be interested in
me, and I would be interested in men. But over and over
again, there was a lot of solidarity. I had a school friend who
came and in those difficult times brought me an egg. First of
all we had . . . I don't know how, no one had an egg, you
know. How did she get this egg? Her uncle had got it somewhere, that egg. And she brought it to me. And she's an eye-
witness for me, she also says in the film, in the film you see
her, she says "During the school assemblies, we stood there,
like this: 'Heil Hitler,' and like that" and tells about how she,
how she came to the kitchen barracks, how the people there
— I don't know if you remember.

TC: I think I . . .

FJ: That was too much. There were always, you know, there
were always people, Germans, white people who helped me.

TC: Hmm. And your contact with the women, the ones who
were in the camp?

FJ: They were bombed. They were put on ships and, they, they,
they were bombed. And the people who wanted to save
themselves, the SS, they got boats, boats to catch them,
right? They [the SS] rowed around and shot them in the
water. There's a film about it.

TC: Mhm.

FJ: Yes.

TC: Were you there for the whole war? Can you . . . ?

FJ: No, I was only, I was only there for a year. That was enough
for me.

TC: Yes. How did you get out?

FJ: Well, I could always go home.

TC: Aha.

FJ: But then I broke down at work and then someone helped me
again. I was, well, I was doing poorly in the last month
before I broke down. I told the woman that I couldn't take
it anymore. It was cold, there was no [heat], only when we

were cooking—then the fire was put out. We sat there in the draft, we had no windowpanes. There was frost, and I collapsed a few times, and this woman just didn't believe it. She said that then we'd have to treat me more severely. Then they took me from work to the hospital in a truck, and there I collapsed. They took me to a hospital, and there was a German woman doctor there. She, she understood the whole miserable situation right away and transferred me [to a hospital] outside of Hamburg. Then I was freed and only [thought], "My God, I hope they come for me." You have to imagine that "Hopefully the Russians will come soon. Hopefully the Americans will come soon. For God's sake, it has to be soon," and so on. A tank meant something completely different for me then than after the war, as a pacifist.[24]

In the preceding passage what engages my attention is the way in which gender and race shape Jansen's descriptions of her experiences in Rothenburgsort. Jansen vividly describes the spaces and her interactions, yet these descriptions are saturated with the ways in which those interactions were structured by her race and gender and by what her blackness and femaleness were seen to mean within this regime. In Jansen's memory narrative, reading race and gender cannot be restricted only to what Jansen says. In fact, it is crucial to engage that which she does not say—that is, the silences in her testimony—as well as how race and gender shape and construct the spaces of social interaction that she describes. As we know, race and gender structure not only the lives of people of color but social interactions in general through material, discursive, and spatial effects. Here Ruth Frankenberg's notion of "racialized social geographies"—a concept that I elaborate to include both the gendering and sexualization of social interactions—is particularly helpful. Frankenberg defines social geographies as the physically and socially "peopled" landscapes of individual interactions in society and the social forms of perception and nonperception entailed in negotiating these landscapes. Racialized social geographies involve considering the racial and ethnic mapping of environments in both physical and social terms.[25] Thus, following Frankenberg's instructive lead, mapping social and spatial geographies of race and gender in Jansen's narrated biography reveals how race and gender structured her interactions both in the Third Reich and beyond. Reading the following excerpt from her memory narrative together with excerpt I offers a particularly powerful illustration of these processes.

EXCERPT J

TC: And among yourselves, you who worked in the kitchen, how was it? Did you — Were you a group or something like that? What kind of relationship did you have to one another? Because you weren't prisoners of — you weren't, you were internees?

FJ: We were the outcasts.

TC: Yes.

FJ: Yes, when I think about it, we got along very well together, although when I went outside, and they, they—well, we had Italians who, who were interned, it was different with them. They got respectable food to eat and they just saw me as a woman. They weren't allowed to have relations with German women, so for that reason, I got grabbed a lot and that was really horrible for me. I never understood, you know, that they had to have that or had to touch someone and all that. That was a really uncomfortable situation. While the others [in the kitchen], where we were together, that kind of thing didn't happen with them—that I, that they only saw me as a woman. . . . Later, after the war was over, [at parties and celebrations, progressive] people, leftist men, would ask me to dance, you know. There were these little peace parties, and they'd say to me, "Listen, Fasia, that doesn't make any difference to me, you know, that you're dark." And then I'd say, "Listen, it doesn't make any difference to me that you're white." They were so out of it then. "You gotta understand me. I didn't mean it like that. You have to . . . I'm for real, you know me. You know? And I didn't want that." I didn't say anything, just looked at them calmly and they'd get angrier and angrier, you know. "Are you offended? Why are you offended? You know how 'international' I am." And so on. You see, so what they [did or said] in anger—well. And I experienced over and over in such circles, even in pacifist circles, that they were used to, before I became, in quotation marks, "this famous singer," I noticed that they were used to seeing people from Africa would come here from poorer situations and receive some little solidarity contribution or project or something, and [such phrases of assurance like], "We're with you" and so on. And it always reminded me of a church or something—they would nod and say, "Thanks for the support," and so on. That's what they were used to. They weren't, they weren't at all used to—I think it's still so today, people taking part in discussions and criticizing them politically or however, or saying, "Listen, what about this and that." They can't take that, right? They're not used to that, right?[26]

The opening lines of this excerpt reinvoke Jansen's memories of her experiences in Rothenburgsort. She reflects on gender's role in Rothenburgsort and on her life as a postwar activist in leftist circles, and in this way she problematizes the inextricability of race and gender in her experience as an Afro-German. The central question posed by this passage of Jansen's memory narrative is what exactly Jansen is saying and is not saying when she comments that they "*just* saw me as a woman." On the one hand, she emphasizes that in the camp, outside of the kitchen, she was treated as an available object, something to be touched. In this context, gender is constituted through race—her blackness—which constructed her availability as a racialized sexual object. As a Black woman and non-Aryan—a racialized gendered Other and threat to the purity of the Aryan race—Jansen was perceived by prisoners in the camp as an available sexual object according to the boundaries circumscribed by NS racial and sexual politics. This construction of her left her open to mistreatment and marginalization even among other non-Aryan prisoners. As a result, Jansen was grabbed or manhandled in the camp.

She implicitly comments on her status as a Black woman when she says "they *just* saw me as a woman." The term *just* ironically emphasizes that which she does not say or does not find it necessary to say: "Black." In the context of her remarks in this sequence, Jansen's reference to herself as a "woman" contrasts with her subsequent reference to "German women" in the next sentence. "German women" were off-limits to internees. Yet Jansen is in fact a German woman, though as a German of African descent her access to this category as it was defined in the Third Reich is limited at best. Jansen's distinction between herself and other "German" women reflects her status at that time in the NS regime, where her Black heritage mitigated her cultural identity because of the elision of Germanness with a racially based concept of national identity, Aryanness.

By contrast, Jansen recalls that within the confines of the barracks kitchen, just outside of the camp, her treatment was different. The other "outcasts" with whom she worked (a separate group of outsiders within the larger group of Others that constituted the camp's population) did not "*only* [see] me as a woman." Here, *only* functions as a paradox similar to that of *just* in the preceding sequence. To be seen only as a woman outside the kitchen meant to be seen as a Black woman and face abuse. To be seen as more than a woman in the kitchen seems to indicate that her blackness, if not also her gender and sexuality, was overlooked. Within the comparatively protected confines of the kitchen, Jansen seemed to regain the status of a human being. In the topography of Rothenburgsort, the marginality of the barracks kitchen appears to have served at least a doubly protective function in Jansen's life: as an alternative to internment or sterilization (which she might otherwise have faced) and as a type of buffer zone in relation to the camp itself. Yet the protective dimensions of this space did not necessarily make it a "safe place." In excerpt I, Jansen describes her interactions with the female NS overseer of the kitchen, who repeatedly remarked on Jansen's adolescent sexual development. These comments were explicit threats aimed at emphasizing the fact that her sexuality as a Black, non-Aryan woman was perceived as a racial challenge to the purity to the NS regime, thereby necessitating her eventual sterilization. Jansen's narrative makes an equally provocative statement regarding the simultaneity and inextricable production of gender and race in the Third Reich. Unlike Hauck, whose access to the category of Germanness (as Aryan) was enabled by the simultaneous privileging of particular forms of masculinity, Jansen's access to Germanness was hindered by the gendering of this category.

For Jansen, femininity did not facilitate access to Germanness because her status as a woman was inextricably produced as Black, a construction diametrically opposed to the privileged racialized construction of white womanhood central to the National Socialist racial state.

In the map of labor in and around the camp that Jansen draws with her memories, an interesting topography emerges. On one level, as I stated earlier, the barracks in Rothenburgsort is situated as a place in the borderlands between the everyday life of the Third Reich and the no-man's-land (or absolute periphery) of Neuengamme. At another level, in the spatial relations of labor in and around the camp, the kitchen in Rothenburgsort functions as a sort of satellite in relation to the inmates and life in the camp, where Jansen's movements again take the form of shuttling back and forth not only between life at the center and the periphery but even within the margins, between the camp and the borderlands of Rothenburgsort. Jansen's memories of her life under the Nazi regime provoke us to rethink the notion of the margins as detached from the center. As her memory narrative demonstrates, even the marginal spaces to which she was supposed to be relegated were themselves porous locations characterized by both distance and distinction from the center while constituting that center through the thoroughly relative and relational interactions of movement and contact with it. Indeed, these spaces of marginality were also sites of complex social interaction.[27]

Jansen's descriptions of her interactions in the camp contrast starkly with those of her work in the kitchen. Although both give a harsh picture of her experiences, her descriptions of the kitchen characterize it as a space of isolation and constrictedness, with an odd sense of intimacy arising from the closeness of these quarters. In this tiny, unheated wooden shack, barely big enough to hold the stove, Jansen, and her male coworkers, they prepared what she describes as a smelly broth for the inmates of the camp. Yet despite the tightness of this space, she describes her situation as protected in comparison to that of the camp. Her description of her interactions in the camp are, by contrast, characterized by openness and exposure, emphasizing her vulnerability because of her race and gender. In each of these spaces, race shapes both the perception of her gender and the sexuality attributed to her, while her gender sexualizes how her race is read and what it is seen to mean. In this way, Jansen's memories of this social landscape power-fully document the inextricability of the racialization of gender and the gendered and sexualized ways that race acquires meaning.

Immediately following her statement that they "only saw me as a woman" occurs what I find to be perhaps the most fascinating narra-tive phenomenon in this passage. In what appears an almost seamless transition from one topic to the next, Jansen sets her experience with the male internees in the camp in relation to her experience as a woman among her leftist male colleagues following the war. In contrast to the "loud silences" that characterize her earlier narration of her experi-ences in the camp, expressing the effects of race in this context, her description of this incident in German leftist circles articulates this issue on a more explicit level. When describing her encounters as a Black German woman among leftist German men, she uses a type of narrative performance, mimicry, to communicate this. (Narrative per-formance will the focus of detailed analysis in the final section of this chapter.) Through mimicry, Jansen acts out her memories of her and her male colleague's remarks in this encounter. In this way, she revives this situation in the present and conveys her experiences in detail. At the same time, setting this performative exchange in the context of her memories of Rothenburgsort, Jansen's narrative technique conveys the parallels and continuities of her perceptions of how she experienced the racialization of gender construction and the gendered construction of race in her interactions in both of these contexts. In the camp, while it might appear that gender was the overt issue she was confronting, race and sexuality implicitly shaped this confrontation. In the second instance, where race seemed to be foregrounded, gender and sexuality were also at stake, shaping and refracting this interaction in compli-cated ways.

As I argued in chapter 3, processes of memory and storytelling are seldom random. For this reason, I struggled with two perplexing ques-tions in reading this excerpt. First, why did Jansen choose to set these two stories in relation to one another? Second, what is the significance of their juxtaposition in her narrative? As I attempted to map the social landscapes of this episode in Jansen's narrative, a graduate student pointed out the role of boundaries in these interactions.[28] In the scene that Jansen describes, expectations regarding the need for boundaries appear to be quite low. In a space such as she recounts—a "peace party," where Jansen is surrounded by her leftist political colleagues—the assumption of a safe space seems implicit. Yet in this context, at precisely the moment when the last boundary of social intimacy is about to be crossed—an invitation to dance—Jansen quite palpably encounters the effects of social constructions of race and gender that profoundly recall the earlier episodes in Rothenburgsort.

Through the initiation of a dance—an interaction of extreme intimacy and absolute proximity—Jansen is confronted with the resilience of a racialized gendered construction of herself as a Black German woman in the context of what seemed to her a quite familiar and protected space.[29] Interestingly, this occurs through an ironic formulation of this remark—that in fact, her race (referred to here as her "darkness") does not matter. The irony of this remark is that not only does her race make a very big difference in how she is perceived even in this "progressive" context but also her own life history and particularly her experiences in the Third Reich show that this has been the case for some time. Moreover, because of the fact that the effects of race as well as those of gender will always have not only discursive but also material and political consequences, this will indeed continue to be the case. Jansen's response to this remark plays off of this irony. When she retorts that her comrade's whiteness similarly "doesn't matter," she effectively states the exact opposite: it in fact makes all the difference in his ability to make a remark that assumes from a position of privilege the prerogative of deciding the salience of race for those who are not white. Jansen's brief remark and, perhaps even more emphatically, her continued silence in the face of her colleague's protestations effectively call into question his energetically helpless attempts to assert the futile argument that "race makes no difference," an argument that implicitly relies on an all-too-familiar liberal discourse of universal equality for all people, who, as we are assumed to know, "are the same under the skin."

As we saw in Hauck's memory narrative, silences often revealed the complex effects of race and gender in the lives of my interview partners. In fact, their articulations of these effects seemed most often to occur at points of resistance in their life histories. In Jansen's case, this occurred when she was faced with racialized and/or gendered constructions of herself as a Black German woman. Jansen's imitation or acting out of both her own and her male colleague's remarks in this encounter revives this situation in the present, vividly conveying her experience. At the same time, setting this performative exchange in the context of her past experience in Rothenburgsort, Jansen's narrative technique also conveys the parallels and continuities of how she experienced the racialization of gender construction in her interactions with men in both of these contexts.

I have emphasized elsewhere in this volume that the richest and most revealing interpretations of oral history texts are those that engage both speech and silence in their analyses. By the same token, the challenge of feminist analyses of such texts lies in reading effects of race and gender as simultaneous and mutually constitutive and locating these articulations in both the silences and utterances of oral texts as well as in the spaces that lie in between. In my informants' memory narratives, silence functions as interstitial space(s) between these individuals' words and statements, framing their articulations by outlining the effects of race and gender and setting them in stark relief. To reiterate my earlier discussion, interstices have been theorized most often as spaces of resistance, creativity, oppositional practice, and articulation. Similarly, in the narratives of Afro-Germans, silences are "loud" interstitial spaces of articulation where my interview partners were able to say that which they often had little capacity to explain.

Unlike Hauck, whose status as an Other within was characterized by his experience of marginalization at the center of NS society, Jansen's experiences as an Afro-German Other within in the Third Reich were characterized by a shuttling movement between periphery and center. On the one hand, as a non-Aryan, Jansen was the object of discrimination and marginalization. On the other hand, as a German she remained a part of NS society. Perhaps most interestingly, as a Black German, her status as both a non-Aryan and a German are rendered ambivalent: as we have seen, as a German of African descent—*Negermischling,* her status under NS law—was ambivalent because the specific legal guidelines for the treatment of Afro-Germans were restricted to marriage laws and school ordinances. Moreover, the experiences of other Afro-German contemporaries of Jansen and Hauck show that these two individuals' experiences cannot be seen as representative, except perhaps for their ever-present fear of persecution based on the ambiguity of their legal status.[30] Such persecution often came to pass, but in many cases it did not. The result was the creation of another curious gap. Blackness was an identifiable basis for discrimination, marginalization, and/or persecution under National Socialism, yet despite the testimonies of both Hauck and Jansen, it is difficult to speak of the systematic persecution of Afro-Germans in the Third Reich.

Despite the fact that the concept of the Other within remains relevant as a metaphor for the situation of Afro-Germans in the Third Reich, it is still important to incorporate a critique of the limitations of the conceptual model of the Other and Otherness into our understanding of the complex processes of racialization and subject formation recounted in the narratives of Afro-Germans and other "marginalized" groups. Otherness implicitly positions individuals wholly on the margins of social interactions. To be Other is to be a subject situated on the periphery with little possibility of movement and minimal explication of the processes through which one comes to inhabit this location. Similarly, the Other offers little if any conceptualization of the contradictions of such positionings, nor of subsequent changes of status, situation, or process. Indeed, the efficacious potential of Otherness/the Other as a conceptual model is in some ways truncated by its inability to account for the subjectivity of those in question. For this reason, rather than concentrating on sites and conditions of marginality, my approach to reading the history of Afro-Germans in the Third Reich has been to focus on examining the processes through which the marginality ascribed to Afro-Germans as the Other has been constructed and the extent to which both marginality and Otherness constitute not a single place or site to which individuals are confined. It is perhaps most instructive to explore how Otherness is inextricably bound up in processes of movement that are intricately linked to the norms of the center. As we have seen in the narratives of both Hauck and Jansen, such an analysis reveals the limitations of two-dimensional, dichotomous geographies of self/Other, margin/center, inside/outside, here/ there and does so in ways that yield a more complicated analysis of subject formation than most models of the Other can offer.

Hauck's and Jansen's narratives of the local politics of race share a description of life between two seemingly exclusive spheres: in Hauck's case, an interiority to the NS state and his simultaneous marginalization therein; in Jansen's case, her movement between an everyday life in the Third Reich and the borderland of labor as a kitchen worker in

Rothenburgsort. The mediation of center and periphery that characterizes Hauck and Jansen's memory narratives maps a topography of the local politics of race in the Third Reich that situates them in a sort of gray zone where the victimization each suffered was neither systematic nor necessarily coherent but rather ambivalent and contradictory.

REJECTION WITH HONOR — *WIEDERGUTMACHUNG* AND THE BUNDESVERDIENSTKREUZ

Jansen's memories construct her position in the Third Reich as characterized by two fascinating tensions: (1) the internal contradiction of being required to labor in Rothenburgsort as a German yet also as an Afro-German (that is, not a "real" German), having to perform this service at the margins of German society without being forced to remain there; and (2) the sociospatial tensions resulting from Jansen's movement between this peripheral location in the barracks of Rothenburgsort and her home at the symbolic center of NS society. These tensions reflect a pattern in Jansen's biography that continues into her later life and is expressed indirectly through her reference to another central recurring theme in her narrative, compensation. This topic serves as an outlet through which Jansen articulates the ambivalence of her status as an Afro-German in the Third Reich. However, the full significance of this issue is discernible only in relation to Jansen's receipt in the late 1980s of the Bundesverdienstkreuz (the German Medal of Merit).

EXCERPT K

FJ: I received the Bundesverdienstkreuz for my work.

TC: I didn't know that.

FJ: Yes, yes. It was also pretty amazing, whether I should actually accept it, right, because I'm against every type of medal.

TC: For what work [did you receive the medal]? You've done so much work.

FJ: Yes it's incredible, right, for exactly the work for which I in principle was condemned. [*Laughter*]

TC: Which do you mean?

[*Laughter*]

FJ: You know, what I otherwise got nothing for, when I—well,

I did once have to get something for this, for peace work, for the fight for this, against the, against the, against the, against the closing of factories here, where I always sang and rallied the women with me and the men's unions and such. [When I received the medal] it amazed everyone and would possibly have . . . although, although I was supposed to have received the award from Weizsäcker, and I wanted that. If at all . . . there were, there was a rally against the Gulf War. We marched in with flags, and at first there were speeches given and all that. But I still have reservations, and I'm considering whether I should give back this medal of honor.

TC: Why? For what reason?

FJ: I'm fighting for my compensation, and one can't on the one hand reward me for my work and on the other hand prevent me, right, from being recognized as a victim of persecution. On the other hand, perhaps I could make that clearer with [the medal]. On the other hand, I haven't used it. But I've heard that some people have done political work using these things. In certain institutions they can just say, "Here, I need this and need this for this and that." But I think that I'll manage it without that.[31]

Jansen received the Bundesverdienstkreuz for her work in the German peace movement from 1960 to 1980.[32] She recounts that she became active in the peace movement directly following the war. Her involvement centered on her role as a singer-activist. Jansen states that she began singing in Rothenburgsort, together with other prisoners and internees. She started singing blues and *Brechtlieder* in 1945 with Holocaust survivors while still in a Hamburg hospital. In 1947, she joined a newly formed choir and began giving street performances in Hamburg of *Brechtlieder* and other socially critical music addressing the postwar political situation in the Federal Republic. In 1970, Jansen spent three months performing with the Brecht Ensemble in Berlin. In our interview, Jansen emphasizes the explosion of the atomic bombs in Japan as a strong motivation for the direction of her music career and for her growing engagement with the nascent German peace movement. Her parents' background as what she calls *stadtbekannte Kommunisten* (locally known communists) was also decisive in her leftist political orientation. A self-defined *rote Schwarze* (Black Red), Fasia

Jansen's career as a singer spans three and a half decades, during which time she earned popular respect as an engaged singer-activist in the peace movement and later, in the labor struggles in the Ruhr valley, where she settled in 1970. Jansen was also active in the women's movement both in the Federal Republic and internationally. She appeared at countless demonstrations, marches, and festivals as well as on German television.

Both Jansen's activism in the peace and labor movements and her career as a singer must be seen in the context of her political orientation as a communist. This issue provides the background for her remark in excerpt K that she received the Bundesverdienstkreuz for precisely the type of work for which she had been condemned—that is, for what she considered peace organizing. For her activism in this area, she neither received nor expected any rewards or privileges. As she comments later, these were group projects involving collective effort and community organization. However, the experience of receiving one of the Federal Republic's highest honors for her activism as a Black Red seems in Jansen's mind to have been undermined by the rejection of her claim for compensation. The paradox that Jansen sees—receiving public recognition for her positive contribution to German society while the same society refused to acknowledge her negative experience as an Afro-German in National Socialist Germany—emphasizes the continuity of contradiction in Jansen's experience. Yet the contrast between the state's rejection of her experiences of persecution during the NS regime and its later affirmation of her work without acknowledgment of these earlier experiences illuminates the narrative of her life. In her memory narrative, this final context allows us to read the larger significance of this recurring pattern of continuity in contradiction, particularly by revealing a dialectic of recognition and rejection, acknowledgment and erasure, sight and oversight that defines the unavoidable presence of an Other situated in a precarious fissure. This Other cannot be completely overlooked but at the same time defies the constructions established to classify her by exceeding the limits of a popular imagination that cannot conceive of her.

CONCLUSION

Our primary association with Nazi Germany is the horrific crimes it perpetrated against humanity—specifically, the persecution and genocide of millions of European Jews. We identify National Socialism with anti-Semitism as its primary motivating force. Yet looking at the effects of this regime on Germany's small population of Black Germans gives us a broader picture of the Nazi state and helps us to understand that although anti-Semitism played a key role in Nazi ideology, it did so as part of a larger system of racism in which race served as the essential biological category that defined an individual's social status and value. Nazi Germany was first and foremost a racial state—one structured around race as the organizing principle of social, political, and economic life in the Reich. As a racial state, the National Socialist regime was founded on its ability to produce specific racialized categories of legitimate and illegitimate subjects. In other words, subjecthood or recognized membership in society was defined in purely racial terms. Legitimate subjects were those who claimed to be of "pure" Aryan heritage and were healthy, productive members of German society. Illegitimate subjects—individuals who had no claim to the rights and privileges of membership in German society—were all those who were not "pure" (for example, Jews, Blacks, and those of mixed racial heritage), those who were "genetically unhealthy" or unproductive (individuals with physical or emotional disabilities, criminals, alcoholics, homosexuals, and epileptics), as well as others.

What is remarkable about the accounts of my Afro-German informants is the ways in which the opposition between and among the categories of race and nation that were fundamental to distinguishing legitimate from illegitimate German subjects in the Reich came to subvert their intended effects in interesting and provocative ways. In spite of the fact that the organizing principle of the Nazi regime aimed to leave no room for any but the pure Aryan German subject, because the racial essences and notions of national purity on which this legitimate German subject was posited were fantastic constructions, not only could they not sustain this system but in the case of some Afro-Germans, these ideas came to have unintended paradoxical effects. The social dynamics of the local are critical for understanding these effects. Afro-Germans' memory narratives provide vivid accounts of the local politics of race in Nazi Germany. Using these accounts to construct a reading of the politics of race in the Third Reich reveals important contradictions among public discourse, state policy, and local social interaction in ways that are consistent with earlier German attempts to confront racial difference in the country's midst. Indeed, attempts to contain race within narrow categories of purity and impurity as a means of delineating privileged and disavowed subject status is a strategy of social management that has consistently had harrowing human consequences and repeatedly has ended in catastrophe. This fact notwithstanding, a critical reading of Afro-German accounts of the local politics of race in the Third Reich constructs a complex picture of why the production of legitimate and illegitimate social subjects in this regime is in fact far more complex than traditional models of exclusion and marginalization might lead us to believe. For although marginalization is usually identified as a phenomenon of the periphery, the narratives of my Afro-German informants urge us to consider the ways in which processes of marginalization in the Third Reich involved more than merely forms of peripherilization of individuals through systematic disenfranchisement and exclusionary practices. Perhaps even more striking are the ways in which these accounts demonstrate that such processes were features of this regime that characterized social interactions at the center as well as at its margins.

Hans Hauck's and Fasia Jansen's narratives of the local politics of race share a description of life in between two seemingly exclusive spheres: in Hauck's case, an interiority to the NS state and his simultaneous marginalization therein; in Fasia Jansen's case, her movement between periphery and center, between her everyday life in the Third Reich and the borderland of labor as a kitchen worker in Rothenburgsort. The mediation of center and periphery that characterized both Hauck's and Jansen's memory narratives maps a topography of the local politics of race in the Third Reich that situates them in a sort of gray zone, where the victimization each suffered was neither systematic nor necessarily coherent but rather ambivalent and contradictory. The memory narratives of Afro-Germans demonstrate that although race and racial difference served as the NS state's mode of defining membership in the larger German collective, this was contested in important ways at local levels of society, where community ties often functioned in oppositional ways to create and enable the recognition, inclusion, and *survival* of subjects deemed unworthy of membership in other social contexts.

These individuals' stories of their lives under this regime attest to the fact that even the most extensive attempts to reduce individuals to only their race and to exclude them from society were unable to account for the essentially paradoxical nature of race—that ultimately, we are all always both far more and far less than our race. Although each of us is marked by our race and experience—the effects of what it means to be Black or white or raced in some way through our interactions in society—we are never only that. In other words, we are always far more than the positive and negative attributes and stereotypes of any racial characterization and at the same time far less than any of these representations by virtue of the fact that none of them can ever capture the complexity of any individual. Paradoxically, this conundrum in the end worked to both Hauck's and Jansen's advantage.

This very important paradox to some extent explains the complicated picture of the Third Reich that emerges from these individuals' memory narratives. Because they were Black, they became objects of the regime's attempts to neutralize the threat they were seen to pose because of their race. Nevertheless, because they were also much more than this and, perhaps most importantly, were Germans who were recognized as members of their local communities, it was possible for them to live within this regime in ways that radically challenged the assumptions of the "place" National Socialism intended him to take up within it—namely, nowhere.

Reading the stories of these two individuals through the lens of a feminist theoretical analysis focused on the minute workings of racialization and gendering allows us to connect the details of lives of ordinary Germans to the larger systems that shaped their lives. Hauck's and Jansen's memory narratives powerfully illustrate the fact that although the system itself was flawed, when it did work through race, race was always constituted through gender, and gender was always racialized through the meanings ascribed to it. Critical to understanding all of these processes are the social dynamics of the local. Being attentive to issues of the local in the stories and memories of ordinary people is a crucial mode of accessing these dynamics and an important site for broadening our understanding of the workings of larger political and social systems such as National Socialism. Only through an understanding of minutely individual effects can we grasp the colossal impact of such a monumental regime.

CHAPTER 5 DIASPORA SPACE, ETHNOGRAPHIC SPACE — WRITING HISTORY BETWEEN THE LINES

A Postscript

This book began with a discussion of a specter with complicated implications for how Black Germans were read and responded to by Germans during the first half of the twentieth century. But in many ways, the chapters presented thus far might be said to be "haunted" by their own ever-so-benign specter of sorts. Then again, perhaps *specter* is far too hyperbolic a term for the phenomenon to which I refer. Perhaps it is better characterized as an insistent, underlying subtext, a nagging assumption or question that cannot be ignored. Although this study has placed the history of Black Germans and the narratives of the lives of two individual members of this group firmly in the context of the history of the Third Reich and the politics of race, gender, and sexuality in early-twentieth-century Germany, the question remains as to how we are to read the history of this community in relation to the similar histories of other Black populations. Indeed, for many, the material presented in this study would pose a different, as yet unanswered question of what links, parallels, and comparisons might be drawn between Afro-German histories of racism, resistance and struggle, and affirmation and identification and those of Black communities in other cultural contexts. Might there be points of similarity and commonality among different Black cultures that connect their historical and cultural trajectories? Might we not view these links as points of comparison that offer us a deeper understanding of the social and political status of Black people more generally?

This closing chapter will respond to this subtext of suggestive and provocative questions about the links and commonalities among different Black communities. Examining the relations between Black communities transnationally and the ways in which these connections can be utilized constructively toward important cultural, political, material, discursive, and analytic ends is at the core of a growing and complex literature on the African diaspora. Yet scholarship theorizing Black community and cultural formations often relies on a discourse of diasporic relation in which similarity and commonality are privileged. In the pages that follow, I hope to complicate and, perhaps more ambitiously, contribute to a rethinking of how the relations of the African diaspora might be conceived more productively. This chapter grows out of a desire to understand the diaspora as a formation that is not solely or even primarily about relations of unity and similarity, but more often and quite profoundly about the dynamics of *difference*. It illuminates these dynamics by thinking about the question of translation among different Black communities, and how difference and translation are themselves crucially constituent elements of the African diaspora. Hence, this final chapter offers a very future oriented end to this historical study of German Blacks in the early twentieth century by considering how this community might refigure the politics of the African diaspora in the twenty-first century.

In his 1994 article, "Diasporas," James Clifford poses the probing question, "What is at stake, politically and intellectually, in contemporary invocations of diaspora?"[1] This question holds continued relevance for current scholarship on Afro-diasporic communities and is central to understanding the links many Black scholars see as significant to an analysis of the transnational relations among Black communities. Reexamining Clifford's question gives us the opportunity to reflect critically on the extent to which the discourse of diaspora has become far more centered, particularly in the fields of Black studies, cultural studies, and African-American history, than it was at the time of the publication of Clifford's essay, just a few years ago. Taking Clifford's provocative query as a starting point is also intended to invite a reflection on whether our stakes in the concept of diaspora in studies of Black communities transnationally have changed as this term has become more centered. At the same time, this question directs our attention toward the less celebratory, less comfortable, more problematic elements of this discourse as well as their implications for our attempts to make sense of the histories, cultural formations, and expressions of Black communities elsewhere.

This final chapter is less a conclusion than a postscript, looking simultaneously both backward and into the future. Linking the narratives of Hans Hauck and Fasia Jansen to scholarly and popular discourses and discussions of diaspora, this chapter explores how the ethnographic exchanges out of which these narratives emerged reflect complex tensions within the relations between Black communities. At the same time, it illustrates some of the exigencies of diasporic relation that make the concept of diaspora something more than an analytic tool—indeed, for many people, it is a practical and political necessity. This chapter explores these issues by way of a particularly rich set of ethnographic phenomena that characterized my exchanges with my Afro-German informants, phenomena that occurred at different times and in different forms in all of my interviews. A complex citational practice that my informants strategically invoked throughout our exchanges, the phenomenon I refer to as "intercultural address" raises fascinating questions about the implicit notions of similarity and relation often assumed between the histories and experiences of Black communities transnationally. The following pages reintroduce several passages from the preceding chapters. These quotations will be returned to the original interview contexts from which they were extracted and reread in relation to the ethnographic settings in which they occurred.

This chapter resituates Clifford's original question, reading it through a very different lens and site of analysis. In so doing, the chapter takes as its starting point a related question, albeit one whose formulation differs from Clifford's in important ways. Specifically, what do invocations of "diasporic relation" do for communities situated at what anthropologist Jacqueline Nassy Brown calls "the margins of diaspora?"[2] Although we may never comprehensively answer this question with any degree of satisfaction, reflecting momentarily on the term *diaspora*—both its more recent genealogy and some of the methodological and theoretical uses to which it has been put—might prove useful as an analytic framework for the study of Black communities, enabling us to begin imagining what such an answer might entail. Following this brief introduction, I offer a reading of some of my encounters with diasporic invocation taken from my work on

Black Germans. The first set of encounters are scholarly ones, the second very rich ethnographic ones. Each offers different insights into the work that diasporic invocation does and the entanglement of intercultural interpellation and interrogation therein. Each asks us in different ways to engage the stakes of the relationships between Black communities in ways that are at times uncomfortable, at times problematic, yet always insightful and instructive.

BORROWINGS, LINKS, AND (BE)LONGINGS

As numerous scholars have made clear, the foundational notion of *diaspora* is the forced dispersal or displacement of a people. A diverse array of social theorists have theorized diaspora in relation to this fundamental notion of dispersal and displacement from an originary homeland, building on the much-cited etymology of the term from the Greek *dia* (meaning "through") and *speirein* (meaning "to sow" or "scatter"). The implicit and often explicit referent in these analyses is what is seen as the defining paradigm (what William Safran, following Weber, terms the "ideal type") of diaspora—the Jewish diaspora.[3] Diaspora traditionally has been associated with a historical event of migration or dispersal whose profound effects come to be inscribed in narratives of displacement. Equally central to this model of diaspora is the maintenance of either a concrete or imagined relationship to an originary homeland and the narratives cultivated and passed down within communities that construct an intergenerational continuity of relationship to such homelands across time and space. Yet, as both Clifford and sociologist Avtar Brah emphasize, the concept of diaspora is not limited to a historical experience. Rather, this idea functions as at once a theoretical concept, a complicated imagined space of relation, and a complex analytic discourse that "invites a kind of theorizing that is always embedded in particular maps and histories."[4] Brah suggests that we conceive of diasporas as "an ensemble of investigative technologies that historicize trajectories of different diasporas, and analyze their relationality across fields of social relations, subjectivity and identity."[5]

Yet when considering the concept of diaspora specifically in relation to African-descended peoples, the question arises of what exactly constitutes the potentially beneficial diasporic connection among Black peoples? Precisely this question has been one focus of the subtle and sophisticated analyses of Black British theorists of diaspora, most prominently Stuart Hall and Paul Gilroy.[6] Many models of African diaspora emphasize the role of African origins, cultural heritage, and legacies, and these models continue to constitute a highly influential discourse both within the academy and beyond it. Both the historical event of migration and at times the residual effects of slavery as a defining moment of inequality whose effects continue to have salience in contemporary social interactions remain elements of these articulations of diaspora. Yet in the European context, Black British scholars such as Hall and Gilroy have theorized diaspora in the British context as multiple complicated processes of positioning in relation to a sense of belonging vis-à-vis the creation of psychic, symbolic, and material communities and "home(s)" in the sites of settlement.

In many ways, Gilroy's conception of diasporic relation might be said to be the privileged model for understanding diaspora among contemporary theorists of Black European culture. Gilroy articulates this relation as a transnational link forged through the mutual perception of a shared, racialized condition and the cultural and political resources Black people use in their struggles against the various and varying forms of racial oppression with which they must contend in their respective contexts.[7] Specifically, Gilroy argues that the ongoing "pursuit of emancipation, justice and citizenship internationally as well as within national frameworks" constitutes a transcultural and historical link between Black cultures.[8] Moreover, an intricate process of borrowing and adaptation is key to Gilroy's diaspora discourse. This dynamic cultural syncretism is central to the relations between Black cultures in the ways that communities such as Black Britain draw on the "raw materials" of Black communities elsewhere. As Gilroy writes in one of his most widely cited formulations,

> Black Britain defines itself crucially as part of a diaspora. Its unique cultures draw inspiration from those developed by black populations elsewhere. In particular, the culture and politics of black America and the Caribbean have become raw materials for creative processes which redefine what it means to be black, adapting it to distinctively British experiences and meanings. Black culture is actively made and re-made.[9]

Through his emphasis on intercultural relations of borrowing, exchange, and adaptation within "settled" Black communities, Gilroy articulates a discourse of diaspora as a complex politics of location and belonging. As Brown asserts, Gilroy's diaspora discourse thus moves beyond a fixation on the consequences of migration, displacement, and relation to originary homelands to focus on the types of raw materials (for example, popular cultural artifacts such as music, shared memories, or cultural narratives) on which Black populations draw in constituting their own cultures and communities.[10] Here, Brown's notion of "diasporic resources" proves particularly useful. In her 1998 article, "Black Liverpool, Black America, and the Gendering of Diasporic Space," Brown engages the stakes of the discourse of Black America in Black British articulations of diaspora and offers an important intervention in the discussion of diasporic relation. Building on Gilroy's notion of raw materials, Brown undertakes a sophisticated analysis of the cultural and political practices of Black Liverpudlians, focusing on their use of "the vast resources of what they construct as the Black world, yet within the political economy of what has been available to them." She continues,

Diasporic resources may include not just cultural productions such as music, but also people and places, as well as iconography, ideas, and ideologies associated with them. . . . I use the term *diasporic resources,* then, to capture the sense that black Liverpudlians actively appropriate particular aspects of "black America" for particular reasons, to meet particular needs—but do so within limits, within and against power asymmetries, and with political consequences.[11]

Emphasizing the African diaspora itself as less a concrete geographical trajectory than a set of relations constructed actively by communities for specific purposes, toward particular ends, Brown contends that "there is no actual space that one could call 'the African diaspora,' despite how commonly it is mapped onto particular locales." Yet she argues that this fact points out the extent to which "social spaces are constructed in tandem with processes of racial formation."[12] Moreover, the complex forms of desire and longing she understands as crucial to the relations between different Black communities are central to her concept of diasporic resources. As we will see, these relations are anything but simple, universal, or egalitarian but rather emerge as the product of past and contemporary histories and hegemonies that require active and self-critical engagement.

DIASPORIC ASYMMETRIES

My interest in fleshing out the limits and tensions of diasporic relation arises out of my increasingly frequent confrontations with diaspora as *the* requisite approach or theoretical model through which one should (or perhaps must) understand all formations of Black community, regardless of historical, geographical, or cultural context. In trying to understand the relationship of the history of Black Germans to the histories of other Black communities, it becomes increasingly apparent that diaspora does not constitute a historical given or universally applicable analytic model for explaining the cultural and historical trajectories of all Black populations. Rather, we must engage this concept with an awareness and articulation of its limits in regard to those Black communities whose histories and genealogies do not necessarily or comfortably conform to dominant models. Indeed, it is worthwhile to recall Gilroy's reminder that diaspora often serves to paper over difficult fissures and gaps within the affiliations constructed between Black communities. As he remarks, "This powerful idea is frequently wheeled in when we need to appreciate the things that (potentially) connect us to each other rather than to think seriously about our divisions and the means to comprehend and overcome them, if indeed this is possible."[13]

Similarly, particularly for a Black community such as Afro-Germans, it is necessary to establish their specific relation to the concept of diaspora before assuming their inclusion within this model on an equal or universal status with other Black communities. Yet such specificity often proves elusive when theorizing the relation of particular Black communities to the African diaspora, as the following example attests. In her 1996 article, "Historical Revelations: The International Scope of African Germans Today and Beyond," Carol Aisha Blackshire-Belay writes:

It is true that the level of awareness of Africa and Africanness among African Germans has increased over the years since the organization of various groups among them. This has also led to a development of consciousness about who they are in European society. Examination of German history and German contacts with African people in Africa, Germany, and in the Americas helps them to identify the obstacles that have historically stood in the way of progress for the African Germans and their situation in German society today. This enables them to understand the ways in which these obstacles have been overcome in places and to draw up a program of action to overcome obstacles where they continue to exist. Indeed consciousness of Africa is a necessary rallying point for the promotion of more fruitful and enduring interactions between continental and diasporic Africans.

The time has come for the African-German community to see itself as a community belonging to the African Diaspora— African-descended people dispersed throughout the world. While the African Germans may perceived [*sic*] themselves as a small, yet visible minority in a white majority society, they are, however, national minorities in the countries of their birth. This becomes much more important when it is considered together with the populations of the African continent, and only then does the balance change. Because as members of the African Diaspora we are all connected by heritage although separated by birth. This connectedness offers us a strength that we can draw from, indeed just as African Americans have discovered over time.[14]

Blackshire-Belay's comments place Afro-Germans in a perplexing and rather awkward space in the discourse of diaspora. On the one hand, Belay describes a reciprocal relation between Afro-Germans' growing awareness of their African history and heritage and the beneficial effects of this awareness in reinforcing their sense of themselves as Europeans. On the other hand, through the emphasis she places on the lessons that might be learned from a closer examination of Germany's historical encounters with Blacks at home and abroad, her comments seem to gesture toward a notion of raw materials or resources that is related to though less well developed than that articulated by Brown and Gilroy.

Yet at this point, Blackshire-Belay's arguments take a distinct turn in a different direction—one that privileges both Africa and African-

Americans in her configuration of the relations of the African diaspora. When she writes that "consciousness of Africa is a necessary rallying point for the promotion of more fruitful and enduring interactions between continental and diasporic Africans," she elides the
benefits of learning from the history of Black peoples' struggles with an
identification with Africa, at the same time making a curiously essential distinction between what she terms "continental" and "diasporic"
Africans. In this way, she seems to invoke the identification with a culturally and nationally transcendent "Africa" as the necessary prerequi-
site to diasporic relation. Blackshire-Belay's notion of the diaspora
thus recenters Africa as a mythic point of origin and a unifying
transnational social and politic adhesive between continental Africans
and their irksome siblings, Afro-diasporics. This recentering of Africa
harkens back to much earlier discourses of diaspora similarly anchored
in sites of origin and notions of cultural heritage as powerful explanatory models for contemporary social and political configurations.

In this context, Blackshire-Belay offers her most strident invocation
to diasporic identification, insisting that the Black German community's identification with the African diaspora is long overdue. Here
she defines *diaspora* quite simply as "African-descended people dispersed throughout the world," where the diasporic relationship
between Black communities is their "common heritage"—a connection
on which, she emphasizes, Blacks can draw for strength. In many ways,
Blackshire-Belay's comments closely resemble the words of African-
American feminist poet and activist Audre Lorde, who, in her 1990
foreword to *Showing Our Colors,* articulates a similar set of issues:
"Members of the African Diaspora are connected by heritage although
separated by birth. We can draw strength from that connectedness."[15]
Yet unlike Blackshire-Belay, who defines a very specific relationship
between Black Germans and Africans in her diaspora discourse, Lorde
formulates this relationship as a question both open to interpretation
and in need of interrogation. In her 1984 introduction to the original
German publication of *Showing Our Colors, Farbe bekennen* (reprinted
in the English edition), Lorde poses this question quite directly:

Who are they, these German women of the Diaspora? Beyond the
details of our particular oppressions—although certainly not outside the reference of those details—where do our paths intersect

as women of color? And were do our paths diverge? Most important, what can we learn from our connected differences that will
be useful to us both, Afro-German and Afro-American.[16]

In her foreword, Lorde refined this formulation to explicitly query
the exact relationship to Africa of Afro-Asians, Afro-Europeans, and
African-Americans.[17] Lorde's persistent efforts to ponder these relations as questions are useful, for in so doing, she foregrounds what she
terms the "connected differences" between different Black communities and cultures such that their moments of divergence become as
salient as their similarities, overlaps, and commonalities.

Blackshire-Belay seems not to give credence to the deeply diasporic
dialogue out of which both the term *Afro-German* and the movement
itself emerged. As the authors of *Showing Our Colors* attest, the thoroughly diasporic, cross-cultural exchange between themselves and
Lorde contributed substantially to their articulation of their identity as
Afro-Germans.[18] Indeed, in many, if not all, of the personal narratives
published in this seminal volume, the reader is struck by Black German
women's recurring stories of fateful visits made to Africa (or Black
communities in the Americas or Britain) and the pivotal role ascribed
to these encounters with Black communities abroad. These experiences
are often not described in positive terms, though they almost always
have substantial implications for the women's later lives. Nevertheless,
while identification with Africa or Black communities elsewhere often
serves as a starting point, such identifications must always be
unpacked and deconstructed to unearth the layers of projection,
desire, and longing that inevitably play a role in these complex relationships. Similarly, privileging Africa within the discourse of diaspora
is equally in need of unpacking and deconstruction.

Yet beyond the tendency of an uncritical invocation of diasporic
relation to diminish the critical capacity of diaspora by reducing this
concept to a descriptive term of identification and similarity through
racialization, Blackshire-Belay's comments also illustrate another perhaps more worrisome dimension of the discourse on the African diaspora that arises from an overemphasis on relations of similarity.
Belay's quotation exemplifies this through the telling role ascribed to
Black America in her articulation of diaspora. The frequent citation of
Black America within scholarly discourse on the African diaspora as

an almost privileged site or referent in the trajectory of diasporic cultural, community, and identity formation, and the increasing use of the African-American context in articulating a politics of diasporic relation, may be read as a discourse that refers not so much to a relation of equity than of hegemony. Blackshire-Belay's less-than-satisfying articulation of transnational diasporic relation embodies this tension, since her reference to the African-American experience seems intended not simply to be relational but rather to be exemplary.

In her compelling critique of Gilroy's conception of the diasporic relationship between Black Britons and Black America, Brown argues that Gilroy's analysis is troubled by the extent to which his attempts to theorize transnational diasporic relationships leave unexamined the asymmetries of power that exist across and between different Black communities and the very different relationships to diaspora that arise as a result. Brown urges us in our engagement of notions of transnational Black diaspora to examine how American hegemonies in particular have contributed to an imbalance in the nature of the transatlantic exchanges that constitute the diaspora. She cautions that

> diaspora may very well constitute an identity of passions; but these passions, and the means of pursuing them, may not be identical within particular communities. These points force the sober realization that, despite invitations to universal identification, not everyone partakes in the privileges of membership to the diasporic community with impunity.[19]

Brown's work highlights a tendency within the discourse of diaspora to assume a kind of equality between Black communities within the diaspora in ways that bracket, ignore, or erase the very different ways in which specific Black communities are situated within the geopolitical relations of power and hegemony. She encourages us to remember that the diaspora is also structured by power asymmetries inscribed both by different histories of racialization, colonization, and imperialism and the more recently accruing forms cultural capital some Black communities, particularly the African-American community, have come to command in the past quarter-century. Indeed, the desire to see such linkages as removed from or outside of these relations is one of the most potentially problematic dimensions of the discourse of diaspora. As Brown also points out, in the relations of the African diaspora, not all Black communities are equal. African-Americans and African-American feminists in particular must be especially mindful of this fact, because the manner in which both Black America and Africa are invoked within African-American discourses of diaspora is also often anything but equitable.

Following Brown, it is important to recognize that the relationships between different Black communities are structured no less by dynamics of power and hegemony than the relationships that came to constitute the diaspora itself. Here, the role of Black America must also be incorporated into any assessment of diasporic relation, less as a concrete history of struggle than as a way in which this history and the increasingly influential cultural capital of Black America travels to and often structures modes of articulation within other communities.[20]

Yet when we set the history of the Black German community in relation to the more complex notions of diaspora discussed in this chapter, it is also important to reflect on the role of an undertheorized element of diasporic relation—namely, the role of memory. Highlighting the function of memory in the writing of history has been one of this text's primary goals. Similarly, the role of memory is an important element in the relations of diaspora and should not be overlooked in its analysis. The status of memory suggests a different process of cultural formation and highlights some important tensions of diasporic relation that must be engaged in any analysis of the Black German community's relation to the African diaspora.

In the German context, the absence of the forms of memory so central to many models of Black diasporic identity and community raises the question of what happens when a community lacks access to such memories, as has historically been the case for Afro-Germans. Until recently, few Afro-Germans had any connection to one another, for most members of this largely mixed-race population grew up as the only Blacks in their surroundings. With the exception of the current generation, most Black German children did not grow up with their Black parents, thus hindering almost any transmission and preservation of memory in a fundamental way. Despite the fact that points of contact and relation among early Black migrants to Germany did exist, the death or departure of these almost always male Black parents often meant that these nascent networks of relation were rarely, if ever, sustained from one generation to the next. Hence, what marks much of this group is the lack of shared narratives of home, belonging, and community that sustain so many other Black communities and on which they draw as "resources" in numerous ways. As a result, Black Germans have never regarded a sense of relation and belonging among themselves or to other Black communities as self-evident. It has come to be negotiated only in the past two decades. Even current attempts to forge political and cultural connections and alliances with members of other Black communities both in Germany and abroad repeatedly falter on this issue, often coming into conflict at the moment when established histories of other Black communities are imposed on Afro-Germans, who are assumed to identify with histories of struggle (most often those of Africans, Caribbeans, or African-Americans) in which Afro-Germans are not seen as active participants. Their struggles often go overlooked, along with the histories and existence of Black Europeans altogether.

Paradoxically, although the preceding chapters have emphasized the importance of memory in reconstructing the history of this population and in understanding the complex and contradictory effects of National Socialism at the local level, this chapter is less about memory per se than about what happens in its absence. In other words, how does the discourse of diaspora play out in a Black diasporic community where memory is quite palpably absent? What must be emphasized here is the extent to which memory plays a central role in constituting forms of diasporic identity and community. The direct and inherited memories of diaspora define and sustain a sense of relation to real and imagined homelands in addition to a sense of relation among and between communities separated spatially in diaspora. As both remembrance and commemoration, this memory technology engages strategic forms of forgetting imposed institutionally from without as well as individually and collectively within specific communities. Memory provides the source of the defining tension of diaspora and diasporic identity: the dynamic play of originary and imaginary homes, and the complex networks of relation forged across national, spacial, and temporal boundaries.

In this way, Afro-Germans are, once again, positioned in a type of interstitial space—implicated and intertwined, though not fully encompassed by such a model of diaspora/diasporic relation. The waves of forced or collective migration that mark other Black communities do not characterize the history of Black Germans. And yet the individual journeys (voluntary except for the children of the postwar occupations and the scattered number of slaves brought by individuals to Germany) that led to the formation of this community might nevertheless be seen in relation to an alternative model of diaspora, albeit in a specifically German manifestation has yet to find full articulation. The lack of recorded historical memories and the consequent difficulty of their public transmission and interpretation in turn further constrains the diasporic function of memory. Thus, the representation of Afro-Germans in larger historical narratives of nation, race, and place has only recently begun to occur, while this community's own work in establishing and claiming a "diasporic memory" still remains in its nascent stages.

DIFFERENCE, DIASPORA, AND *DÉCALAGE*

In an article that echoes a number of concerns similar to my own, Brent Edwards offers a brilliant intellectual history of the uses of diaspora as an analytic framework to do what he terms "a particular kind of epistemological work."[21] Edwards's essay, "The Uses of Diaspora," carefully excavates the history of this term's emergence within Black scholarly discourse, drawing lines of continuity and distinction from the Pan-Africanist movement and Negritude, through contemporary Black British cultural studies, and forward toward the future implications of theorizing the diaspora in Black scholarship. What emerges from Edwards's genealogy is a nuanced conception of diaspora that foregrounds a notion of difference that is constituent to its formation and, at the same time, its most productive analytic potential. Edwards contends that the dynamics of difference he posits as diaspora's most salient feature and founding logic is one that can only be understood through an exploration of the necessary and inescapable moments of translation that accompany it. Translation, as both bridges and gaps of meaning produced in the interstices of converging differences within the diaspora, is indicative of necessary divergences, as well as points of linkage, contestation, and communication that construct any relation that might be articulated as diasporic. As Edwards contends:

If a discourse of diaspora articulates difference, then one must consider the status of that difference—not just linguistic difference but, more broadly, the trace or the residue, perhaps of what resists translation or what sometimes cannot help refusing translation across the boundaries of language, class, gender, sexuality, religion, the nation-state.[22]

What is particularly useful about the concept of diaspora that emerges in Edwards's piece is a provocative notion of diaspora as *décalage* that he develops so masterfully in the final pages of the essay. Borrowing from Negritude poet Leopold Senghor, Edwards resignifies *décalage* to engage differences among and between Black communities as a necessary and inevitable negotiation of a kind of "gap" or "discrepancy" between them. Reading Senghor's invocation of *décalage* against the grain, Edwards deploys the term as an innovative model for reasserting the unevenness and diversity of the African diaspora. Edwards argues for an analytics of diaspora that accounts for and attends to difference by conceiving of this formation as always inherently involving complex moments of *décalage* that structure relations among communities in diaspora. He concludes:

> *[D]écalage* is the kernel of precisely that which cannot be transferred or exchanged, the received biases that refuse to pass over when one crosses the water. It is a changing core of difference; it is the work of "differences within unity." . . . *[D]écalage* is proper to the structure of a diasporic "racial" formation, and its return in the form of *disarticulation*—the points of misunderstanding, bad faith, unhappy translation—must be considered a necessary haunting. . . . [P]aradoxically, it is exactly such a haunting gap or discrepancy that allows the African diaspora to "step" and "move" in various articulations.[23]

The final sections of this chapter offer a series of readings of what Edwards might term moments of "diasporic *décalage.*" These sections examine a rich selection of ethnographic encounters during which I came to engage such uneven and discrepant processes of translation, quite literally, "face-to-face." My focus is on the dynamics of a series of interpellative exchanges—specifically, moments when I and my Black

German interlocutors felt ourselves to be "hailed" and recognized in ways that we identified with, despite the fact that these references and citations were not always accurate translations of those identifications, nor necessarily ones that we shared. The aim of my analysis is to explore what kinds of insights might be gained from engaging otherwise unremarkable gaps in the translation of blackness within the diaspora, and how understanding these moments of translation as simultaneously also sites of interpellation might help to articulate not only the specificities of the diaspora and diasporic relations, but also racial and gendered formation, cultural identity, and the effects and implications of the nation in compelling and productive ways.

The phenomenon I refer to as "intercultural address" will serve as a revealing point of entry for exploring these dynamics. This term describes a series of eruptions/interruptions that I encountered repeatedly in the process of interviewing: as an African-American, I often became the object of "address," directly and indirectly spoken or referred to—at times even becoming the topic of our conversation—by my Afro-German interview partners in their attempts to explain and describe their experiences as Black people in German society. These unexpected exchanges were moments when I became aware of gaps of translation and moments of interpellation between us, as well as how we actively produced Black identity in our dialogues. My informants repeatedly made strategic use of Black America to articulate their assumptions of our similarities and commonalities as Black people while always emphatically insisting on the specificity of our culturally distinct experiences of race in our respective societies. As we will see, in Fasia Jansen's narrative, intercultural address most often took the form of cross-cultural queries that challenged me to situate myself in relation to the issues of race and identity that I unintentionally attempted to impose on her through my questioning. In Hans Hauck's narrative, intercultural address was expressed through his use of repeated references to me and to the African-American context in a series of narrative comparisons and contrasts that reflect and refract important aspects of how the relations among diaspora Blacks are configured. In this way, intercultural address illuminates important tensions of diasporic relation through the ways in which it simultaneously contests and affirms the assumptions of similarity between Black communities that were negotiated discursively in our interviews.

As a way of contextualizing the articulations of intercultural address that follow, it seems both pertinent and necessary to include some degree of ethnographic detail (or "thickness") in my analysis. I do this as a way of suggesting how each of my informants' comments was situated within the larger interview and to fill in some of the contours of the ethnographic space of my encounters with Hauck and Jansen. Despite the fact that the oral histories I conducted were intended to produce alternative historical sources, engaging these interviews as an ethnographic space proves important not only to understand the eruptions of intercultural address that emerged therein but also as a self-conscious attempt to acknowledge the extent to which the space of the interview constitutes a complex and loaded terrain shaped by dynamic interpersonal negotiations that reflect many of the complicated processes of social and cultural formation unearthed in and through the narratives they produce.

"SPÜRST DU DENN, DAT DU SCHWARZ BIST?": FEELING BLACK AND THE DIFFERENCE IT MIGHT MAKE

My conversations with both Hans Hauck and Fasia Jansen took place in Germany in 1992. At the time, I was a graduate student living in Berlin, on a research fellowship working on my dissertation. It was the second of what would eventually be a six-year residence in Berlin, at a volatile time in this city and country's more recent history. It was a crucial moment in postreunification Germany: between 1989 and 1992, Germany experienced a dramatic increase in racist and xenophobic violence. In April 1991, a twenty-eight-year-old Mozambican man was killed by a group of neo-Nazi youth who pushed him in front of a moving tram in the East German city of Dresden. In September of the same year, right-wing youth firebombed a residence for asylum seekers and assaulted Vietnamese and Mozambican residents in Hoyerswerde. According to the Federal Office for the Protection of the Constitution (Bundesverfassungsschutz), 1992 marked the height of these violent attacks. In August 1992 seven nights of violence occurred in the East German port city of Rostock, while in November of that year three Turks were killed in an arson attack in the small town of Moelln.[24] In response, Germans staged a series of candlelight marches in Berlin, Munich, Hamburg, Bonn, and other cities, with more than three million people voicing protests against the violence. My interviews with Hauck and Jansen occurred against this disturbing background of resurgent racist violence and resounding reminders of eras past.

As with all of my informants, my initial contact with both Hauck and Jansen was facilitated informally, through a third party and mutual acquaintance. I received their names from a woman journalist whose documentaries on the history of Blacks in Nazi Germany had been an important starting point for my research. My initial contact with both Hauck and Jansen followed what would probably be described as the most conventional rules of ethnographic or oral historical formality and etiquette—an initial contact letter followed by a phone call. I explained that I was interested in speaking to them as part of my dissertation research. As discussed in chapter 4, Jansen was a well-known activist living in a small industrial town in the Ruhr valley. Over the years, she had become a public figure of sorts and had developed a following among German trade unionists and in leftist, pacifist, and feminist circles, both within the region and in the Federal Republic more broadly, through her music and her dedicated work on these causes. Jansen agreed to speak to me after receiving my letter and on what I later learned was the enthusiastic recommendation of our mutual acquaintance. I conducted two interviews with Jansen over a two-day period; one of these was planned, while the other was a spontaneous follow-up interview that occurred a day later.

Our first interview took place in a political café near Jansen's home. The location was familiar to me not because I had ever visited it before but because I had been in countless cafés like it in other German cities. It was familiar as a result of my political biography and activist work with feminist and antiracist groups in Berlin and in the cities to which my colleagues and I had traveled as part of this work. It was a place one could find in almost any German city. The café was part of a larger *Projekt,* one of the countless publicly funded local political projects that at the time were subsidized by agencies of the German federal, state, and local governments. The café was attached to a larger set of rooms used for meetings and other activities of the different political groups and alliances that worked out of the center. The café served as an informal *Treffpunkt* (meeting place) for activists and community members affiliated with or affected by the project's work. Unfortu-

nately, Jansen and I never got around to discussing the specific nature
of the work of this particular project—we were engrossed in her story
from the moment I arrived.

Jansen had suggested that we meet at the end of her shift in the café
and do the interview there. The café would be closed, and it was one of
the few times she was available to speak to me. Jansen was a busy
woman. She struck me as hectic on the phone, and I was intimidated by
her assertiveness. I jumped at this small window of opportunity to
speak with her and agreed to do the interview at the café, disregarding
my own reservations about the potential noise and disruption of such
a public place. As it turned out, the noise of café cleanup and the com-
ings and goings of the project and café staffers were indeed quite dis-
tracting, but only to me—she was completely unfazed by it all. Until
then, I had always conducted interviews in my informants' homes, a
setting that I felt put them at ease and made them more comfortable
speaking with a stranger. As I found out when I arrived at the café,
location made no difference to Jansen, a gregarious, vivacious, witty,
and outgoing woman who felt as much at home here as at her residence. It seemed somehow almost more appropriate to interview her
here, since, as she later explained to me, she spent more time in such
places and traveling between these and other sites of her activism than
she did at home. In fact, in this semipublic place, only I felt awkward—
an out-of-place young American academic at a site of working-class
struggle, asking this fascinating woman to reveal her innermost
reflections on her complicated life.

But Jansen put me very much at ease. She had an easy way, and her
charming manner allowed us to quickly establish an warm and open
rapport. In fact, Jansen caught me quite off guard when, shortly after
we met, she went so far as to correct my use of the formal *Sie,* traditionally used in German by a younger person to address an elder or
stranger. She insisted that I address her with the informal *du.* Yet it
would be misleading to represent our exchange as a comfortable
process of mutual and transparent comprehension, despite the warmth
and honesty of our rapport. Indeed, in many ways, Jansen insisted
quite strenuously on mutual respect as the basis of our dialogue, and in
quite specific ways, she defined the terms and delineated the boundaries of our relationship in the interview. One example of this is the fact
that at the beginning of our second interview (which took place in her

home), Jansen informed me that she preferred that we use the more formal *Sie*. I had never experienced such a reverse shift from informal back to the formal, and I immediately thought I had done something to offend her. But Jansen explained that in her experience, *Sie* conveyed a mutual respect that is quite often lost with the *du* form, even among good friends, and she recounted an instance with a close friend when such had been the case. In making this shift, Jansen established a particular form of formality between us. At the same time, it was also a gesture of control in that she effectively defined the terms of the level of intimacy and respect in our exchange.

Perhaps because of the fact that our rapport was so good, the seams and gaps in our communication became that much more visible, in ways that I found extremely revealing of the deeper texture of our dialogue. As we will see, this complex interaction can be read as a compelling commentary on the tensions within the relations of the African diaspora in ways that urge us to consider the extent to which such relations are actively constituted at multiple levels in our cross-cultural dialogues and thus can never be assumed as a simple fact of similarity, affinity, or commonality. Intercultural address is one important site where both the texture of this complex ethnographic space and the dynamics of cross-cultural diasporic relation were made manifest in provocative and compelling ways.

The following example of intercultural address in Jansen's testimony adds an interesting dimension to my earlier discussion of the status of Africa in the discourse of diaspora. In this excerpt, Jansen and I discuss our relationship to "Africa" as Black women of different Western societies. We negotiate a popular construction of blackness that attributes to us a nonexistent relationship to Africa, a place that is foreign to both of us, whose social and cultural backgrounds lie outside the African continent.

EXCERPT L

FJ: Later, [my sister] continued her studies in America. I don't
     know what happened then. We met again after the war.
TC: Mhm, after the war.
FJ: Yes, —
TC: Was that —

FJ: I met all my brothers and my siblings then.

TC: Here in Germany?

FJ: In Germany.

TC: How did that come about?

FJ: One of them is director of geo-, geology—he does research
      on rocks and stuff like that and had some contacts, business
      contacts, in Hamburg. And then he heard that I was there
      and absolutely wanted to meet me. It was a terrible shock
      when a man came toward me who looked exactly like me.
      Exactly! It was my face. Yes. And it was so incredibly won-
      derful for me. He wanted to take me back to Africa. But I
      grew up here, and that's very, very hard. You see, I had no
      yearning for Africa.

TC: Um-hmm. Um-hmm. And —

FJ: I don't know how it is for you, if you have a yearning for
      Africa?

TC: Not at all. [*Laughter*] I understand what you mean, because
      I'm American.

FJ: Right.

TC: That's it. Nothing else.

FJ: That's it.[25]

In this passage, Jansen discusses one of her few encounters with her
African siblings. In Jansen's comments, *Africa* represents our common
heritage as Black women. However, in the German context in which
we at the time both resided, *Africa* is constructed as implicitly opposed
to Germanness, and as the place where all Blacks come from, belong,
and/or should have some mythical longing to be. Both of us reject this
construction of *Africa*. But what constitutes the "yearning" or "longing" (*Sehnsucht*) to which Jansen refers? Jansen's comments put an
interesting spin on the issues of relation and affiliation to Africa suggested by Blackshire-Belay. Whereas Blackshire-Belay emphasizes the
necessity for "diasporic Africans" such as Jansen to gain a greater
appreciation of the significance of Africa and African culture in the
development of their identities, communities, and social and political
struggles, Jansen's remarks highlight the tenuous nature of external
attempts to define what this relationship should be, how it should look,
and/or the terms on which it is or should be based.

The importance Jansen attributes to her contact with her African brother certainly affirms some part of the significance Blackshire-Belay attributes to contact with her African heritage. Yet Jansen's reaction to her brother's assumption that she would necessarily feel a natural connection to or affiliation with Africa seems equally worthy of comment. Jansen's brother's insistence that she return with him posits Africa as a lost homeland of sorts and intrinsically assumes either a return or, at the very least, identification and affiliation. As in Blackshire-Belay's comments, Africa is again constituted as a mythic, transcendent signifier of diasporic relation, the site to/through which all routes lead as the link between Black peoples. But in fact, it is less a site—that is, location—than a symbol that signifies connection in Jansen's case, anchoring a relation of kinship that begins with blood and for her brother ends with return. Yet for Jansen, like many Afro-German members of her generation, kinship with her African relations and culture is substantiated not by presence but by absence. For her, there were no shared memories or rituals of connection and few if any resources on which to draw in establishing any links of culture or heritage. Diaspora itself constructs such a relation, and Africa is its wholly symbolic vehicle. In her reaction to her brother's suggestion, Jansen asserts the limits of such a notion of diasporic relation. Her response engages *Africa* not as a symbol but as a peopled place of cultures and histories, a place to which, she emphasizes, she has no concrete relation: "But I grew up here, and that's very, very hard. You see, I had no yearning for Africa." Although links of kinship and heritage are important, Jansen underlines that hers are in Germany, rather than in Africa.

At this point, Jansen's engagement of the limits of diasporic relation broadens when she transposes this thorny issue onto me by querying my understanding as an African-American of my relationship to Africa. Her question, "I don't know how it is for you, if you have a yearning for Africa?" addresses me as a Black woman who, like her, is also from a culture outside of Africa. Her query articulates a request for confirmation or rebuttal of her own sense of the limits of diasporic affinity/affiliation. Yet the effect of her question is to establish an ambivalent connection. By addressing me directly as a Black woman and querying whether I have a relationship to Africa similar to that which she has just recounted in the story about her brother, Jansen initiates a process of interpellation that hails and thus produces me as a Black woman, a hailing to which I respond with immediate affirmation. Not only do I feel (cited and) recognized through her addressing me, but I also identify quite palpably with the awkwardness of the diasporic relation in which she is situated by her brother. Addressing her question to me effectively enables her to enact within the interview the same dynamic she has just described between herself and her brother. By asking me as another "sister" to position myself on the topic of my sense of my relationship to Africa—a place of tremendous symbolic significance in the discursive geography of the African diaspora, yet a place to which I have no "real" substantive connection—her use of intercultural address puts me in the position of having to recognize the gap that exists between the two of us and a notion of diasporic relation that centers on Africa as a site of origin and an assumed identity arising out of this site. In the process, her query effectively forces me to perform the same kind of positioning she did in relation to her brother, thereby beautifully making her point.

Intercultural address both points to necessity of making this symbolic relation and concrete nonrelation explicit and makes clear the extent to which they remain present as an assumed underlying relation in need of clarification. The fact that she asks me so pointedly where I "stand" in this relation strikingly attests to the truth of this paradox. In the end, we negotiate in this passage our relation to the diaspora, comparing our respective conceptions of what it means to be Black and to not come from Africa—that is, have a European or American socialization. In our exchange, the classic subject-object relation of interviewer-interviewee or speaker-listener dissolves almost completely in the context of our common rejection of a preexisting relation to Africa by virtue of race. In our discursive negotiation of the limits of diasporic relation, *Africa* at once signifies and facilitates the existence of our relationship to one another as Black people and at the same time highlights the need to translate and specify such gaps in the diaspora rather than assume those relations, as well as their limits, on the basis of both commonality and, even more importantly, distinction.

The intercultural relations of diaspora are quite decidedly the everpresent (sometimes explicit, at other times implicit) subtext of my interviews, both in the content of my questioning and woven through the fabric of our interpersonal interaction. Furthermore, intercultural address provides the vehicle through which this latent subtext repeatedly erupts into our interviews. A second and particularly evocative example of this from my interviews with Jansen is the following exchange, a sequence discussed briefly at the beginning of chapter 3.

EXCERPT M

TC: But what motivated you to do all this, all these political things and activities?

FJ: You shouldn't ask me about motivations and such things— you can't do that. It had to do with my being Black.

TC: What exactly?

FJ: All the things that I experienced must never again [be allowed to] happen. I've seen too much misery, and [I] throw all the strength that I have into [political work]. But you mustn't think that I always—that I wanted to run around and play the heroine for justice. Instead it was always, always whatever was there, "Listen, you have to come," like that, right? Always pushing for something, now I've got it— did you see, with the mills, get that through, he wants mills, all sorts of things, like that. And then in the women's initiatives, the ones that fought for their husbands' jobs. They always came and got me.

TC: Came and got you?

FJ: And that's why — or went there — and that's why I didn't need a psychologist. I was able to get rid of all the anger that I stored up, you know, all of it.

TC: But what —

FJ: I've brought people to tears, but I've also made them laugh, and the reverse. And then, finally, I ended up in the women's movement. Good. Now you ask the questions.

TC: [*Laughter*] May I?

FJ: You have to now. It costs too much money in tapes.

TC: Yes. The question about being Black. What exactly was it that, that connects your political work with your being Black? How did you express it, or what did it give you?

FJ: *You have to imagine, there was no Black movement here. I was all alone with this, and I myself never felt that I'm Black.*

> *The others have their problems [with it]. That was never my*
> *problem. [Laughter]*

TC: *Uh-huh. You never felt this yourself?*

FJ: *Do you feel that you're Black?*

TC: *Yes!*

FJ: *How?*

TC: *Yes. Yes, I mean —*

FJ: *Yes, when you look at yourself.*

TC: *Well, you're right.*

FJ: *I said to the children, I say, "Imagine, I know that I don't have*
> *this racial problem with myself. If I have a problem with being*
> *Black, then it's your problem, or your parents' problem."*[26]

The sequence of intercultural address in this excerpt is embedded in
our discussion of Jansen's political work. I begin by asking Jansen to
describe her motivations for her activism. Her reply is unequivocal: it
has to do with being Black. She explains that her activism comes from
a commitment never to allow what she experienced to happen again
and that her political activism served as an outlet for her to work
through many of her experiences. Later in the passage, I attempt to follow up on Jansen's original statement by asking for the exact nature of
the connection between her blackness and her political activism. My
intention was to obtain a more precise description of her personal
understanding of this relationship. In response, Jansen initiates a subtle shift in our discussion, eliding the issue of blackness by referring to
the absence of a Black movement in Germany ("You have to imagine,
there was no Black movement here"). At first glance, Jansen's remarks
seem almost to contradict her original statement that her political
engagement was related to her being Black. A superficial reading of
this passage might lead one to interpret Jansen's reply as a misunderstanding, where Jansen mistakenly interprets my question to refer to
her engagement in a Black political movement. However, a closer reading of this passage offers a more plausible interpretation of her
remarks.

Jansen emphasizes that she could not participate in a Black movement because no such movement existed in Germany. As a consequence, she had no opportunity to work through her experiences as a
Black person in Germany with other Blacks in Germany. Here her

implicit reference seems to be the U.S. civil rights movement of the 1960s and '70s. Jansen's emphasis on the absence of a Black movement in Germany is a direct response to my question, despite the discursive shift with which she introduces the topic into our conversation. The lack of a Black movement plays a primary role in explaining the necessity for Jansen's political engagement because the situation forced her to come to terms with her blackness alone ("I was all alone with this [*Ich war doch ganz alleine auf so was*]").

In many ways, Jansen's comments in this passage echo both Gilroy and Brown's discussions of the diasporic resources and raw materials they describe as marshaled by Black communities transnationally and used in strategic ways in the cultural, community, and identity formation of populations such as Black Britons. Yet Jansen's comments also speak to her sense of the lack of availability of such resources to her in Germany at a key point in her life. Her awareness of and engagement with the struggles of Blacks and women elsewhere, which she articulates throughout her narrative, makes clear that she did in fact draw inspiration from them. Still, Jansen seems to mourn the extent to which, regardless of their tremendous value to her, these struggles remain models and resources that are foreign and thus applicable only by extrapolation. Here again, the work diaspora seems to do is ambivalent, affirming the significance of access to transnational cultural and political models and resources while at the same time highlighting the extent to which they can always only be partial in their ability to satisfy the particular tasks, longings, and desires of specific communities in their equally specific cultural contexts. The kinds of borrowing and adaptation so central to Gilroy's model of the syncretism of Black expressive cultures are certainly important. Nevertheless, his model may not sufficiently account for the situations of populations like Black Germans, whose very different historical trajectory and consequent marginality in the discourse of diaspora perhaps demand a different formulation.

Just after Jansen's reference to the absence of such resources for potential borrowing and adaptation, a more substantial shift occurs in our discussion via the phenomenon of intercultural address.

FJ: I myself never felt that I'm Black. The others have their problems [with it]. That was never my problem.

TC: Uh-huh. You never felt this?

FJ: Do you feel that you're Black?

TC: Yes!

FJ: How?

TC: Yes. Yes, I mean . . .

FJ: Yes, when you look at yourself.

TC: Well, you're right.

FJ: I said to the children, I say, "Imagine, I know that I don't have this racial problem with myself. If I have a problem with being Black, then it's your problem, or your parents' problem."

In this sequence, our exchange moves away from the issue of the connection between Jansen's politics and her experience of blackness, beginning with her statement that she has never "felt" Black. As an African-American, I initially respond with skepticism to this remark. I am curious about why and how Jansen does not "feel" her blackness. Without reflecting on the implications of this statement, I implicitly attribute this phenomenon to Jansen's German cultural context. This assumption, along with my skepticism and curiosity, is expressed in my response to Jansen's statement, when I pose to her the question, "You never felt this?" My question effectively sets up an implicit relation of difference between the two of us—a difference between two Black women's understandings of the effects of blackness as more than "just" skin color. In response to this submerged level of my question, Jansen shifts the focus away from herself and directly addresses me, challenging me to reflect on the issue I have just directed at her. Jansen's counterquestion, "Do you feel that you're Black?" rejects the assumptions of difference underlying my question, for Jansen directly takes issue with the subtext of my question: if I must ask why she does not feel her blackness, then by implication I (unlike her) must indeed be able to feel this aspect of myself. What follows is a fascinating exchange during which Jansen reverses the roles of the ethnographic encounter to query me on Black identity and in the process foils my attempts to interpellate her as a Black woman. Yet this role reversal also reveals an equally compelling process in which she comes to interpellate me on this same issue.

My comments to Jansen are made in response to her earlier statements that she grew up with little or no exposure to Black people and that she lacked either a movement or community of Blacks with whom to identify. I assume, based on these remarks, that her comments are indicative of a lack of identification with blackness. I want to understand her comments in this way because, as an African-American, I equate a lack of contact with Blacks to a lack of identification of blackness. Indeed, as an African-American, I have to acknowledge that my model of Black identity fixes identity to a domestic community with whom one shares concrete ties of culture, history, and socialization. I also assume that the absence of these things as Jansen describes them in our interview would make such an identification improbable for Jansen, and I conclude all too quickly that her comments in this sequence are a direct reflection of that lack.

But Jansen's query as to my own sense of feeling Black interpellates me to the extent that I feel called on to articulate this feeling as part of my identification as a Black woman. From the moment Jansen begins to describe her experience of blackness in this sequence, I feel hailed to situate myself in relation to what I want to understand as our shared identity as Black women. Unlike in the previous example (excerpt L), though, this time it is a hailing to which I respond with suspicion, somewhat defensively. Although I feel directly addressed and recognized as a Black woman by her comments, I am not quite comfortable with her particular citation (rendition) of the experience of blackness/Black identity. When I attempt to relate (translate) Jansen's articulation of her understanding of what it means to be Black to my understanding, this translation fails because I want to see her concept of blackness as identical to my own. I again confront an inevitable gap of translation—in this case, the gap between related notions of blackness and Black identity that may share similarities but are far from identical.

But more important than the rapidity with which I jump to these conclusions are the assumptions that underlie them with regard to the relationship between my construction of blackness as an African-American and Jansen's as an Afro-German. Equally significant is Jansen's response to my clumsy attempts to impose my own conception of blackness on her. The persistent skepticism I express, through my insistence on the fact that I, unlike her, can and do feel my blackness, functions as both an attempt to dispute the extent to which one can claim not to feel her race and an implicit attempt to impose an

African-American model of Black identity on our exchange by contrasting my feeling with her lack. Indeed, by disputing her claim not to feel blackness, I seem intent on either exposing her denial or convincing her to acquiesce to the veracity of my position. Yet Jansen's response exposes my motives as well as the limitations of my narrow understanding of the dynamics of racial formation. Jansen articulates a complex sensitivity to processes of racial subject formation: she alludes to the fact that blackness has never been intrinsically problematic for her but rather has constituted a problem in what it is understood to mean by others and in how both we and others act on and thus produce it. Her counterquestions and challenges in this way school me, provoking me to recognize the ways in which I take for granted that blackness is a physical or material experience and one on which I act like I have cornered the market.

Jansen's questions forced me to understand the real message of her initial comments: that race and racial difference are the products of social interaction and interpretation, and that those interactions occur not just in Germany between whites and blacks, and not only during the war, when race in Germany was an individual's defining feature. They also occur among Blacks from different social and national contexts in our contemporary transnational encounters. In many ways, our exchange undeniably reproduces important tensions that might be seen as inherent to any cross-cultural dialogue between Black people from different backgrounds. What is perhaps most instructive about our exchange is how the negotiation of our assumptions about our differences and similarities becomes manifest within the interview in ways that make them available to analysis and interpretation. Such analysis nevertheless brings us back to the question of whether these negotiations can or should be seen as a reflection or expression of relationships that might be termed diasporic, and if so, in what ways and toward what ends. The question of what work conceiving of such negotiations as diasporic does forces us to consider the extent to which the type of queries and contestations that characterized my exchange with Jansen are both necessary for and inherent to the relations between members of different Black communities and never in and of themselves either an explanation or an endpoint of such an analysis. The paradoxical open-endedness of the relations of diaspora is an issue to which Hauck's articulations of intercultural address also speak in equally compelling ways.

"MAN BRAUCHT EIGENTLICH EINER SCHWARZEN AMERIKANERIN NICHT ZU ERZÄHLEN": BLACK AMERICA, BLACK GERMANY, AND THE "CROWDED SPACE" OF DIASPORA

As with Jansen, my initial attempt to contact Hauck occurred in the form of a letter. I sent off my letter feeling confident that our mutual friend had alerted Hauck to the fact that I would be contacting him and hopeful that he would be receptive to my request for an interview. She had encouraged me to get in touch with him and assured me that he would respond positively. This was not a cold call, and I entered into our encounter optimistic, though anxious and experiencing the inevitable sense of terror and strangeness that accompanies the initial stages of ethnography and interviewing. The initial personal contact certainly marks one of the greatest moments of anxiety for ethnographers and oral historians, and in my interaction with Hauck, this was a phone call. Almost immediately on receiving my letter, however, Hauck phoned me in Berlin. I had feared both that he would turn down my request for an interview and perhaps worse, that if he granted me the opportunity to speak with him, my German would fail me in the midst of our conversation. Neither of these scenarios came to pass. But what did occur proved no less off-putting, albeit far more complex in ways that I see as emblematic of the tensions of diaspora among African-Americans and Black Germans that are the focus of my analysis in this chapter.

In our phone conversation, Hauck and I discussed the details of where and how the interview would transpire, and I offered to travel to his home to conduct it. We agreed on this, and it eventually proved a very comfortable setting for the interview. Yet toward the end of our conversation, Hauck posed a quite pointed question, one that I would come to see as characteristically direct and revealing regarding our future interactions. He began with an apology, explaining that he did not mean to offend me, but he needed to ask: "Are you Black? I mean, I know you're American, but are you a Black American or a white American?" My letter had described my interest in understanding his experiences and my desire to have them accounted for within the larger narrative of German history and the history of National Socialism, and I had introduced myself as an American, a historian, and a Ph.D. candidate. His comments made me realize that I had neglected to say that I was Black. I am still unsure about why I did not mention this in my letter, and was only made aware of the implications of this omission later—by Hauck himself.

Hauck's question pierced the anonymity of our phone exchange in ways that would become familiar to me in our interview and our many subsequent conversations. The directness of his question also characterized my conversations with all of my Black German interview partners. It was a direct invitation to me to situate myself in the same ways and with the same degree of specificity that I asked and implicitly assumed of them. When I replied to Hauck's query that yes, I was African-American, he responded that he had thought so and that that was good. He agreed to do the interview with me and later told me that had I been white, he would not have consented.

Hauck's comments disarmed and confounded me. I was perplexed by the idea that Hauck talked to me on the condition of my blackness and by the assumptions that this seemed to reveal. Was my blackness assumed as the basis of empathy? Solidarity? Identification? An essential commonality and capacity to understand his experiences? More important, I was far more daunted by my uncertainty that I could live up to any of the expectations that I imagined his remarks to imply. Similarity and identification seemed to me the implicit point of reference for his remarks, and I felt wholly inadequate to such expectations. Indeed, I found my reply and affirmation that I was an African-American to be the source of greater unclarity than clarity. For what that statement did not name was the fact that I am an African-American born in New York City and raised in the suburbs of Washington, D.C. It did not say that I am a middle-class African-American raised by parents from working-class families in one of the most class-stratified Black communities in the United States. My response did not indicate that I am a graduate of a Seven Sisters college and an Ivy League university or speak to the vast problems of translation and interpellation that African-Americans experience within our own communities, as well as our even more vexed problems in communicating these complexities in our dialogues with Black communities outside of the United States, particularly in Europe. My answer did not address the ways in which these tensions undergo constant negotiation, deferral, and displacement in each and every one of the relations that Black people refer to as diasporic, ways that sometimes get talked about but very often do not. I did not address any of these issues, but Hauck did—perhaps not always as directly but nevertheless, all too explicitly.

The phenomenon of intercultural address is even more provocatively expressed in my interview with Hauck. The following exchange is a continuation of a passage cited in chapter 3 in which Hauck discusses the effects of his membership in the Hitler Youth and of his subsequent sterilization on his social interactions as a youth in Nazi Germany.

EXCERPT N

HH: Of course after my sterilization, it was clear that it was over for me with the [Hitler Youth], with the whole spirit of it, which I more or less understood at fifteen or sixteen—in contrast to the thirteen-year-old.

TC: I don't quite understand what you mean.

HH: In contrast to the thirteen-year-old, who enjoyed the whole the Hitler Youth game, the fifteen-year-old didn't anymore. He was able to think more about it, but he had to go along.

TC: "Had to"?

HH: Well, what should I have done? No one forced me. But the circumstances forced me. I had to. I was an apprentice with the railroad. Without being in the Hitler Youth, I wouldn't have been allowed to do that. We appeared at all sorts of different occasions in uniform, in Hitler Youth uniform.

TC: Did that make a difference in how you were treated? When you wore this uniform?

HH: Yes. No one saw any more that I didn't really belong.

TC: No one?

HH: No, no one. And those who did know said nothing. It wasn't at all like that. There were many who knew. [But] as far as I can remember, it never caused me any problems.

TC: With the uniform?

HH: With the uniform.

TC: *And without it? Would that then have —*

HH: *Without it, I wouldn't have been able to participate. One can't even imagine it anymore.*

TC: *Yes, I'm asking —*

HH: *I just find — Yes, well, your question alone expresses a lack of knowledge of the situation back then.*

TC: *Exactly.*

HH: *That's quite clear. I understand it, because one can't at all imagine it, especially not as an American. Though, as far as I'm concerned, America is certainly no heaven on earth. So actually, one doesn't have to tell a Black American in what way this difference [racial differentiation] was expressed— even though it's legally forbidden in America. For us this differentiation was compulsory by law. And in spite of this, not everyone did it. You certainly know many Americans who behave impartially toward you [deal with you without prejudice]. You also have others. You see, that's how it is. Even in a democracy like America, that's the case. How much more so in a dictatorship like Hitler's Germany.*[27]

In this excerpt, I am intent on clarifying the specific role that the Hitler Youth uniform played for Hauck and make three consecutive attempts to pose this question in various formulations. As discussed at length in chapter 3, in this excerpt Hauck explains that the Hitler Youth served a protective function in his life that enabled him to participate in spheres of German life to which he would otherwise not have had access because of his African heritage. At this point, I intervene to make a first attempt at clarifying the role of the Hitler Youth uniform in this process. In response, Hauck replies that the uniform concealed his heritage. When I attempt a second, follow-up question, Hauck interrupts. Because of this interruption, my question remains unclear. Hauck nevertheless responds by offering his interpretation of what he assumes would have been my question. He concludes by commenting that his situation is difficult to imagine in the present. When I make a third attempt to obtain a clearer articulation of Hauck's interpretation of the significance of the Hitler Youth uniform, he again interrupts, expressing irritation with my query. In this case, he responds by remarking on what he sees as my inability to understand his situation as a result of my apparent lack of knowledge. What was previously seen as a general phenomenon is now specifically attributed to me. Confronted with this situation, I am left no alternative but to acknowledge the correctness of his assessment, for although I am

familiar with the historical context of these events, Hauck's experience
therein is indeed something of which I am truly ignorant. My persistence in asking my question in this exchange results not only from
curiosity and stubbornness but also from my belief that Hauck has not
answered me. In this interchange, I seem to resist or be incapable of
accepting Hauck's explanations. In fact, Hauck does respond to my
questions but does so in a way that I could neither recognize nor
acknowledge at the time.

Hauck's answers to my question are made from within his own
frame of reference, which, because it is based on his Afro-German cultural context, is unfamiliar to me. Initially in our exchange, Hauck and
I attempt to communicate from two distinct standpoints, as an
African-American and an Afro-German. The misunderstanding that
develops between us is one effect of this phenomenon. In essence, it is
a problem of translation, specifically my desire to translate his experiences into the familiar terms of my own cultural context. Here intercultural address delineates the gap that exists between us—one that
requires translation across the specificity of our respective cultural
backgrounds. At the point where this misapprehension becomes manifest, Hauck makes an important shift in his narrative technique in an
attempt to resolve this conflict. Hauck's statement, "Your question
alone expresses a lack of knowledge of the situation back then," articulates his recognition of the limits of his previous narrative strategy in
achieving the comprehension of his African-American interlocutor.
When it becomes clear that his initial mode of presenting his experience
is not effective, he switches to an alternative one that directly targets
my frame of reference as an African-American: comparison. Here
Hauck uses me and the African-American context as the point of reference for his comparison.

Hauck responds to my admission of difficulty in understanding his
situation by reiterating his earlier statement that a lack of knowledge
regarding his experiences is understandable as a general phenomenon.
Unlike his statements in the previous sequence, he goes a step further
in this instance to specifically address this phenomenon to me as an
American: "I understand it, because one can't at all imagine it, especially not as an American." Hauck's remarks ascribe my inability to
understand him to a gap that he urges me to bridge through reference
to my own, more familiar cultural context. His comments can be seen

as a gesture of pardon, excusing my lack of knowledge as not necessarily my fault but rather a cultural phenomenon, related to the fact that
my cultural context is the United States. By bringing the general "lack
of knowledge" or ignorance (*Unkenntnis*) to which he refers earlier in
relation to a specifically American lack of knowledge, Hauck seeks to
explain the temporary disruption of our communication in the interchange that preceded it. But directly thereafter, he qualifies this pardon, moving from describing a phenomenon of unfamiliarity among
Americans to remarking on the specific relation that I, as an African-
American, am assumed to have to this issue: "So actually, one doesn't
have to tell a Black American in what way this difference was
expressed." The implication of his statement is that as an American,
my unfamiliarity is understandable, but as a Black American, it is not
acceptable. Hauck again uses comparison and juxtaposition to illustrate and clarify his situation, a clear statement of his assumptions of
the applicability to his situation of my cultural knowledge as an
African-American as a necessary tool for translating our differences.[28]
His comments take the form of a truism, indicating his belief in the
self-evidence of what he is saying. Two different forms of juxtaposition
follow: a comparison and a contrast between the American and German contexts. In each case, Hauck uses either me or the African-American context to further specify the complexities of his situation as a
German of African descent in the Third Reich as well as this experience's similarities to and differences from my cultural context—that is,
the dominant model of the "Black experience" in the so-called First
World. Each is an attempt by Hauck to make the differences in our
respective experiences and knowledge of blackness apparent and in the
process, to facilitate my translation and comprehension of these differences.

Hauck's use of intercultural comparison strategically names the gap
that is emerging in our conversation while attempting to bridge this
gap by invoking his own limited knowledge of the aspects of my cultural context that might enable me to understand his. Addressing me
through this comparison at once invokes a relationship of similarity
between our communities and demands attention to their distinctions.
His comparison sets up a relation that vividly recalls Lorde's articulation of the "connected differences" between Black communities situated in very different locations within the diaspora. Yet as Brown

reminds us, it is important to keep in mind that the distinctive ways that so-called marginal Black communities such as Afro-Germans are positioned in relation to Black America are not always equal, nor do these relationships stand in a neutral space outside of or immune to power and social hegemony. Thus, particularly with regard to Hauck's comments and his use of intercultural address, it is important to consider the question of what Hauck's invocation of Black America tells us about the relationships between Black communities in the diaspora if we conceive of these relations to be as much shaped and affected by structures of power and hegemony as any other social formation.

The following excerpt offers much insight into this question. In an earlier chapter, this passage ends with Hauck's return to work at the railroad and his statement that the Nuremberg Laws prohibited him from marriage. In the interview itself, though, his comments continue. The passage begins with Hauck's recollections of his sterilization. What begins as a straightforward recounting of those painful events takes an interesting turn as Hauck attempts to communicate its significance to me, his African-American interlocutor.

EXCERPT O

> HH: After the judgment, they immediately loaded us up and took us to hospital. There we were operated on, and in ten days I was released. And there I stood, back on the job. They had been informed at the railroad. And they informed me too, I wasn't allowed to marry, I could marry no German girl. That was clear. It was part of the Nuremberg Laws. And the same people ask me today, "Hey, why didn't you marry?"
>
> TC: And why didn't you marry?
>
> HH: Whom could I have married?
>
> TC: And after the war?
>
> HH: Well, after the war, it was too late.
>
> TC: Yeah?
>
> HH: After the war, it was too late. When I returned from the POW camp, I was thirty years old. Certainly, a person can also get married at thirty. But I didn't want to any more. Before that, no girl would have taken me. Even if the girls

had wanted to, their parents wouldn't have allowed it. *I don't know if I have to explain to you — If you wanted to marry a white American man somewhere in a particular area, one doesn't have to ask you why you don't want to marry him. Maybe you do; maybe he does, too. But it's still impossible. And here, aside from that, it was forbidden. It wasn't even worth mentioning.*[29]

In the final sequence of this excerpt, Hauck attempts to clarify his situation on the issue of marriage by means of comparison. "Addressing" me directly as a Black person via his conception of my African-American cultural background, the point of reference for his comparison is once again, me. He begins with a gesture of hesitation, remarking on the potential superfluousness of explanation: "I don't know if I have to explain to you." This phrase appears initially to indicate a moment when Hauck seems about to defer to what he assumes to be my "obvious" cultural knowledge of such a situation by drawing on an example from my cultural context to which I am assumed to be able to relate. Using as his example his image of what it would be like for me in the United States if I decided to marry a white man, Hauck sets up a relation of similarity between us by drawing on the potential commonality of our experiences as Black people. His statement, "One doesn't have to ask you why," introduces a second assumption of commonality between the Afro-German and African-American contexts. His references appear to negate any discrepancy in our understanding of the consequences of interracial marriage. Yet in this second instance, though, he is less hesitant. His statements in this last sequence appeal for intercultural reciprocity, urging me to draw on my own cultural knowledge as an African-American to answer the question I just posed.

The exchange in this excerpt offers a second example of the process of negotiating our respective experiences as Black people that transpired at a discursive level during our interview. In this passage, intercultural address takes the form of an attempt to establish both discursive and intercultural reciprocity through comparative references. But Hauck's use of comparison has a second dimension that does more than establish a dialogue of similarity, functioning at the same time as a gesture of distancing and respect, as an attempt to probe the boundaries of our communication and to explain the ways in which experiences of race and racialization exceed an simple discourse of similarity.

Directly following his allusion to interracial marriage in the United States, Hauck defines the limits of his comparison. He uses the relation of similarity that he established through his reference to the African-American context to explain the differences between the two situations. The statement, "And here, aside from that, it was forbidden," signifies an end of the similarities between Hauck's experience as an Afro-German and those of African-Americans. Despite the fact that as an African-American, I may recognize the similarities between Hauck's experiences and those of my cultural context, our experiences as Black people differ considerably. As he shifts from using comparison as a means of establishing similarity to using it as a marker of difference, intercultural address becomes a form of critical juxtaposition. His insistence on simultaneously alluding to both the differences and the similarities between his experiences and those of African-Americans is neither random nor contradictory, for he intends the similarities he emphasizes to reinforce my ability to translate the differences in our respective experiences of blackness. Like his comments in excerpt N, Hauck's use of comparison and juxtaposition provoke me to reflect critically on my African-American context, as his repeated references to me and my cultural context effectively interpellates me as an African-American woman, in the process implicating and drawing me into his narrative more directly. In both instances, I am continually forced to critically assess the relationship between our two communities and to acknowledge the significant differences between them.

Yet Hauck's use of comparison and juxtaposition must also be seen in relation to the existence of another kind of discursive gap in representing the situation of Afro-Germans. Here, comparison and juxtaposition function as modes of conveying an experience that lies in space left out by available modes of representing Blacks in Germany, as well as being largely overlooked in the discourse of diaspora. On the one hand, the hegemonic discourse of German identity remains a largely homogenous and homogenizing discourse of whiteness that often conflates Germanness with whiteness as a form of racial identity. On the other hand, the discourse on Blacks in contemporary Germany defines its Black residents primarily as immigrants and foreigners in German society—individuals most often seen as Third World economic and political refugees in pursuit of the wealth and opportunity the First World promises. At the same time, representations of African-American culture as the dominant point of reference for First World Black populations permeate this discourse. At the level of visual representation, Black America—particularly through the proliferation of hip hop, house, funk, and R&B through music videos—has made African-American cultural styles and expressions a focal point of identification for Blacks in Germany. In addition, the African-American civil rights movement serves as a model for Black liberation struggles around the world. The dominance of these representations of African-American history and culture in Germany have come to define popular perceptions of Blacks in the First World. One effect of these representations is the perception of Afro-Germans (as well as all other Blacks in Germany) as either Third or First World Others.

Here I would elaborate on Wright's assertion that Black Germans are read primarily as Africans and thus constructed as "Others-from-Within from Without" by proposing that we also consider the status of the Black American as a construction that exerts significant and competing discursive, conceptual, and ideological power over how blackness is read in Germany. This "First World Other" figures prominently in the contemporary construction of blackness in Germany both because of the legacy of the post–World War II occupation and because of its circulation in popular culture. In the German context, the Black American represents a mobile figure of the Black whose status outside of the United States is frequently neither abject nor marginal. On the contrary, in Germany this figure is often privileged, exoticized, and commodified as a complex vector of cultural appropriation and interpellation. Understanding this additional dimension of the construction of blackness in Germany helps to explain why the discourses of Black and German identity that define *German* as white and *Black* as either African or African-American leave little, if any, discursive space for Black German articulations of self, space that might allow individuals such as Hauck to describe the experiences of Germans of African descent in ways that might not necessitate reference to Black America.

In both of the excerpts from his narrative cited in this chapter, Hauck's use of intercultural address renders his experience in relation to the constraints of these discourses of race and ethnicity for Blacks in

Germany. Moreover, these excerpts illustrate the way in which the articulation of an experience that overlaps supposedly distinct forms of identity necessitates not only a dialogical relation of similarity (or at the very least, direct or indirect "reference") to these dominant discourses but also a differential and contestatory stance beyond them. The construction of alternative forms of identity such as Afro-German also involves direct engagement with the dominant forms of identity that bound and consequently circumscribe them. Hauck's narrative practice, as well as the experiences he recounts, reflect the negotiation of these positions—between that which is sayable within or in relation to existing and/or available terms of Black and German identity and that which remains unsayable and therefore unsaid.

Intercultural address points to the discrepancies we encountered understanding our respective experiences of race in the diaspora; the insistent need for the translation of these differences; the modes of diasporic interpellation enacted in these exchanges; and the at times inequitable resources available to communities situated in very different spaces within the diaspora. The moments of intercultural address examined in this chapter illustrate some of the asymmetries within the diaspora and some of the ways in which communities such as Afro-Germans must consistently reckon with Black America and its hegemony as an "always already there" primary referent for the African diaspora through which they must speak in their attempts to articulate these experiences. For this reason, it is perhaps all the more important to interrogate the contradictory manner in which this ever-present referent shapes these articulations and mediates their relation to the diaspora. The question we must ask is what the use of Black America as a mode of articulation limits or prevents Hauck and individuals like him from saying at the same time that it enables him to speak.

In both Hauck's and Jansen's narratives, intercultural address can be seen as a challenge that encourages us to reflect on the status of Black America in relation to other Black populations involved in the process of articulating their experiences and constructing alternative forms of Black identity and community. Intercultural address asks us to take a closer look at the influence of representations of African-American culture in these constructions. Each of these exchanges raises the question of whether these intercultural negotiations can or should be seen as a reflection or expression of relationships that might be termed diasporic, and if so, in what ways and toward what ends. And yet, although it presents itself as an obvious model for explaining the sense of relationship postulated through such cross-cultural querying and citation, the question remains whether we can or should understand such citational imperatives as "diasporic" or as an expression or consequence of a "diasporic relation"? Should the ways in which Afro-Germans draw on the African-American context be seen as their use of some of the few diasporic resources available to them as Black people lacking other indigenous narratives of belonging, community, and struggle—or, for that matter, access to the forms of collective or individual memory that sustain other Black communities? In other words, can or should such references to Black America be understood as necessary attempts to draw from elsewhere that which is lacking, though essential, to the constitution of very different notions of Black identity and community at "home"? Or might such references also have everything to do with Black America's emergent cultural capital, which increasingly allows it an almost endless capacity to proliferate and travel to many different global locations and thus become an available referent? In Hauck's case, as well as for many members of other Black European communities more generally, I believe that the latter is the case.

Although the concept of diaspora invites us to use it as an obvious model for explaining the sense of relationship postulated through such cross-cultural querying, in some ways, this invitation seems almost too seductive to be believed. One might ask whether part of the work diaspora does is to hold out a promise it cannot quite keep, the promise of transparent forms of relation and understanding based on links forged through shared histories of oppression and racialization. Indeed, the concept of the African diaspora seems sometimes to invite us to forget the subtle forms of interpellation and incumbent gaps of translation that are a crucial part of all transnational dialogues.

Edwards's compelling articulation of *décalage* as a haunting gap and necessary discrepancy in the African diaspora, and his insistence that there will always be some remainder that continually resurfaces within the diaspora as points of misunderstanding, bad faith, and unhappy translation is a cogent reminder that both translation and translation gaps are inherent elements of all diasporic formations by virtue of the ever-present diversity of Black culture and community. Their gaps in particular can neither be negated, resolved, nor erased. On the contrary, they are that which enables, rather than hinders, both community and communication.

Each of the discrepant moments of diasporic invocation presented in this chapter asks us to think about the stakes of diasporic relation and how those relations are structured as much through difference as through similarity, and enunciated through complex modes of translation and interpellation that are anything but transparent. Engaging the tensions of diasporic relation as processes of translation and interpellation helps to explain how the diaspora/diasporic links are produced both actively and strategically; how the discourse of diaspora circulates in uneven ways geographically, and within and between different communities; and how diaspora does indeed do interesting and important "epistemological work." The processes and practices of citation, translation, and interpellation that I have examined here are extremely illuminating and instructive when engaged with an eye toward understanding how they reveal the necessary if not crucial forms of distinction and commonality that characterize all transnational dialogues. But what is most essential to the future of African diaspora studies is the project of making more explicit what exactly constitutes the links and relations between us and how they necessarily require translation. For those of us interested in reconstructing the histories out of which communities and identities emerge, the ways in which intercultural and transnational links, bonds, and affiliations between different communities are invoked and produced through nuanced articulations both by scholars and by individual members of these communities is a dimension of the study of the diaspora that should not be overlooked. Indeed, articulations like those explored here urge us to rethink the discourse of diaspora and the diasporic relations it references. We might more productively think of them as less a common trajectory of cultural formation or as a set of cultural and historical links that either precede or call into being particular community formations or identifications. Following Judith Butler, I would conceptualize the diaspora as space in which the relations, definitions, and identifications within and between communities come to materialize and to matter as "real" in ways that are strategically useful; these phenomena in turn "hail" and thus interpellate us in important political, symbolic, and often quite material forms. Indeed, the links and relations of the dias-pora are themselves enacted in and through such transnational exchanges in ways that are thoroughly strategic and deeply embedded in intricate social webs of power and hegemony. Hence, I propose that we think of the diaspora as less an answer or explanation than as itself a persistent question—in fact, the question posed at the beginning of this chapter. What work does diaspora do?

My conversations with Black Germans about their memories of their lives in the Third Reich forced me to contend with their often very different understandings of race and their status as raced social sub-jects, understandings that were not always compatible with my own. My status as an African-American often became the site of challenge, as the ground on which complex contestations of difference and not simply similarity were waged. It is important to continually keep in mind that, like the category of race itself, our relation as Black people to the diaspora is not something we all have or are born with. On the contrary, these relations are constructed through negotiations and contestations in specific ways that are not always or easily translated/translatable into our respective cultural contexts. Relations of diaspora forged on the basis of similar experiences of racialization are not transparent links between Black people; rather, these relations are the products of highly constructed processes of cultural reading and interpretations that shape, define, and often constrain our ability to understand the differences between our histories and cultures. Although our experiences of living blackness may in some ways be sim-ilar, it is also necessary to consider the differences between our cultures and histories and to recognize how their specificities have come to bear on the ways in which the effects of race are lived and read.

APPENDIX

Original German Interview Excerpts

TC: Was sind deine[1] Erinnerungen an diese ersten acht Jahren mit deiner Mutter?

HH: Daß ich mich immer gefreut habe, daß ich sehr verschmust war, dann mit meiner Mutter. Das war ja klar. Ich habe sie nur so selten gesehen. Ich war ja nicht den ganzen Tag bei ihr. Ansonsten war das eine Kindheit wie alle anderen auch. Das Zurücksetzen habe ich ebenso schnell vergessen. Es wurde mir nur immer wieder in Erinnerung gebracht. Das ist kein Einzelfall. Es gibt andere Kinder, die von — wo der Vater beispielsweise im Gefängnis war oder so irgendetwas, denen es so ähnlich geht. Nur bei mir war alles eben wegen meiner Herkunft oder der Herkunft meines Vaters.

TC: Habt ihr in der Familie jemals darüber geredet?

HH: Ich — in meinem Beisein nie. Das war ein Tabu. Das war ein Thema, da wurde nicht darüber gesprochen. Obwohl als ich klein war, habe ich oft mal gehört—wo ich schon größer war und in der Schule war—wenn sie sich darüber unterhalten haben, aber wenn ich in die Nähe kam, war das Gespräch immer erledigt.

TC: Daß sie immer über dich geredet haben, aber nicht in deinem Beisein? Was für einen Eindruck hat das auf dich gemacht?

HH: Daß ich gemerkt habe, das/was heißt [unclear], daß irgendetwas anders ist als sonst. Aber ich kann nicht sagen, daß

---

1. At Hauck's request, I use the informal *Du* form to address him.

es anderen unehelichen Kindern vielleicht genauso gegangen ist.

TC: Aber diese Herkunftsfrage, das war nicht so ein —

HH: Das war kein Thema. Das Thema war Tabu. Das kann man sagen mit großem Gewissen.

TC: Mit wem bist du aufgewachsen, im Haus? Deiner Mutter und deiner Großmutter?

HH: Bei meiner Großmutter. Und eine Tante war noch immer da. Manchmal kam auch mein Onkel—die Geschwister meiner Mutter. Die wohnten zwar nicht hier oder nicht immer hier. Eine hat geheiratet, und der andere war auswärts beschäftigt, aber wenn sie da waren, war die ganze Familie zusammen. Das beweisen die Fotos. [Here Hans refers to childhood photographs of himself and his family that he had shown me earlier in our conversation.]

TC: Und hattest du das Gefühl, daß du gut aufgenommen wurdest, innerhalb von der Familie?

HH: Doch/Das [unclear]. Das kann man nicht sagen, daß ich nicht gut aufgenommen wurde. Ich selbst habe — Ich war auch dadurch, daß man doch immer so etwas gehört hat, aber niemals was Richtiges, sensibilisiert darauf, sensibler als andere Kinder, schon früh. Ich hatte auch damals schon eine gute Aufnahmefähigkeit dadurch. Das ist, was mir in der Schule zustatten kam. Hat mir im Leben vieles schwerer gemacht, nicht leichter.

TC: Wie würdest du das beschreiben? Zum Beispiel —

HH: Wenn man — einfach — leichter über etwas hinwegkommt, oder man ist weniger motiviert oder meist weniger aufnahmefähig. Dann kriegt man auch weniger mit. Wer ein bißchen — manche Menschen sind ein bißchen borniert. Und die haben doch vieles leichter im Leben. Die machen sich weniger Gedanken. Mit Recht oder Unrecht, das ist eine andere Frage. Ich habe mir sehr früh Gedanken gemacht über meine Herkunft und das. Aber ich war immer noch zu klein mit meiner Mutter zu sprechen darüber.

TC: Und was für Gedanken hast du dir über deine Herkunft gemacht? Wie hast du das irgendwie begriffen oder genannt oder bezeichnet? Hattest du mit jemandem darüber geredet?

HH: Das wurde mir ja gesagt. Das wußte ich, daß mein Vater

Algerier war. Aber wir haben nie darüber gesprochen. Das wurde auch mal so fallengelassen im Gespräch: "Du kannst deine Herkunft nicht verleugnen"—absolut nicht im Bösen gemeint. Wenn ich geschrieen habe oder Blödsinn gemacht habe, wurde mir das immer wieder gesagt.

TC: Was war deine Reaktion darauf?

HH: Ich konnte mir doch gar nicht vorstellen, daß Algerier anders sind. Ich wußte doch gar nicht, was das ist. Erst viel später, als ich das begreifen lernte. Dann war meine Mutter lange tot. Da konnte ich nicht mehr mit ihr darüber sprechen.

TC: Wie alt warst du, als du das begriffen hast?

HH: Achteinhalb Jahre war ich, als sie gestorben ist—achteinviertel Jahr.

TC: Und als du erstmals begriffen hast, was es heißt — [schwarz zu sein].

HH: Das haben die Nachbarkinder mir beizeiten beigebracht.

TC: Wie?

HH: Das kann man ganz schwer begreifen, daß in Äußerungen wurden mir Schimpfwörter an den Kopf geworfen, die Herkunft meines Vaters betreffend. Das war kurz nach dem Krieg. Und die Väter aller anderen Kinder waren ja deutsche Soldaten. Und meiner war ein Feind.

TC: Das war nach dem Krieg?

HH: Das war nach dem Krieg. Der Krieg war ja 1918 zu Ende. Und der war hier als Besatzungssoldat. Der hat den Krieg mitgemacht und war nachher hier als Besatzungssoldat.

TC: Und wie hast du darauf reagiert, als dir das vorgeworfen wurde?

HH: Am Anfang habe ich mich immer gewehrt, und nachher war ich immer schuld an allem. Und das war irgend etwas, was sich mir im Leben sehr nachteilig ausgewirkt hat. Unbesehen war ich schuld. Die Menschen waren damals noch weit, weit zurückgeblieben. Das habe ich so oft festgestellt bei anderen Besatzungskindern nach dem Zweiten Weltkrieg.

TC: Kanntest du andere Besatzungskinder — ?

HH: 25 Jahre später. Natürlich kannte ich. Nach dem Zweiten Weltkrieg kannte ich viele.

TC: Von dem Ersten kanntest du einige?

HH: Die habe ich erst kennengelernt, als ich sterilisiert wurde.

TC: Wann wurdest du sterilisiert?

HH: 1935. Eigentlich, die Schwierigkeiten gingen erst los, als ich aus der Schule kam.

TC: Wie alt warst du da?

HH: 14 Jahre war ich, als ich aus der Schule kam, und dann, ich war mit 13, das ist wieder die Zeit, in der Hitler kam, war ich in der Hitler-Jugend.

TC: Ohne Schwierigkeiten kamst du da rein?

HH: Ohne Schwierigkeiten!

TC: Obwohl es bekannt war, daß dein Vater —

HH: Obwohl es bekannt war, ohne Schwierigkeiten. Und das war für mich etwas Neues, ohne — mit 13 Jahren macht man sich keine politischen Gedanken. Aber das Ganze, das Spiel und das Antreten und das Soldatenspielen, das hat mir Spaß gemacht. Aber —

TC: Und deshalb bist du eingetreten?

HH: Deshalb bin ich eingetreten. In der Katholischen Jugend hatte ich viel mehr Schwierigkeiten.

TC: Wegen deiner Herkunft?

HH: Wegen meiner Herkunft.

TC: Woran liegt das?

HH: Woran das liegt? Das müßte man die Geistlichen fragen, die zu der Zeit hier waren. Das — mit unserem damaligen Pfarrer, [er] hat mir das vorgehalten. Das mag ihm manchmal Leid getan haben nachher, aber er hat es gemacht.

TC: Wie hat er sich dir gegenüber verhalten?

HH: Ja, das ist im Einzelnen so schwer zu sagen, nur — Er hat, obwohl er gewußt hat, daß ich Waisenkind war, hat er mich wegen meiner Kleidung gerügt und, und — Das kann man so schlecht sagen, wie. Nur [es] ist öfters die Bemerkung gefallen: "Du hat's gerade nötig"—was immer er damit gemeint hat.

TC: Ziemlich subtil.

HH: Ich habe doch aber immer das alles vielleicht auch übersensibilisiert, habe ich alles auf mich bezogen. Das ist die andere Seite. Aber ich habe mich nicht selbst so gemacht.

EXCERPT B

TC: Wie lange warst du bei der Hitler-Jugend?

HH: Mit 13 und 14 Jahren, und 15. Und hatte nachher immer das Recht gehabt, die Uniform zu tragen. Man darf nicht vergessen, daß ich auf der Eisenbahn gelernt habe. Und das habe ich dem zu verdanken, dem vorhin erwähnten SS Offizier. . . .

TC: Und was hat er für dich konkret gemacht?

HH: Ich bin niemals angezeigt worden. Auch als ich nicht mehr in der Hitler-Jugend war. Es hat auch niemanden mehr danach gefragt. Es hatte mich niemand mehr bedrängt. Und das war schon viel wert.

TC: Im Vergleich zu der Zeit, bevor du in der HJ warst.

HH: Im Vergleich zu anderen, die deutschen Jungen, die hätten sich nicht so drücken können, davon.

TC: Und versuchtest du während dieser Zeit für dich klarer zu kriegen, was der Unterschied innerhalb von dieser Organisationen war, in der HJ oder der Wehrmacht, wie du das beschreibst "aufgenommen zu werden," statt wenn du nicht dabei wärst, "Schwierigkeiten" zu haben. [The interviewer's question here was unclear both to the interviewer and her interview partner.]

HH: Daß natürlich nach meiner Sterilisation mit der HJ, mit dem Geist, den ich auch mit 15–16 Jahren schon einigermaßen begriff, vorbei war, war doch ganz klar. Im Gegensatz zu dem Dreizehnjährigen.

TC: Ich verstehe nicht genau, was du meinst.

HH: Im Gegensatz zu dem Dreizehnjährigen, der Freude hatte am ganzen Hitler-Jugend Spiel, hatte das der 15-jährige schon nicht mehr. Der konnte schon mehr denken, aber der mußte da mitmachen.

TC: Mußte?

HH: Ja, was hätte ich denn machen sollen? Es hat mich niemand gezwungen. Aber die Umstände haben mich gezwungen. Ich mußte ja. Ich habe ja gelernt auf der Eisenbahn. Ohne in der Hitler-Jugend zu sein, hätte ich gar nicht lernen können da. Wir sind ja zu allen möglichen und unmöglichen Gelegentheiten in Uniformen angetreten. In Hitler-Jugend Uniformen.

TC: Hat das einen Unterschied gemacht? Wenn du diese Uniform getragen hast, [in bezug] auf wie du behandelt wurdest?

HH: Ja, hat ja niemand mir angesehen, daß ich eigentlich gar nicht dazugehörte.

TC: Niemand?

HH: Nein. Und die das gewußt haben, haben nichts gesagt. Es war beileibe nicht so. Es waren etliche, die das gewußt haben. Mir hat das, so weit wie ich mich zurückerinnern kann, niemals eine Schwieriegkeit bereitet.

TC: Mit der Uniform?

HH: Mit der Uniform.

EXCERPT C

Vielleicht bin ich im Verzweiflungsfällen auch viel verzweifelter als andere. Ich war das einmal. Ich habe ein Suizidversuch gemacht. . . . Ich habe auf mich geschossen, und der Vater meines Freundes ist dazwischen gesprungen. Ich habe nachher im Krankenhaus gelegen, und das wurde vertuscht, von einem Kriminalbeamten. . . . Da war ich 21. Da wollten sie mich dauernd nehmen zur vormilitärischen Ausbildung. Und ich hatte immer Angst davor. Die vormilitärische Ausbildung wurde von der SA durchgeführt. Mit der hatte ich nie was zu tun. *In der HJ hier kannte mich jeder.* Hatte mich auch keiner — ich kann es nicht anders sagen, böse gewollt. Manche gut sogar. Aber dort, wo wir hin evakuiert waren, während des Krieges, konnte man nichts garantieren. . . . Saarbrücken war geräumt, — weil es war doch Krieg. . . . Die Grenze war drei Kilometer weg. Und hier hatte die französische Artillerie hereingeschossen. Hier waren keine Menschen. Und unsere Dienststelle von der Eisenbahn war in das Innere Deutschlands verlegt . . . in verschiedenen Orten. Ich selbst war mit einem Teil Arbeitskollegen in Paderborn. Und nachher in Schneidemuhl und dann in Opladen. Und in Opladen habe ich den Suizidversuch gemacht, weil ich mich nicht mehr retten konnte, von den Benachrichtungen zur vormilitärischen Ausbildung bei der SA. Und dahin wollte ich nun bei keinen Umständen. Das hätte zu Komplikationen geführt, vor denen ich Angst hatte. . . . Der Nachweis der arischen Abstammung und den ganzen Krempel. *Die kannten mich ja dort nicht.* Und ich konnte ja unmöglich eine arische Abstammung nach — wo soll ich die herbringen. . . . Hier war ich davon selbst unter- [unclear]. Ich habe vorher schon einmal gesagt, daß ich hier auch Leute hatte, die mir geholfen haben. . . . *In der Fremde—da kannte mich keiner.* Und da war ich unzweifelhaft da irgendwie, gegenan. Das wollte ich ja nun vermeiden. Denn damals hatten wir schon Krieg mit Rußland, und es war abzusehen, wenn sie uns als Soldaten holen werden. In der Zwischenzeit sind schon viele, viele, die vorher nicht Soldaten werden mußten, Soldaten worden. Und so kam es dann auch bei mir. Ich wurde gefragt, ob ich Soldat werden wollte. Habe ich gesagt, ja. Und da habe ich jetzt die Chance die normale—habe ja vorher schon erklärt—die normale Chance gehabt, so halt 50 zu 50; entweder komme ich durch oder nicht. Und ich bin durchgekommen.

EXCERPT D

HH: Außerdem bin ich mit 19 Jahren gemustert worden, wie alle anderen auch.

TC: Gemustert? Was ist gemustert?

HH: Gemustert. Das heißt für die Wehrmacht, für den Wehrdienst gemustert untersucht. Das nennt man Musterung.

TC: Das war mit 19. Das war 2 Jahre, nachdem du sterilisiert wurdest.

HH: Das war 2 Jahre ja, nachdem ich. . . . Ich war nicht ganz 17 Jahre, ich war 16 Jahre, als ich sterilisiert wurde. Und bei der Musterung, 1939, das heißt nun mal Musterung zum Militärdienst, war ich "wehrunwürdig."

TC: "Unwürdig"?

HH: Ja. Arbeiten durfte ich, aber ich durfte damals kein Soldat werden. Erst im Laufe des Krieges, 1941, hat sich das gelockert. Und 1942 wurde ich eingezogen, mit meiner Einwilligung. Da kam es darauf an, da hätte ich jetzt sagen

können: "Ihr wolltet mich nicht, und jetzt will ich nicht."
Dann würde ich heut' hier nicht mehr sitzen. Das ist ganz
einfach. Wir haben Beispiele dafür.

TC: Aber damals mußtest du das machen, mußtest du in die
Wehrmacht eintreten. Oder?

HH: Ja. Vielleicht hätte ich mich weigern können. Dann könnte
ich heute nicht mehr darüber reden. Von einem Fall weiß
ich das. Ein Kamerad, der mit mir sterilisiert worden ist, der
ist nicht mehr wiedergekommen. Der kam ins Lager. Und
ich bin gegangen, weil ich das als eine Chance ansah. Das
war das erste Mal, wo ich mit anderen gleichgesetzt wurde.
Denn die anderen "arischen" deutschen Jungen, meine
Kameraden, meine Schulkameraden, die wurden auch
eingezogen. Und das wollte ich, und dann bin ich eingezogen worden. Und jetzt hatte ich ganz bewußt vom Schicksal
die Chance, 50 zu 50. Entweder überlebe ich's oder ich überlebe es nicht. Und ich habe es überlebt.

EXCERPT E

HH: Ich wurde eingezogen und wurde Soldat, und bin 1945 in
russische Gefangenschaft gekommen. Ich war fünfmal verwundet. Ich war zweimal zu Hause gewesen, im Urlaub und
als ich verwundet war. Und bin '45 im Januar in russische
Gefangenschaft gekommen. . . .

TC: Wie lange warst du in Gefangenschaft?

HH: Bis zum 23 April 1949. . . . Die Gefangenschaft kann ich
nicht schildern. Gefangenschaft ist nicht leicht. Das ist —
hat doch jeder gewußt. — Aber ich bin von den Russen
mehr als Mensch behandelt worden als wie vorher von
meinen eigenen Landsleuten.

TC: Inwiefern?

HH: Inwiefern? Weil dort wegen meiner Herkunft niemand ein
Trara gemacht hat.

TC: Und die anderen deutschen Soldaten, haben sie das auch
mitgekriegt? Daß du anders behandelt wurdest?

HH: Ich wurde ja nicht anders behandelt.

TC: Aber mehr menschlich?

HH: Ich wurde genauso behandelt wie die anderen Deutschen auch. Nur es wurde gar kein Unterschied gemacht. Mein eigenes Vaterland hat das nicht gemacht. Das hat mich benachteiligt. Erst als Soldat hat es mich gleich behandelt.

TC: Und hattest du das Gefühl während deiner Soldatenzeit, daß du gut wirklich gut aufgenommen wurdest?

HH: Bei der Wehrmacht hat man keinen Unterschied gemerkt.

TC: Trotzt deiner —

HH: Ich wurde nach den ersten fünf Monaten Gefreiter, d.h. erster Dienstgrad befördert. Da hat man keinen Nachteil gemerkt bei der Wehrmacht. Es waren viele Wehrmacht-Offiziere, die mit dem System nicht einverstanden waren und nichts gesagt haben. Aber das hat man wohl gemerkt. Bei der Wehrmacht wurde ich nicht benachteiligt.

EXCERPT F

TC: Hast du Aversion wegen deiner Herkunft in den anderen Ländern empfunden?

HH: Nee. Wegen meiner Herkunft, nee. Wegen der deutschen.

TC: Es war Deutschsein und nicht — ?

HH: Ja! N'ich meine — Ich bin ja nicht damit gereist oder ich habe ja nicht damit posiert, daß ich es — unter den Nazis minderwertig. — Ich bin dann in russischer Gefangen-schaft, hätte ich als Saarländer viel eher nach Hause fahren können.

TC: Warum?

HH: Wenn ich mich mit den anderen Saarländern, denen ich gar kein Unrecht geben kann, die haben sich als Franzosen gemeldet, und sind damit 'rummarschiert, obwohl sie kaum ein Wort Französisch konnten. Sie sind eher nach Hause gekommen. Das ist verständlich von Menschenstandpunkt. Aber ich wurde zu einem Standpunkt nicht selber. — Für mich brauchte ich den Standpunkt. Nicht gegenüber den Russen, um heimzukommen. Ich brauchte den mir persön-lich gegenüber, "Was bin ich jetzt?" Ich habe dadrauf nie gehört. Ich bin Deutscher und war so entgegen der Ansicht Hitlers oder der Nazis, bin ich Deutscher und auch [in

Russland]. Mehr wollte ich gar nicht sein. Deshalb hätte ich da nie mitgemacht in Ungarn. Ich gebe den Kameraden, die das gemacht haben, kein Unrecht. Die haben Recht gehabt. Sie sind früher nach Hause gekommen. Aber die haben den inneren Widerstreit nicht vorher erlebt, wie ich ihn erlebt habe. Und das ist der Unterschied. Deshalb konnte ich das nicht, aber im Ausland irgendwie daraus. — Opportunist war ich noch nie, in meinem Leben nicht. Hätte ich's leichter gehabt. Das war ich noch nie. Ich war in der Hitler-Jugend nicht aus opportunistischen Gründen.

EXCERPT G

TC: Und mit deiner, mit deinem Vater hast du ja direkt über Rassismus geredet? Das du vielleicht wegen deiner Hautfarbe abgekriegt hast?

FJ: Also meine Familie hat mich besonders geliebt vielleicht deswegen.

TC: Meinste?

FJ: Ich wollte gerne Tänzerin werden, und mein Vater [stepfather] schwärmte für Josephine Baker.

TC: Aha.

FJ: Das war'ne Steptänzerin, und ich wollte absolut Tänzerin werden, und dann hat er, eh hab' ich, eine Tanzausbildung bekommen, so mit etwas über elf war ich da und ich mußte mit dreizehn von der Tanzschule, wo denn der, der Direktor der Tanzschule gesagt hat also eh: "Sie kann keine Tänzerin werden" und "Ich hab Schwierigkeiten mit den Reichskult(-) mit der der Reichskulturamt, Reichskulturkammer, und man müßte sich mal vorstellen, wenn die eh der Vorhang aufgeht, und da steht eine Schwarze, und ich krieg Schwierigkeiten, wenn ich Fasia hier auf der Schule behalte." Also mußte ich von der Tanzschule, das war so schlimm für mich.

EXCERPT H

FJ: Ich habe Wiedergutmachung beantragt.

TC: Haben Sie das gekriegt? Hast du —

FJ: Nein, das ist zigmal abgelehnt worden. Erstmal konnte man nicht feststellen, daß eh Neger unter unter Rassengesetze fielen, und dann gibt es natürlich eh auch widersprüchliche Angaben, die gemacht wurden, weil Unrecht mir geschehen ist, als ich ein kleines Kind war, ab acht, neun, zehn. Und dann müssen, nicht wahr, Verwandte aussagen so wann, die wissen nicht, war das dann und dann, oder war es so, also diese diese Komplikationen, die da die dazwischen kommen, nicht? Aber zum Beispiel so einwandfrei ist festgestellt, daß ich die Tanzschule, ich wollte Tanz- Tänzerin werden, daß ich die verlassen mußte aus rassischen Gründen, das hat die die eh Tanzschule auch dann nach dem Krieg bestätigt, daß sie mich entfernen mußte, weil sie sonst Schwierigkeiten gehabt haben, und zwar aus rassischen Gründen mußten sie mich entfernen. Aber ich frage mich manchmal auch, wieso habe ich das eigentlich aushalten können? Ich frage mich manchmal, habe ich versucht deutsch zu sein, was ich ja auch bin eh. Ich komme aus Hamburg, ich spreche diesen deutschen Dialekt, was wieder Leute aus Hamburg verblüfft und wo man denn so 'nen kleinen Zuschuß hat, wenn man Hamburger Platt spricht.

EXCERPT I

TC: Was hast du gemacht, nachdem du nicht mehr da [in die Tanzschule] kommen durftest?

FJ: Das war für mich ganz schlimm, das war für mich, ich wurde dann verpflichtet, von den Nazis. Es gab ein Pflichtjahr, alle deutschen Mädchen mußten mit vierzehn Jahren ein Pflichtjahr machen, das heißt, bevor sie irgendwo in Familien reingingen, wo sie so Arbeiten machen mußten, Familien unterstützen mußten und so weiter im Haushalt, da kam das für mich nicht in Frage. Ich landete in einer Baracke in Hamburg in einem Stadtteil, wo nichts, fast nichts stehen geblieben war, in Rothenburgsort, in dem Stadtteil wurden polnische Judenfrauen eingesetzt.

TC: Wo, was für ein Stadtteil war das nochmal?

FJ: Rothenburgsort. Eh und ich wurde in einer Barackenküche, wurde verpflichtet in einer Barackenküche zu arbeiten, ist so ein kleines Ding gewesen mit einem großen Herd mit, ich begreif's heute noch nicht, daß da also vier und fünf und sechs Leute drin sitzen und mußten also zwischen, ich war zwischen Kriegsgefangenen Franzosen, also Internierten, zwischen eh ukrainischen, zwischen Ostarbeitern, eh Ukrainer, zwei, also der Franzose, die zwei eh, —

TC: Ukrainer.

FJ: Ukrainer eh und ein italienischer Internierter, Internierter, werde ich Ihnen später was von erzählen, also so auch zwischen zwischen diesen Männern. Und wir sollten angeblich, sollte ich Kartoffeln schälen, aber es war stinkende Brühe, stinkender verfaulter Kohl, der kam, wo du nur ein paar Kohlblätter reinschmeißen konntest. Die Brühe, die stank also, und das mußte ich dann in Eimern mit einem ukrainischen Jungen dann zu den Frauen bringen, zu den polnischen Judenfrauen, die auch interessant diese, diese, aber du willst ja was von mir hören und nicht von den polnischen Judenfrauen.

TC: Nee, ich würde auch noch gerne deine Eindrücke hören.

FJ: Na ja, also ich will es ganz kurz machen, ich habe schreckliche Sachen gesehen: Frauen, denen sie die Haare abgeschnitten hatten. Hab erlebt, wie man in ein paar Monaten aus Menschen Tiere machen kann, wenn man ihnen kaum was zu essen gibt, und wenn man dann mit 'ner Brühe vorbeikommt, wo die Menschen sich also gegenseitig angreifen, bloß um ein bißchen was in den Magen zu kriegen. Diese polnischen Judenfrauen sind alle vernichtet worden. Keine am Leben geblieben.

TC: Welchen, welchen KZ war das? Das war ein KZ?

FJ: Neuengamme.

TC: Neuengamme?

FJ: Ja. Aber ich, dieses, diese Lagerküche, diese Küche, diese Baracke, die stand in Rothenburgsort, da wo sie arbeiten mußten.

TC: Und warst du, mußtest du da bleiben?

FJ: Ich kann, konnte nach Hause gehen. Ich konnte nach Hause gehen.

TC: Ah, du konntest, mhm.

FJ: Ich konnte nach Hause gehen.

TC: Das war irgendwie so ein Job, könnte man sagen, aber schrecklicherweise war das so überhaupt nicht?

FJ: Nein, nein. Ich, in der Zeit, wo ich also, hab, ich zwischen denen gesessen und ich wurde so behandelt, wie, ich war unter Kontrolle der, einer Frauenschaftsleiterin, Frau Kappler, aus Rothenburgsort, NS-Frauenschaftsleiterin. Und die kontrollierte mich, ob ich da war, wie ich arbeitete, wie ich gearbeitet habe, und immer so Geschichten, so was Drohendes ja ich müßte ja bald sterili-, sterilisiert werden. Ich bekam ja meine, meine Mensis, wollen mal sagen, das bekam ich und die hatten natürlich Angst, denn unser Führer will 'ne weiße Rasse haben, und um Gottes Willen, ich wär, ja auch jetzt in dem Alter, wo sich auch Jungens für mich interessierten, wo ich mich auch für Männer inter-essiere. Aber es gab dann immer wieder eine unheimliche Solidarität. Ich hatte eine Schulfreundin, die kam in dieser schweren Zeit und brachte mir ihr Ei. Erstmal hatten, ich weiß gar nicht wie dat, kein Mensch hatte ein Ei, weißt du, wie kam die jetzt zu diesem Ei, du? Ihr Onkel hat dat irgend-wie dahin gebracht, ein Ei. Und das brachte sie mir. Und sie ist für mich die Zeitzeugin, sie sagt auch im Film, in diesem Film erkennst du sie wieder, wo sie sagt: "bei dem Schult-reffen, wir haben da so gestanden: 'Heil Hitler!' und so" und — erzählt denn wie die, wie sie in diese Barackenküche kam, wie die Leute da so. Ich weiß nicht, ob du dich erin-nerst in dem —

TC: Ich glaub' ich —

FJ: Das ist zu viel gewesen. Also es gab immer, du es gab immer wieder Leute, Deutsche, Weiße, die mir geholfen haben.

TC: Hmh und deine Kontakt mit den eh Frauen, die in dem Lager waren.

FJ: Die sind also bombardiert worden, die sind auf Schiffe gekommen, und die die eh sind dann eh ja sind bombardiert worden und die Leute, die sich retten wollten, sind dann von der SS, die also mit Booten Auffangbooten, nich wahr, rumfuhren dann, abgeknallt worden im Wasser. Da gibt es auch ein Film drüber.

TC: Mhm.

FJ: Ja.

TC: Warst du den ganzen Krieg da in diesem — kannst du da — ?

FJ: Nein, war ich war nur, also ich war ein Jahr da. Das genügte für mich.

TC: Ja. Wie kamst du raus?

FJ: Also ich konnte ja immer nach Hause gehen.

TC: Aha.

FJ: Aber ich bin dann bei der Arbeit zusammengebrochen, und dann bin ich wieder geholfen worden. Ich bin so'n, also es ging mir immer schlecht so im letzten Monat, bevor ich zusammengebrochen bin, ich hab es dann auch gesagt, dieser Frau gesagt, daß ich nich mehr kann. Es war kalt, es war also keine, nur wenn also da also gekocht wurde, dann wurde das Feuer ausgemacht. Dann saßen wir im Durchzug, wir hatten also keine Fensterscheiben. Es war Frost und eh ich bin auch ein paar mal zusammenge- brochen, und diese Frau hat das einfach nicht geglaubt. Die hat denn gesagt, ja dann müssen wir andere Saiten aufspan- nen. Und dann haben sie mich also mit dem Blockwagen von der Arbeit aus, da bin ich zusammengekracht, in ein Krankenhaus gefahren und da war eine deutsche Ärztin, die det die ganze Misere also sofort gesehen hat und die mich dann nach außerhalb Hamburgs verlegt hat. Und dann bin ich befreit worden und dann hab ich immer nur: mein Gott hoffenttlich kommt für mich, das mußt du dir mal vorstellen, für mich, hoffentlich kommen die Russen bald, hoffentlich kommen die Amerikaner bald, um Gottes Willen, das muß doch schnell gehen und so weiter. Ein Panzer hatte für mich 'ne ganz andere Bedeutung als nach dem Krieg als Pazifistin.

EXCERPT J

TC: Und unter euch, die in dieser Koch-, Kochküche gearbeitet haben, wie war das dann? Hast du dich als eine — Wart ihr eine Gruppe oder so was — Was war dieses Verhältnis zwischeneinander, weil ihr nicht Kriegesge- nicht nicht, ihr wart diese KZ-lerinnen — ?

FJ: Wir waren die Ausgestoßenen.
TC: Ja.
FJ: Ja. Wenn ich mir das überlege, war es ein sehr gutes Verhältnis, wobei ich, also wenn ich rausging schon und die die, wir hatten also Italiener, die die interniert waren, da war das anders, die kriegten auch noch anständig zu essen und die haben mich eben als Frau gesehen. Und durften also mit deutschen Frauen nicht verkehren und von da aus bin ich schon unheimlich also eh angepackt worden, und und das war also für mich ganz furchtbar. Und ich hab das nie eingesehen, nich wahr, also daß die das nu haben müßten oder jetzt jemand berühren müßten und all dat so ist, das ist schon 'ne sehr unangenehme Sache gewesen. Während die, wo ich mit zusammen gesessen hatte, eh eh da kamen also diesen diese Sachen nich vor, daß ich, sie irgendwie in mir nur so die Frau gesehn haben, die unbedingt. . . . Nachher als der Krieg zu Ende war, da kamen denn immer so (fortschrittliche) Leute auch so linke Männer, die haben dann, haben mich zum Tanzen geholt, ne? Waren schon so kleine Friedensfeste, und haben zu mir gesagt: "Hör mal Fasia, dat macht mir überhaupt nichts aus, ne, dat du dunkel bist." Und dann hab ich gesagt: "Du hör mal, aber es macht mir auch nichts aus, dat du weiß bist," ne? Dann waren die so fertig: "Du mußt mich doch richtig verstehen, das hab ich nicht so gemeint. Du hast doch, ich bin ganz echt, du kennst mich doch." Weißte, und "ich wollte das gar nicht." Ich hab nichts gesagt, nur ruhig geguckt und die wurden immer wütender, ne? "Bist du beleidigt? Warum bist du beleidigt, du weißt doch, nicht wahr, international wie ich da stehe" und so. Verstehst du, also was die in Wut nun also, und hab' dann auch immer wieder in solchen Kreisen erlebt auch in Friedenskreisen, daß sie gewöhnt waren, bevor ich jetzt in (Anführungsstrichen) diese "bekannte Sängerin" wurde, daß sie immer gewöhnt waren, das hab ich mitgekriegt, Leute aus Afrika, die als arme Teufel hierherkamen und die irgendwie in einem Projekt oder 'ne Solidaritätsspende in die Hand bekamen, und "Wir sind mit euch" und so weiter und der dat dann so, kam mir dann so wie in der Kirche vor, dann genickt und sich

bedankt dann für die Unterstützung und so weiter. Dat waren sie gewöhnt. Sie waren, sind überhaupt nicht gewöhnt, ich denke, das geht bis heute noch, daß man sich in Diskussionen einschaltet, und wo man sie auch politisch oder irgendwie angreift und sagt: "Ja, hör mal, was ist denn mit das und das also?" Das können sie gar nicht verkraften, ne? Die sind also, das sind sie nicht gewöhnt, ne?

EXCERPT K

FJ: Ich hab das Bundesverdienstkreuz gekriegt für meine Arbeit.

TC: Wußte ich nicht.

FJ: Ja. Ja. Es waren auch so stark, ob ich es überhaupt annehme, nich, weil ich gegen jede Art von Orden bin.

TC: Für welche welche Arbeit, du hast so viele Arbeiten gemacht?

FJ: Ja es ist Wahnsinn, nicht, gerade für die Arbeit, wo ich also im Grunde genommen für verurteilt worden bin, nicht? [*Lachen*]

TC: Welche meinst du? [*Lachen*]

FJ: Weißte, wo ich anderwo keine Zuschüsse für gekriegt hab, wenn ich also, ich hatte ja mal Zuschüsse haben müssen für diese jene, für Friedensarbeit, für für ja Kampf um um diese eh gegen die gegen die für die gegen die Schließung der Fabriken hier, wo ich immer Lieder gemacht hab, und die Frauen da mitgezogen hab, und die Männergewerkschaft und so. Das war für alle sehr erstaunlich . . . obwohl obwohl ich sollte vom Weizsäcker ausgezeichnet werden und ich wollte das, wenn überhaupt so, es sind, es war 'ne Kundgebung wegen des Golfkrieges. Wir zogen mit Fahnen ein, und es wurden erstmal Reden geschwungen und all so wat. Aber ich habe nach wie vor Bedenken und ich überlege mir, ob ich dieses Bundesverdienstkreuz nicht wieder abgebe.

TC: Warum? Aus welchem Grunde?

FJ: Ich kämpfe zum Beispiel um meine Wiedergutmachung und man kann mich nicht einerseits auszeichnen für meine Arbeit und andererseits eh verhindern, nicht wahr, daß ich überhaupt, nicht wahr, anerkannt bin als eben Verfolgte.

Andererseits auch ja vielleicht so das das könnte ich damit deutlich werden machen. Andererseits, ich habe es bisher nicht ausgenutzt, aber ich habe gehört, daß einige, die politische Arbeit machen mit diesem Ding in bestimmte Institutionen also da mal sagen können: hier ich brauche dies und brauche das für dieses und jenes, wo man, weiß ich, man gerade gemacht hat. Aber ich denke, daß ich das auch so erreiche, ohne. . . .

EXCERPT L

FJ: Sie [Fasia's sister] ist dann nachher hat in Amerika weiterstudiert, ich weiß nicht, was da passiert ist, wir haben uns nach dem Krieg nochmal getroffen.

TC: Mhm, nach dem Krieg.

FJ: Ja —

TC: War das —

FJ: Da habe ich meine ganzen Brüder und meine Geschwister kennengelernt.

TC: Hier in Deutschland?

FJ: In Deutschland.

TC: Wie kam das so?

FJ: Eh, der eine war, ist Direktor of Geo-, Geologie, der also Gesteinsforschung und so was und hat so Beziehungen, Handelsbeziehungen gehabt und war denn in Hamburg, und dann hat er gehört, daß eh ich da bin und wollte mich unbedingt kennenlernen. Ich habe einen unheimlichen Schock gekriegt, als ein Mensch mir entgegenkam, der genau so aussah wie ich, genau, das war mein Gesicht, ja. Und das war so unheimlich schön für mich, und der wollte mich auch, die wollten mich nach Afrika holen, aber ich, ich bin hier groß geworden, das ist sehr, sehr schwer, also ich hatte keine Sehnsucht nach Afrika.

TC: Tja. Und —

FJ: Ich weiß nicht, wie es dir da geht, ob du Sehnsucht nach Afrika hast?

TC: Überhaupt nicht. [*Lachen*] Ich, ich versteh dich ganz gut, weil ich Amerikanerin bin.

FJ: Ja, ja.

TC: Basta.

FJ: Basta.

EXCERPT M

TC: Aber was hat dich motiviert alles, alle diese politischen Sachen und Aktivitäten zu machen?

FJ: Du mußt mich nich nach Motivation und so wat fragen, dat kannste nich. Das hat was mit meinen Schwarzsein zu tun.

TC: Was genau?

FJ: Alles, was ich erlebt habe, das darf nich mehr wieder passieren, ich hab' zuviel Elend gesehen und alles reinschmeißen, was überhaupt an Kraft ist so, aber du mußt nicht vorstellen, daß ich mir das jetzt ständig, dat als Heldin nun wollt' ich rumrennen und Gerechtigkeit, sondern hat sich immer, immer war wat da, du mußt kommen und hör mal und so, ne? Für immer für wat einsetzen, jetzt hab' ich ja, haste gesehen, mitte Spinnen, dat durchzuboxen, er will Spinnen haben, all so'n Kram. Aber dann in diese Fraueninitiativen, die um die Arbeitsplätze ihrer Männer gekämpft haben. Ich bin immer geholt worden.

TC: Geholt?

FJ: Und deshalb oder auch hingegangen, und deshalb brauchte ich im Grunde genommen keinen Psychologen. Ich konnte die ganze Wut, verstehst du, alles, was ich gespeich[-ert], konnt ich loswerden.

TC: Aber was —

FJ: Ich hab Leute zum Weinen gebracht, aber auch zum Lachen und umgekehrt auch. Und dann bin ich zuletzt bin ich in der Frauenbewegung gelandet. Gut. Jetzt fragst du weiter.

TC: [*Lachen*] Darf ich?

FJ: Du mußt jetzt. Das kostet zuviel Geld an Tonband.

TC: Jaa. Die Frage mit dein — Schwarzsein. Was genau war das, was eh dein Schwarzsein mit dieser politischen Arbeit verbunden hat? Wie hast du das reingebracht oder was hast du da rausgekriegt von dieser Arbeit?

FJ: *Es hat doch hier überhaupt keine Schwarzenbewegung gegeben hier, mußt du dir mal vorstellen. Ich war doch ganz alleine auf so was, und ich selber hab' nie für mich selber nie gespürt, daß ich Schwarze bin, dat haben, die anderen haben ihre Probleme. Dat war ja nich mein Problem. [Lachen]*

TC: *Aha. Du hast das nie selber gespürt?*

FJ: *Ja, spürst du denn, dat du schwarz bist?*

TC: *Ja!*

FJ: *Wo an?*

TC: *Ja, ja, ich meine, —*

FJ: *Ja, wenn du dich selber anguckst.*

TC: *Na ja, du hast schon recht.*

FJ: *Ich hab', ich hab' zu den Kindern gesagt, ich sag, "Stell dir doch mal vor, ich weiß doch, ich hab' doch diese Rassenprobleme überhaupt nicht mit mir selber, dat ich jetzt ein Problem hab', daß ich jetzt so also schwarz bin, das ist euer Problem, oder die Probleme euer Eltern."*

EXCERPT N

HH: Natürlich nach meine Sterilisation mit der HJ, mit dem Geist, den ich auch mit 15–16 Jahren schon einigermaßen begriff, vorbei war, war doch ganz klar. Im Gegensatz zu dem Dreizehnjährigen.

TC: Ich verstehe nicht genau was du meinst.

HH: Im Gegensatz zu dem Dreizehnjährigen, der Freude hatte am ganzen Hitler-Jugend Spiel, hatte der Fünfzehnjährige schon nicht mehr. Der konnte schon mehr denken, aber der mußte da mitmachen.

TC: Musstest?

HH: Ja, was hätte ich dann machen sollen? Es hat mich niemand gezwungen. Aber die Umstände haben mich gezwungen. Ich mußte ja. Ich habe ja gelernt auf der Eisenbahn, ohne in der Hitler-Jugend zu sein, hätte ich gar nicht lernen können da. Wir sind ja zu allen möglichen unmöglichen Gelegenheiten in Uniformen angetreten. In Hitler-Jugend Uniformen.

TC: Hatte das einen Unterschied gemacht? Wenn du diese Uniform getragen hast, auf wie du behandelt wurde?

HH: Ja, hat ja niemand mir angesehen, daß ich eigentlich gar nicht dazugehörte.

TC: Niemand?

HH: Nein. Und die die das gewußt haben, haben nichts gesagt. Es war beileibe nicht so. Es waren etliche, die das gewußt haben. Mir hat das, so weit wie ich mich zurückerinnern kann, niemals eine Schwierigkeit bereitet.

TC: Mit der Uniform?

HH: Mit der Uniform.

TC: *Und ohne? Wäre das dann —*

HH: *Ohne hätte ich ja gar nicht mit machen können. Das kann man sich überhaupt nicht mehr vorstellen.*

TC: Ja, ich frage jetzt —

HH: *Ich finde nur — Ja, aus der Fragestellung geht schon die Unkenntnis der damaligen Situation voraus.*

TC: *Genau.*

HH: *Das ist ganz klar. Ich verstehe das. Weil man sich das gar nicht vorstellen kann, schon gar nicht als Amerikaner. Obwohl bei euch ja nun auch nicht, nach meinem Empfinden, der Himmel auf Erden ist. Also, man braucht eigentlich einer schwarzen Amerikanerin nicht zu erzählen, in was sich der Unterschied nun ausdrückt. Obwohl es gesetzlich verboten ist in Amerika. Bei uns war das Unterschiedmachen zu Nichtariern gesetzlicher Zwang. Und trotzdem haben es nicht alle Menschen gemacht. Du hast bestimmt viele Amerikaner, die du kennst, die dir unbefangen gegenüber treten. Du hast auch andere, siehst du. Und das ist doch etwas was selbst, wenn es jetzt demokratisch zugeht, wie in Amerika, ist das der Fall. Wieviel mehr in einer Dikatur wie das Hitler-Deutschland war.*

EXCERPT O

HH: Nach dem Urteil wurden wir sofort verladen und ins Krankenhaus, und da wurde am nächsten Tag operiert, und nach 10 Tagen wurde ich entlassen. Und da habe ich auf der Arbeit gestanden. Die wurden verständigt auf der Eisenbahn. Und mir wurde das auch mitgeteilt. Ich durfte ja nicht heiraten, kein deutsches Mädchen heiraten. Das war klar. Spielt unter den Nürnberger Gesetzen. Und heute fragen mich die selben Leute, "Ach, warum hast du nicht geheiratet?"

TC: Und warum bist du nicht geheiratet?

HH: Wen hätte ich heiraten können?

TC: Aber nach dem Krieg?

HH: Ja, nach dem Krieg dann war es zu spät.

TC: Ja?

HH: Nach dem Krieg war es zu spät. Als ich zurückkam aus Gefangenschaft, war ich 30 Jahre alt. Ich weiß, man kann auch mit 30 Jahren noch heiraten gehen. Aber jetzt wollte ich nicht mehr. Vorher hätte mich kein Mädchen von hier genommen. Auch wenn die Mädchen gewollt hätten. Aber ihre Eltern hätten das nicht zugelassen. *Ich weiß nicht, ob ich dir erklären muß, wenn du einen weißen Amerikaner irgendwo in einer ganz bestimmten Gegend heiraten wolltest, braucht man dich jetzt gar nicht zu fragen, warum willst du den nicht heiraten. Vielleicht willst du, vielleicht will auch er. Aber es ist trotzdem unmöglich. Und hier war es außerdem verboten. Das war gar nicht spruchreif —*

NOTES

INTRODUCTION

1. These difficult issues of context and representation raise another equally important question: What are the implications of the process of archiving such memories with regard to both access to and use of them by Afro-Germans in the writing of their history? This question invites us to consider the role of the physical recording of individual memories and recollections of the past experiences of members of earlier generations of Afro-Germans as the basis for establishing a history for this group, which, in turn, enables their entry into Germany's official history (or histories). To what extent is access to these recorded memories an integral part of the process of constructing national and cultural identity, and how does the potential lack of access to such memories—or the limitations imposed on that access by locating them in the United States rather than Germany—facilitate, reify, and affirm gaps in the construction of national histories, collective memory, and identity? Although the process of archiving such material makes it available to a larger audience, in this case, doing so would at the same time effectively remove the material from this community and in some ways, hinder access to these important historical voices. Finally, in what ways are such processes served by preserving such memories in a location like the Holocaust museum? The questions raised by this anecdote certainly cannot be answered with any degree of satisfaction in the space of an introductory essay. Yet I raise them with more than merely rhetorical intentions, for they illustrate important aspects of one level on which this study engages the issue of representation—specifically, the status of memory in historical analysis.

2. *Hitler's Forgotten Victims: Black Survivors of the Holocaust,* directed by David Okuefuna and produced by Moise Shewa (59 min., Afro-Wisdom Productions, United Kingdom, 1997).

3. Carol Aisha Blackshire-Belay, ed., *The African-German Experience: Critical Essays* (Westport, CT: Praeger, 1996). Chapter 5 of this book undertakes a detailed analysis of some of the broader implications of these tendencies for the study of the African diaspora.

4. Susanne Zantop, *Colonial Fantasies: Conquest, Family, and Nation in Precolonial Germany, 1770–1870* (Durham, NC: Duke University Press, 1997); Sara Friedrichsmeyer, Sara Lennox, and Susanne Zantop, eds., *The Imperialist Imagination: German Colonialism and Its Legacy* (Ann Arbor: University of Michigan

Press, 1998); Pascal Grosse, *Kolonialismus, Eugenik und bürgerliche Gesellschaft in Deutschland, 1850–1918* (Frankfurt: Campus, 2000); Lora Wildenthal, *German Women for Empire, 1884–1945* (Durham, NC: Duke University Press, 2001).

5. For some studies of note, see Hans Debrunner, *Presence and Prestige, Africans in Europe: A History of Africans in Europe before 1918* (Basel: Basler Afrika Bibliographien, 1979); Sander Gilman, *On Blackness without Blacks: Essays on the Image of the Black in Germany* (Boston: G. K. Hall, 1982), Sander Gilman, *Difference and Pathology: Stereotypes of Sexuality, Race, and Madness* (Ithaca: Cornell University Press, 1985); Sander Gilman, "Black Bodies, White Bodies: Toward an Iconography of Female Sexuality in Late Nineteenth-Century Art," in *Race Writing and Difference,* ed. Henry Louis Gates Jr. (Chicago: University of Chicago Press, 1986); Rosemarie K. Lester, *Trivialneger: Das Bild des Schwarzen im westdeutschen Illustriertenroman* (Stuttgart: Akademischer Verlag H.-D. Heinz, 1982); May Opitz, Katharina Oguntoye, and Dagmar Schultz, eds., *Farbe bekennen: Afro-deutsche Frauen auf den Spuren ihrer Geschichte* (Berlin: Fischer, 1986) (translated as *Showing Our Colors: Afro-German Women Speak Out,* trans. Anne Adams [Amherst: University of Massachusetts Press, 1992]); Fatima El-Tayeb, *Schwarze Deutsche: Der Diskurs um 'Rasse' und nationale Identität, 1890–1933* (Frankfurt am Main: Campus, 2001); Clarence Lusane, *Hitler's Black Victims: The Historical Experiences of Afro-Germans, European Blacks, Africans and African Americans in the Nazi Era* (New York: Routledge, 2002); Reinhold Grimm and Jost Hermand, eds., *Blacks and German Culture: Essays* (Madison: University of Wisconsin Press for Monatshefte, 1986); Robert Kesting, "Forgotten Victims: Blacks in the Holocaust," *Journal of Negro History* 77 (1992): 30–36; Peter Martin, *Schwarze Teufel, Edle Mohren: Afrikaner in Bewußtsein und Geschichte der Deutschen* (Hamburg: Junius, 1993); Tina Campt, "Afro-German Cultural Identity and the Politics of Positionality: Contests and Contexts in the Formation of a German Ethnic Identity," *New German Critique* 58 (1993): 109–26; David McBride, Leroy Hopkins, and C. Aisha Blackshire-Belay, eds., *Crosscurrents: African Americans, Africa, and Germany in the Modern World* (Columbia, SC: Camden House, 1998); Blackshire-Belay, *African-German Experience;* Annegret Ehmann, "From Colonial Racism to Nazi Population Policy: The Role of the So-Called Mischlinge," in *The Holocaust and History: The Known, the Unknown, the Disputed, and the Reexamined,* ed. Michael Berenbaum and Abraham J. Peck (Bloomington: Indiana University Press in association with the U.S. Holocaust Memorial Museum, 1998). See also the following Afro-German autobiographies: Hans J. Massaquoi, *Destined to Witness: Growing up Black in Nazi Germany* (New York: W. Morrow, 1999), and Ika Hügel-Marshall, *Invisible Woman: Growing up Black in Germany,* trans. Elizabeth Gaffney (New York: Continuum, 2001).

6. Some of the most important of these are the works of Stuart Hall, particularly "Cultural Identity and Diaspora," in *Identity: Community, Culture, Difference,* ed. Jonathan Rutherford (London: Lawrence and Wishart, 1990); and "Minimal Selves," in *Black British Cultural Studies: A Reader,* ed. Houston A. Baker Jr., Manthia Diawara, and Ruth H. Lindeborg (Chicago: University of Chicago Press, 1996), and those of Paul Gilroy, especially *"There Ain't No Black in the Union*

Jack": The Cultural Politics of Race and Nation (Chicago: University of Chicago Press, 1991); *Small Acts: Thoughts on the Politics of Black Cultures* (London: Serpent's Tail, 1998); *The Black Atlantic: Modernity and Double Consciousness* (Cambridge: Harvard University Press, 1993); and *Between Camps: Race, Identity, and Nationalism at the End of the Colour Line* (London: Allen Lane/Penguin, 2000). Noteworthy recent elaborations of diaspora that build on these early seminal works include Brent Hayes Edwards, "The Uses of Diaspora," *Social Text* 66 (2001): 44–73; Jacqueline Brown, "Black Liverpool, Black America, and the Gendering of Diasporic Space," *Cultural Anthropology* 13 (1998): 291–325; Avtar Brah, *Cartographies of Diaspora: Contesting Identities* (London: Routledge, 1996). See also Barnor Hesse's articles: "Reviewing the Western Spectacle: Reflexive Globalization through the Black Diaspora," in *Global Futures: Migration, Environment, and Globalization,* ed. Avtar Brah, Mary Hickman, and Maírtín Mac an Ghaille (London: Macmillan, 1999); "Black to the Front and Black Again," in *Place and the Politics of Identity,* ed. Michael Keith and Steve Pile (London: Routledge, 1993): 162–82.

7. The two accounts presented here were part of a larger interview project undertaken between 1991 and 1998, during which I conducted a total of twenty-one interviews with eleven individuals—ten women and one man—born between 1919 and 1946. With two exceptions, interviews were conducted in the homes of my informants in cities across Germany (Berlin, Oberhausen, Frankfurt, Dudweiler-Saarbrucken, Düsseldorf, and Gelsenkirchen, among others). All interviews were conducted in German.

8. Ronald Grele, "Movement without Aim," in *Envelopes of Sound: The Art of Oral History* (New York: Praeger, 1991), 138–39. See also Louis Althusser and Etienne Balibar, *Reading Capital* (London: Verso, 1979), 24–30.

9. Among many other works, see Lawrence Langer, *Holocaust Testimonies: The Ruins of Memory* (New Haven: Yale University Press, 1991); Geoffrey Hartman, *The Longest Shadow: In the Aftermath of the Holocaust* (Bloomington: Indiana University Press, 1996), and Geoffrey Hartman, ed., *Holocaust Remembrance: The Shapes of Memory* (Oxford: Blackwell, 1994); Shoshana Felman and Dori Laub, *Testimony: Crises of Witnessing in Literature, Psychoanalysis, and History* (New York: Routledge, 1991); James Edward Young, *Writing and Rewriting the Holocaust: Narrative and the Consequences of Interpretation* (Bloomington: University of Indiana Press, 1988); Luisa Passerini, *Fascism in Popular Memory: The Cultural Experience of the Turin Working Class,* trans. Robert Lumley and Jude Bloomfield (New York: Cambridge University Press, 1987); Luisa Passerini, *Autobiography of a Generation: Italy 1968,* trans. Lisa Erdberg, foreword by Joan Wallach Scott (Hanover, NH: University Press of New England, 1996); Michael H. Frisch, *A Shared Authority: Essays on the Craft and Meaning of Oral and Public History* (Albany: State University of New York Press, 1990); Alessandro Portelli, *The Death of Luigi Trastuilli and Other Stories: Form and Meaning in Oral History* (Albany: State University of New York Press, 2001).

10. One noteworthy example of the work of writing the postwar history of the Afro-German community that has already begun is Yara-Colette Lemke Muniz de

Faria's book, *Zwischen Fürsorge und Ausgrenzung: Afrodeutsche Besatzungskinder im Nachkriegsdeutschland* (Berlin: Metropol, 2002).

11. Teresa de Lauretis, *Technologies of Gender* (Bloomington: Indiana University Press, 1987). See also Michel Foucault, *The History of Sexuality,* vol. 1, *An Introduction,* trans. Robert Hurley (New York: Vintage, 1980), 180.

12. Pierre Nora, "Between Memory and History: *Les Lieux de Memoire,*" in *History and Memory in African-American Culture,* ed. Genevieve Fabre and Robert O'Meally (Oxford: Oxford University Press, 1994), 290.

13. Maurice Halbwachs, *On Collective Memory,* ed., trans., and intro. Lewis A. Coser (Chicago: University of Chicago Press, 1992), 40.

14. De Lauretis, *Technologies,* 25.

15. Ibid.

16. Ibid., 18.

17. Joan Scott, "Experience," in *Feminists Theorize the Political,* ed. Judith Butler and Joan Scott (New York: Routledge, 1992), 27, 37.

18. Young, *Writing and Rewriting,* 37.

19. Ibid.

20. Ibid., 10.

21. Saul Friedländer, *Memory, History, and the Extermination of the Jews of Europe* (Bloomington: Indiana University Press, 1993), 130.

22. As cited in S. Friedländer, *Memory,* 131. See also Jean-François Lyotard, *The Differend: Phrases in Dispute,* trans. Georges Van Den Abbeele (Minneapolis: University of Minnesota Press, 1988).

PART I

1. "*Ich wußte, daß mein Vater Algerier war. Aber wir haben nie darüber gesprochen. Das wurde auch mal so fallengelassen im Gespräch: 'Du kannst deine Herkunft nicht verleugnen'—absolut nicht im Bösen gemeint. Ich konnte mir doch gar nicht vorstellen, daß Algerier anders sind. Ich wußte doch gar nicht, was das ist. Erst viel später als ich das begreifen lernte. (. . .) Das haben die Nachbarskinder mir beizeiten beigebracht. (. . .) In Äußerungen wurden mir Schimpfwörter an den Kopf geworfen, die Herkunft meines Vaters betreffend. Das war kurz nach dem Krieg. Und die Väter aller anderen Kinder waren ja deutsche Soldaten. Und meiner war ein Feind.*" (Hans Hauck, interview by author, Dudweiler, Germany, 20 April 1992. All translations by the author.)

2. For the experiences of Afro-Germans more generally, see, for example, Tina Campt, Pascal Grosse, and Yara-Colette Lemke Muniz de Faria, "Blacks, Germans and the Politics of Imperial Imagination, 1920–1960," in *Imperialist Imagination,* ed. Friedrichsmeyer, Lennox, and Zantop, 205–29; Katharina Oguntoye, *Eine Afro-Deutsche Geschichte: Zur Lebenssituation von Afrikanern und Afro-Deutschen in Deutschland von 1884 bis 1950* (Berlin: Hoho Verlag Christine Hoffmann, 1997).

3. Gilman, *On Blackness,* xii.

4. In *On Blackness without Blacks,* Gilman asserts that what is characteristic

of the German conception of blackness is the fact that it developed in the virtual absence of a black presence. He maintains that in Germany, the image of blackness developed independently of an "external reality," composed rather "of elements taken from external traditions and altered to fit certain needs of a radically different culture" (xi). Gilman describes this image as "an accretion of borrowings which were altered and shaped to create patterns into which these projections were cast" (xi). This resulted in what he refers to as a "mirage of blackness," a phenomenon that altered German responses to Blacks when the latter were eventually confronted "in reality." See also Gilman, *Difference and Pathology;* Gilman, "Black Bodies," 223–61.

CHAPTER I

1. *"Ich bin in Frankfurt [August 1920] geboren. Weil meine Mutter hier es sehr schwer hatte, als man sehen konnte, daß sie schwanger war, ist sie nach Frankfurt [gegangen]. Mein Vater wurde nach Frankfurt versetzt. Obwohl sie nicht verheiratet waren, hatte sie ja sonst niemand mehr auf der Welt und da ist sie [ihm] nachgereist. (. . .) Schwierigkeiten hat es schon gegeben nach den Aussagen von den noch lebenden Nachbarn. (. . .) Schwierigkeiten, mit einem Besatzungssoldaten, mit einem farbigen Besatzungssoldaten, das muß man dabei sagen. Und dann in einer gut katholischen Familie, erstmal schon der Makel der 'unehelichen Geburt' und dann noch das Schlimmste mit 'so einem,' mit einem Farbigen. Das war damals ganz schlimm."* (Hans Hauck.)

2. Hans-Jürgen Lüsebrink, "'Tirailleurs Sénégalais' und 'Schwarze Schande'— Verlaufsformen und Konsequenzen einer deutsch-französischen Auseinandersetzung (1910–1926)," in *"Tirailleurs Sénégalais": Zur bildlichen und literarischen Darstellung afrikanischer Soldaten im Dienste Frankreichs,* ed. Janos Riesz and Joachim Schultz (Frankfurt: Lang, 1989), 57. See also Grosse, *Kolonialismus,* 199–209.

3. Keith L. Nelson, "'The Black Horror on the Rhine': Race as a Factor in Post–World War I Diplomacy," *Journal of Modern History* 42 (1970): 612.

4. Ibid., 613. See also Grosse, *Kolonialismus,* 199–205.

5. "Elles sont précisément les qualités que réclament les longues luttes de la guérre moderne: la rusticité, l'endurance, la tenacité, l'instinct du combat, l'abscence de nervosité, et une imcomparable puissance de choc. Leur arriveé sur le champ de bataille produira sur l'adversaire un effet moral considerable. Ces précieux advantages du nombre et de qualité sont les facteurs importants qui entreront en ligne des la premiére bataille; mais si la lutte se prolonge, nos forces africaines nous constituent des réserve presque indéfinies dont la source est hors de la portée de l'adversaire et que permettent de continuer la lutte jusqu'a ce que nous obtenions un premier succes, et, le succes obtenu, de la pour suivre au triomphe définitif." (Charles Mangin, *La Force Noire* [Paris: Hachette, 1910], 342f, as cited in Grosse, *Kolonialismus,* 202.)

6. "Die französischen Militärstrategen setzten hierbei in erster Linie auf eine 'natürliche Befähigung' der im europäischen Verständnis minder zivilisierten

Völker in militärischen Konflikten, verglichen mit den schwäachlichen und nervösen europäischen Männern. Diese Anschauung beruhte auf dem konstruierten Gegensatz zwischen Natur- und Kulturvölkern, wonach die europäische Kulturentwicklung die natürlichen Triebe, einschließlich der Aggression, domestiziert habe. Dieser Einschätzung schloß sich auch ein deutscher Kommentator der französischen Militärpolitik an, demzufolge 'der westafrikanische Neger bei seiner . . . urgesunden Kraft, bei seinen ererbten und wachgehaltenen kriegerischen Anlagen zum Soldatenhandwerk sich mehr eigne als der in einer abgearbeiteten Stadtbevölkerung erwaschsene Europäer' (*Die Zukunft* 76 [1911]: 297)" (Grosse, *Kolonialismus,* 203). Grosse states that this article was translated and published in France in *Révue des Tropes Coloniales* in February 1912.

7. "Vielmehr ist die Dämonisierung der potentiellen Gegner im Rahmen der psychologischen Kriegsvorbereitung zu verstehen. Die 'schwarze Gefahr' wurde so zum Symbol für die antizipierte Grausamkeit des kommenden Krieges. . . . Die sprachliche Verrohung, die die Charakterisierung der 'schwarzen Gefahr' insgesamt hervorbrachte, projizierte das Gewaltpotential des Krieges auf das Bild dehumanisierter französischen Kolonialtruppen als vermeintliche Ursache. Unter diesen Prämissen ließ sich das wehrbereite deutsche Volk zum einzigen wahrhaften Hüter der europäischen Kultur bzw. Der 'weißen Rasse' stilisieren, das 'die Würde Europas vor . . . afrikanischen Barbaren' bewahrte und den Rückfall in die Zeiten des 30jährigen Krieges verhindere" (Grosse, *Kolonialismus,* 204–5).

8. "Im Kontext der deutschen Kampagne gegen die 'Schwarze Schande' erhielten diese u.a. von Mangin verwendeten Beschreibungsmuster der 'obéissance aveugle,' der 'agressivité innée' des 'penchant matériel pour la guerre' sowie der 'Unzivilisiertheit,' die afrikanischen Soldaten zugeschrieben wurden, jedoch radikal entgegengesetzte Bedeutungsdimensionen: statt—wie in der kolonialen Anthropologie des Vorkriegsfrankreichs—als positiv gewendete Charaktermerkmale der Afrikaner zu gelten, die als zu erziehende 'grands enfants' und 'âmes simples' galten, wurden sie in der deutschen Öffentlichkeit der Zeit zu Zeichen barbarischer Wildheit umgewertet" (Lüsebrink, "'Tirailleurs Sénégalais' und 'Schwarze Schande,'" 61).

9. Before the war, Solf had succeeded Bernhard Dernberg as colonial secretary. Bethmann Hollweg appointed Solf to the post in 1911. Solf had previously served as colonial governor for the German colony of Samoa. Both Friedrich von Lindequist, civilian governor of German Southwest Africa, and Solf (both of whom were part of what came to be known as the era of colonial reform) later played central roles in drafting and implementing the decrees banning racially mixed marriage that prompted the parliamentary debates regarding the legality of *Mischehen* in the colonies and the Reich.

10. Nelson, "Black Horror," 609.

11. See Gisela Lebzelter, "Die 'Schwarze Schmach': Vorurteile—Propaganda—Mythos," *Geschichte und Gesellschaft* 11 (1985): 37. In her study of the Rhineland campaign, Schüler quotes official French figures that set the number of colonial troops at twenty-three thousand. U.S. General Henry Allen of the Interallied Rhineland High Commission, who investigated the reports of atrocities

committed by the black troops, also set the number colonial troops at an average of twenty-five thousand between January 1919 and June 1920, when France withdrew the majority of its Senegalese troops (Anja Schüler, *The "Horror on the Rhine": Rape, Racism, and the International Women's Movement,* John F. Kennedy Institute for American Studies Working Paper 86/1996 [Berlin: Free University of Berlin, 1996]: 3).

12. Nelson, "Black Horror," 616.

13. Ibid., 625.

14. Edmund Dene Morel, "Black Scourge in Europe: Sexual Horror Let Loose by France on the Rhine," *London Daily Herald,* 10 April 1920.

15. Edmund Dene Morel, *The Horror on the Rhine,* 8th ed. (London: Union of Democratic Control, 1921).

16. "Unsere Jugend in der Pfalz und im Rheinland wird geschändet, unser Volk verseucht, die Würde des Deutschen und der weißen Rasse zertreten. Der englische Journalist nennt dies 'eine wohl überlegte Politik.' Ist diese für unser Volkstum im Rheinland verderbliche, für die Ehre und Würde des deutschen Volkes und der weißen Rasse schändliche, von einem Engländer als wohl überlegt bezeichnete Politik unserer Feinde der Reichsregierung bekannt?" (Verhandlungen der verfassungsgebenden Deutschen Nationalversammlung, 1920, Bd. 343, Anlagen zu den Stenographischen Berichten Nr. 2676 bis 3076, no.2771, p. 3081, as cited in Reiner Pommerin, *Sterilisierung der Rheinlandbastarde: Das Schicksal einer farbigen deutschen Minderheit, 1918–1937* [Düsseldorf: Droste, 1979], 13).

17. Here I must acknowledge a cogent point suggested to me by Michelle Maria Wright. Although Gobineau's *Essai sur l'inégalité des races humaines* ("Essay on the Inequality of the Human Races"; the first secular argument for racial hierarchization) became a popular reference for a wide variety of late-nineteenth- and twentieth-century white supremacist movements, the *Essai* is far from consistent in its argument. While Gobineau's thesis asserts, on the one hand, that civilizations collapse because of miscegenation when inferior blood pollutes that of the superior race, elsewhere in the *Essai* he argues that a civilization cannot become a great artistic culture, nor its people adequately vigorous *without* intermixture, specifically mixing with Blacks. This is less surprising if one considers, as Michael Biddiss has noted, that the ultimate goal of the *Essai* was to prove that French civilization would collapse if power were not returned to the aristocracy whom, he maintained, were racially distinct from the middle class and peasant class. At one point in the *Essai,* Gobineau reminds his readers that he is well aware that an African chieftain is easily superior to the French peasant or even the French bourgeosie. See Arthur comte de Gobineau, *Essai sur l'inégalité des races humaines,* 2d ed. (Paris: Firmin-Didot, 1884); and Michael Biddiss, *Father of Racist Ideology: The Social and Political Thought of Count Gobineau* (London: Weidenfeld & Nicolson, 1970).

18. My discussion in this section is based in large part on the analysis undertaken in Tina Campt and Pascal Grosse, "'Mischlingskinder' in Nachkriegsdeutschland: Zum Verhältnis von Psychologie, Anthropologie und Gesellschaftspolitik nach 1945," *Psychologie und Geschichte* 6 (1994): 48–78. See also Grosse,

Kolonialismus, 176–92, as well as Ehmann, "From Colonial Racism to Nazi Population Policy"; William Tucker, *The Science and Politics of Racial Research* (Urbana: University of Illinois Press, 1994).

19. For a more extensive discussion of these and other studies of racial mixture, see Campt and Grosse, "'Mischlingskinder'"; Pascal Grosse, "Kolonialismus und das Problem der 'Rassenmischung' in Deutschland: Zur Geschichte der anthropologischen Psychologie 1920–1940," in *Psychology im soziokulturellen Wandel— Kontinuitäten und Diskontinuitäten,* ed. Siegfried Jäger et al. (Frankfurt: Peter Lang, 1995), 75–85.

20. On the other side of the Atlantic, one of the leading U.S. eugenic scientists, Charles Benedict Davenport, conducted a second study of racial mixture during World War I. Davenport's primary concern was with the potentially negative results of racial mixture. Concurring with Fischer, Davenport asserted that the most important effect of these mixtures was not physical but rather psychological. Published in 1917, the study used the same methodology as Fischer's: anthropometric measurements and family genealogies. Davenport provided scientifically sophisticated arguments for much older claims about the psyche of the mulatto, arguing that mulattos combined "ambition and push . . . with intellectual inadequacy which makes the unhappy hybrid dissatisfied with his lot and a nuisance to others." Ambition was an attribute assumed to have come from the white parent, and inadequacy was assumed to have come from the Black. Davenport concluded that miscegenation necessarily meant disharmony and that "hybridized" people were inevitably badly put together, dissatisfied, and ineffective. See Tucker, *Science and Politics of Racial Research.* Between 1921 and 1927, German, American, Norwegian, Dutch, and Chinese scientists undertook at least nine subsequent studies on racial mixture. See Campt and Grosse, "'Mischlingskinder,'" 51–58; see also Ehmann, "From Colonial Racism to Nazi Population Policy," 115–330.

21. Mary Douglas, *Purity and Danger: An Analysis of Concepts of Pollution and Taboo* (London: Routledge, 1991).

22. Elizabeth A. Grosz, *Volatile Bodies: Toward a Corporeal Feminism* (Bloomington: Indiana University Press, 1994), 193

23. For a detailed analysis of the gendered politics of racial mixture in the German colonies, see Grosse, *Kolonialismus,* 145–53; Wildenthal, *German Women,* 79–130.

24. "Solche Verbindungen die Rasse nicht erhalten sondern verschlechtern. Die Abkömmlinge sind in der Regel sittlich und körperlich schwach, vereinigen in sich die schlechten Eigenschaften beider Eltern" (Bundesarchiv Koblenz, R 151 FC 5180, as cited in Cornelia Essner, "Zwischen Vernunft und Gefühl: Die Reichstagsdebatten von 1912 um koloniale 'Rassenmischehe' und 'Sexualität,'" in *Zeitschrift für Geschichtswissenschaft 6* [Berlin: Metropol, 1997], 503).

25. "Jeder, dessen Stammbaum auf väterlicher oder mütterliche Seite auf einen Eingeborenen zurückgeführt werden kann, muß selbst als Eingeborener betrachtet und behandelt werden" (Bundesarchiv Koblenz, R 151 FC 5180, as cited in Essner, "Zwischen Vernunft und Gefühl," 503–4).

26. Lora Wildenthal, "Race, Gender, and Citizenship in the German Colonial

Empire," in *Tensions of Empire: Colonial Cultures in a Bourgeois World,* ed. Frederick Cooper and Ann Laura Stoler (Berkeley: University of California Press, 1997), 267. See also Wildenthal, *German Women,* 84–85.

27. Wildenthal, "Race," 266–67.

28. Ibid., 267.

29. Oskar Hintrager, *Südwestafrika in der deutschen Zeit* (Munich: R. Odenbourg, 1955), cited in Wildenthal, "Race," 267.

30. Helmut Walser Smith, "The Talk of Genocide, the Rhetoric of Miscegenation: Notes on Debates in the German Reichstag Concerning Southwest Africa, 1904–14," in *Imperialist Imagination,* ed. Friedrichsmeyer, Lennox, and Zantop, 116.

31. "Sie senden Ihre Söhne in die Kolonien: Wünschen Sie, daß Sie Ihnen wollhaarige Enkel in die Wiege legen?" (Stenographische Berichte über die Verhandlungen des Deutschen Reichstages, Band 285, S 1648, as cited in Essner, "Zwischen Vernunft und Gefühl," 509).

32. Ibid.

33. Essner remarks that unbeknownst to Ledebour, the Landesrat in Windhuk had already begun drafting a proposal for what she refers to as a *Mischlingsverordnung* that sought to impose sanctions on interracial sex during periods of fertility and proposed a scheme of state-regulated bordellos (ibid., 510).

34. "Wo bleibt da die Logik, weil wir keine Mischlinge in den Kolonien haben wollen, verbieten wir die Mischehe? . . . Wenn Sie so vorgehen, dann müßten Sie doch den Beweis dafür erbringen, daß die meisten Mischlinge aus den Mischehen hervorgehen. Es ist dies aber nicht der Fall, sondern gerade umgekehrt: 99 Prozent aller Mischlinge in den Kolonien Stammen aus dem außerhelichen Geschlechtsverkehr, und nur 1 Prozent stammt aus Mischehen" (Stenographische Berichte, Band 285, 1649f, cited in ibid.).

35. Ibid.

36. Wildenthal, "Race," 264.

37. For a more exhaustive analysis of the participation of the German women's movement in the discourse of this campaign, see Sandra Maß, "Die 'Schwarze Schmach': Der Diskurs über die afrikanischen Kolonialsoldaten im Rheinland, 1919–1925," master's thesis, University of Bochum, 1998.

38. "Die Eingeborenen in Samoa werden . . . diese Verbot mit Freuden begrüßen. Unter den Samoanern ist die Zahl der Weiber leider eine erheblich geringere als die der Männer, und beinahe bei jedem Versuch von Weißen, eingeborene Frauen zu heiraten—und sie heiraten am liebsten in die Häuplingskreise hinein—. . . können leicht Umbequemlichkeiten zwischen dem Clan der Eingeborenen und den Weißen entstehen" (Stenographische Berichte, Band 283, S. 98f, as cited in Essner, "Zwischen Vernunft und Gefühl," 507).

39. Essner, "Zwischen Vernunft und Gefühl," 511.

40. Wildenthal's 2001 study, *German Women for Empire, 1884–1945,* offers a comprehensive and detailed analysis of the manifold forms through which German women utilized and engaged the discourse of womanhood in strategic ways to achieve a number of different feminist and political ends.

41. See Wildenthal, "Race," 267–81; Wildenthal, *German Women,* 79–130.

42. "Mein Vater war aus dem sogenannten farbigen Afrika, wie eben Marokkaner oder, oder Algerier. Und meist sind, die sind ja nicht schwarz. Sie . . . gehören zu den Farbigen. Also sie waren keine Arier. [Aber] in der Behandlung waren keine Unterschiede. Ich bin unter dieselben Gesetze gefallen wie die. Der 'Arierparagraph' bestimmte ganz eindeutig, wer Deutscher ist oder artverwandten Blutes ist. Wenn man es streng nimmt, durfte ich keinen Gesangvereinen und keinen Turnvereinen beitreten. Ich bin ja auch nicht beigetreten. Weil du überall unterschreiben mußtest, daß du deutsch oder artverwandten Blutes bist. . . . Und die oftmals gestellte Frage: Warum hast du nicht geheiratet? Während der Zeit durfte ich nicht von vornherein. Ich hätte nur unter uns, Mädchen, unter den dreien, die ich kannte, auswählen dürfen. Wir hätten heiraten dürfen. Beide sterilisiert. Wir hätten so mit dem deutschen Volk keinen 'Schaden' mehr angerichtet" (Hans Hauck, interview by author, Dudweiler, Germany, 20 April 1992).

43. Gilman, *On Blackness,* xiii.

44. "Auf die französichen Ableugnungen einer 'schwarzen' Besetzung im Rheinland stellen wir folgendes fest: . . . Die 17 farbigen Regimenter . . . sind zwar im Winter teilweise nach Südfrankreich gebracht worden, seit Februar 1921 aber wieder größtenteils nach Deutschland verlegt. . . . Nach unbedingt zuverlässigen Nachrichten setzt sich diese Streitmacht zusammen wie folgt: 9–10 Regimenter Eingeborene aus Algier, 2 Regimenter Eingeborene aus Tunis, 3 Regimenter Eingeborene aus Marokko, 1 Regiment Eingeborene aus Madagaskar. Dazu kommen kleine Kommandos von Senegalesen (Negern) und eine Anzahl Anamiten (Indochinesen). . . . 'Neger' also im strengen Sinne des Wortes, sind sonach in geschlossenen Verbänden nicht mehr anwesend, jedoch sind die Braunen von Nord-Afrika, die Algerier, die Tunesen und Marokkaner stark mit Negern vermischt und die Madagassen, die Eingeborenen von Madagaskar, haben vielfach einen negerähnlichen Typus. Aber es handelt sich auch gar nicht um die Schattierungen in der Hautfärbung, sondern um die schmähliche Demütigung, die Frankreich durch die Verwendung unzivilisierter farbiger Truppen geflissentlich dem deutschen Volke im besetzten Gebiet antut. Dagegen allein wendet sich der deutsche Protest" (Bundesarchiv Berlin-Abteilung Potsdam, Germany, Records of the Reichskommissar für die besetzten rheinischen Gebiete [hereafter RBRG], Abteilung I/1755, Bestandssignatur 16.02, no. 48, Band, 109). These files contain 1920–22 German newspaper clippings on the Black occupation troops.

45. "Was das europäische Empfinden verletzt bei der Verwendung schwarzer Truppen, liegt nicht in der schwarzen Farbe, sondern in der Tatsache, daß Wilde dazu verwendet werden, ein Kulturvolk zu überwachen. Ob diese Wilden nun ganz schwarz oder dunkelbraun oder gelb sind, macht keinen Unterschied. Das Prestige der europäischen Kulturgemeinschaft ist in Gefahr. Darauf kommt es an. Und gerade die Völker, die wie England und Frankreich darauf angewiesen sind, über farbige Völker eine unbezweifelte Herrschaft auszuüben, sollten daran denken, daß sie mit der Erniedrigung Deutschlands in den Augen der Farbigen, die weiße Rasse erniedrigen und damit ihr eigenes Prestige schwer gefährden.

Auf Anfragen ist nun in Frankreich, sowie auch im englischen Parlament die

Antwort erteilt worden, daß keine schwarzen Truppen mehr in Deutschland stehen. In dieser Antwort, die, wenn man das Schwarz als Farbbezeichnung betont, formell richtig ist, liegt aber doch ein böses Stück Sophismus. Im Frühjahr 1920 standen noch zwei Negerregimenter in Deutschland, die im Mai des gleichen Jahres nach Syrien abtransportiert wurden. Heute steht keine geschlossene Negertruppe mehr auf deutschem Boden, das ist richtig. Aber dafür braune Truppen, und zwar: 9 bis 10 algerische Regimenter, 2 tunesische und 3 marokkanische Regimenter, dazu 1 Regiment Madagassen, im ganzen, wie das 'Echo de Paris' berichtet, 45 000 Mann.

Die Tatsache also ist unverändert, daß ein Kulturvolk wie Frankreich ein anderes europäisches Kulturvolk wie Deutschland durch Wilde überwachen läßt. Ob diese Wilden ein wenig mehr schwarz oder braun oder gelb sind, spielt gar keine Rolle. Sie müssen das Empfinden haben, die Polizisten eines Volkes der weißen Rasse zu sein, und darin liegt das Empörende für das deutsche Volk und gleichzeitig das Gefährliche für die weiße Rasse überhaupt" (ibid., 120).

46. "Die Hauptgefahr bei der Verwendung farbiger Truppen im Herzen Europas liegt vielmehr in der systematischen Weckung und Aufzucht ihres Machtgefühls der weißen Rasse gegenüber. . . . Für die militärische Ausbildung der Schwarzen hat Frankreich durch ihre Verwendung im Weltkrieg und als Besatzungstruppen hinreichend gesorgt. Die französischen Miliärs jedoch wollen in ihrem Siegerwahn die furchtbare Gefahr immer noch nicht sehen. So wurden erst kürzlich wieder Senegalneger vor Abtransport zur Heimat in Paris als die 'Helden von Dirmuiden, der Marne, der Dardanellen und der anderen Orte, wo man anbeissen [illegible] mußte, koste es, was es wolle,' in überschwenglichster Weise gefeiert. . . . Auf diese Weise wird das Machtgefühl der farbigen Rasse gegen die Weißen von den französischen Militärs nur gestärkt" (ibid., 146).

47. "Die weiße Frau . . . nahm bei den Europäern immer eine sichtbar bevorzugte Stellung ein. Aus diesem Grunde zollte ihr auch der Neger meist unbedingte Achtung und oft unterwürfigen Gehorsam. . . . Die weiße Frau war für ihn aber etwas ganz anders, das er nicht mit dem Begriff Weib belegte, sondern ein ihm etwas unerreichbar Hohes, das er sicher nur in sehr seltenen Fällen bewußt begehrte. . . . Dieser Neger nun, der in ungezählten Millionen Afrika und Teile der übrigen Welt bewohnt und im Allgemeinen noch auf einer der tieferen Sprossen der Leiter vom Tier zum Menschen steht, wird nach Europa gebracht, wird nicht nur im Lande des Weißen zu seiner Bekämpfung verwandt, sondern wird auch noch systematisch dazu abgerichtet, das zu begehren, was ihm früher unerreichbar war, die weiße Frau! Wird dazu angehalten und angetrieben, diese wehrlosen Frauen und Mädchen mit seinem tuberkulosen und syphilitischen Pesthauch zu begeifern, in seine stinkenden schwarzen Affenarme zu reißen und in der denkbar bestialischsten Weise zu mißbrauchen! Ihm wird gelehrt, daß . . . er alles tun kann, was sein tierischer Instinkt auch nur im leisesten fordert, ohne irgendwelche Schranken zu finden, ja daß er sogar noch Unterstützung beim 'Sieger' findet" (ibid., 182).

48. "Die 'Schwarze Schmach' ist jedoch—wie lange soll man es noch einer tauben Welt in die Ohren schreien—nicht nur eine Schmach für Deutschland, sie ist viel mehr, sie bedeutet die Schändung der weißen Kultur überhaupt, sie ist

gleichbedeutend mit dem Anfang vom Ende der Vorherrschaft des weißen Mannes" (ibid., 120).

49. "Ist es Ihnen denn nicht bewußt, daß durch die ständige Vermehrung der französischen schwarzen Truppen, Englands heutige Weltstellung noch weit mehr gefährdet ist als das Leben der deutschen Nation? Wenn wir gerade von ihrer Seite besonderes Verständnis für unseren Kampf gegen die französischen schwarzen Truppen erhoffen, so geschieht dies nicht aus pazifistischen Illusionen, sondern aus der Überzeugung heraus, das hier unsere Interessen sich decken, weil wir von der gleichen Seite her bedroht sind. Ihr Volk, in dem sich seit jeher normannischer Herrenstolz und angelsächsisches Gerechtigkeitsgefühl so wundersam gemischt finden, wird endlich begreifen müssen, daß die Stütze seiner heutigen Weltgeltung durch die Emanzipation der schwarzen Rasse, wie sie Frankreich betreibt, erschüttert werden mußte. Ahnen Sie . . . die Gefahren, welche die von Frankreich vertretene Gleichberechtigung der schwarzen Rasse mit der weißen Rasse nach sich ziehen kann? Ahnen Sie, welche Folgen bei ungehinderter Fortsetzung dieser französischen Politik für die Haltung der englischen Kolonialneger entstehen werde? Überdenken Sie . . . diese Gedankengänge und [Sie werden meinen] es handelt sich vielmehr um eine Angelegenheit des Selbstbewußtseins und der Selbsterhaltung der weißen Rasse" (ibid.).

50. "Zu spät werden diese erkennen, daß sie durch Verwendung der farbigen Truppen im Rheinlande eine Katastrophe für ganz Europa heraufbeschwören. Bleibt die Hoffnung auf die übrigen europäischen Staaten und auf Amerika. Hoffentlich bricht das Solidaritätsgefühl der weißen Rasse noch rechtzeitig Bahn, um der aufsteigenden afrikanischen Gefahr noch in letzter Stunde wirksam zu begegnen" (ibid., 146).

51. Beveridge was one of the most outspoken figures involved in the Rhineland campaign, second perhaps only to Morel and Henry Distler, editor of the *Berliner Zeitung* and other publications on the extreme right, including *Die Nacht am Rhein*. During the campaign, Beveridge gave numerous speeches protesting the "Horror on the Rhine." It is unclear, however, whether she was a German or U.S. citizen. She had apparently worked for the German embassy in Washington and claimed to be an American, yet she is also said to have held a German passport. Schüler cites conflicting reports from the U.S. chargé d'affaires in Helsingfors, Magruder, who was convinced that Beveridge was German, and the American consul in Berlin, who believed her to be an American (*"Horror on the Rhine,"* 8).

52. *Münchener Neuste Nachrichten,* 24 February 1921, Jrg. 74, no. 81, RBRG, 54.

53. "Dann tritt Frau Beveridge ans Podium; wer kennt ihn nicht, den Namen dieser mutigen Amerikanerin, dieser selbstlosen, für wahre Menschlichkeit begeisterten und begeisternden Frau, dieser Mutter aller elenden und hungernden deutschen Kinder? Stürmischer Beifall empfängt sie, stürmischer Beifall folgt fast jedem ihrer prägnant formulierten, die Dinge beim richtigen Namen nennenden Sätze. Mehr als Worte aber wirkt es auf die Versammlung, als die Rednerin zwei Kinder, ein sechjähriges, unterernährtes deutsches Kind, erbarmungswürdig anzusehen, und ein neun Monate altes, fast ebenso großes Mischlingskind aus dem

besetzten Gebiet vorgestellt. . . . Dramatischer, ergreifender, als diese Gegenüberstellung vermag kein Mensch der Welt zu sprechen!" (ibid., 56).

54. *Fränkische Kurier Nürnberg,* 24 November 1920, ibid., 27.

55. "Neben der entsetzlichen Not, unter der die weißen Frauen im besetzten Gebiet leben, droht dem deutschen Volk eine außerordentlich große Gefahr durch gewaltsame Vermischung mit Farbigen, durch Vermischung mit Geschlechts- und anderen Krankheiten, durch eine Nachkommenschaft aus den unglücklichen Opfern der Farbigen, deren mindestens stets ein Dutzend verschiedener Rassen am Rhein stehen.

Berechnet man auf Grund der sogennanten Mendelschen Regeln, daß ein menschlicher Stammbaum von einer einmaligen Mischung mit artfremden Blut, in 300 Jahren sich reinigt, dann ergibt sich, daß durch eine so vielmalige und vielseitige Mischung wie sie die farbige Besetzung bewirkt, die deutsche Rasse auf Jahrtausende verunreinigt wird. Nicht die deutsche Rasse allein, sondern auch die ganze weiße Rasse. Denn es werden zwar alle Anlagen der Eigenschaften beider Eltern vererbt; nicht jede Anlage braucht sich aber in jedem Nachkommen zur äußerlich kenntlichen (also bei der Zuchtwahl vermeintlichen) Eigenschaft zu entwickeln. Ganze Generationen können scheinbar ganz—[illegible] sein, ein junges Paar aus solchen 'seit Menschengedenken' rein weißen Familie heiratet, freut sich auf den Sprößling, und es kommt ein erbärmlicher Mischling. Denn gerade derartig spätfolgende Bastarde sind gewöhnlich noch übler, als die aus unmittelbarer bewußter Rassenmischung. Wehe der weißen Rasse, wenn das dichtbevölkerte Rheinland der Mulattiosierung im Herzen des rein weißen Europas verfällt!

Lange nachdem die Besetzung vorbei ist, werden Züge und Hautfarbe dieser sonderbaren Geschöpfe, welche sowohl von Ost als West verabscheut werden, laut für jeden Beobachter nach Rache gegen das Volk schreien, das im Namen des Sieges hierfür verantwortlich ist" (ibid., 210).

56. See also Maß's discussion of Beveridge's discourse in "Die 'Schwarze Schmach,'" 96–115.

57. See Omer Bartov's masterful interpretation of the power of the discourse of victims and enemies in the constitution of German national identity in "Defining Enemies, Making Victims: Germans, Jews, and the Holocaust," *American Historical Review* 103 (1998): 771–816. Bartov's analysis focuses specifically on anti-Semitism and the role of Jews as scapegoats in Germany, demonstrating how the construction and glorification of victimhood and its inextricable link to locating enemies both from without and within have functioned as a "national adhesive" in the history of Germany since World War I. His explication is illuminating in the broader context of understanding how these constructions function similarly with regard to the concept of race more generally.

CHAPTER 2

1. Pommerin, *"Sterilisierung der Rheinlandbastarde,"* 29–30. See also Proctor, 112.

2. It is also important to distinguish between the status of Afro-Germans in the Third Reich and that of non-German Blacks living in Germany at the time. Unlike Afro-Germans, the African immigrant populations in Germany's metropoles were the object of complex domestic policies of containment and instrumentalization aimed primarily at achieving Nazi aspirations toward the eventual reestablishment of a colonial empire that exceeded the Kaiserreich's earlier colonial holdings (see Campt, Grosse, and Lemke Muniz de Faria, "Blacks, Germans, and the Politics of Imperialist Imagination," 214–22; see also Oguntoye, *Eine Afro-Deutsche Geschichte*). For this and other reasons related to their different statuses as citizens and noncitizens and the respective symbolic/strategic value or lack thereof, these two subpopulations should not be conflated into a broader group of "Blacks in Germany."

3. I will not be presenting an in-depth or extensive analysis of National Socialist eugenic programs, because such is not the primary focus of this study. This chapter will be devoted primarily to Nazi sterilization programs. Sterilization under the National Socialist regime and Nazi eugenic programs in general have been quite thoroughly documented in several outstanding historical works that form the basis of my discussion in this chapter. In addition to Pommerin, *"Sterilisierung der Rheinlandbastarde,"* the most notable among these are Michael Burleigh and Wolfgang Wipperman, *The Racial State: Germany 1933–1945* (New York: Cambridge University Press, 1991); Henry Friedlander, *The Origins of Nazi Genocide: From Euthanasia to the Final Solution* (Chapel Hill: University of North Carolina Press, 1995); Saul Friedländer, *Nazi Germany and the Jews,* vol. 1, *The Years of Persecution, 1933–1939* (New York: HarperCollins, 1997); Robert Proctor, *Racial Hygiene: Medicine under the Nazis* (Cambridge: Harvard University Press, 1988); Gisela Bock, *Zwangssterilisation im Nationalsozialismus: Studien zur Rassenpolitik und Frauenpolitik* (Opladen: Westdeutscher, 1986); Gisela Bock, "Anti-Natalism, Maternity, and Paternity in National Socialist Racism," in *Nazism and German Society, 1933–1945,* ed. David F. Crew (London: Routledge, 1994), 110–40; Paul Weindling, *Health, Race, and German Politics between National Unification and Nazism, 1870–1945* (Cambridge: Cambridge University Press, 1989); Peter Weingart, Jürgen Kroll, and Kurt Bayertz, *Rasse, Blut und Gene: Geschichte der Eugenik und Rassenhygiene in Deutschland* (Frankfurt am Main: Suhrkamp, 1988).

4. See Jeremy Noakes, "Nazism and Eugenics: The Background to the Nazi Sterilization Law of 14 July 1933," in *Ideas into Politics: Aspects of European History, 1880–1950,* ed. R. J. Bullen, H. Pogge von Strandmann, and A. B. Polonsky. (Totowa, NJ: Barnes and Noble, 1984), 75–94.

5. Bock, "Anti-Natalism," 111.

6. Beyond Noakes's insightful analysis of the nexus of race, gender, and class in Nazi eugenic ideology and population policy, feminist historians of the Third Reich have been instrumental in articulating the role of gender in Nazi racial politics. The groundbreaking work of these scholars demonstrates the fact that, as Bock has aptly put it, "Just as National Socialist race policy was not gender-neutral, so National Socialist gender policy was not race-neutral . . . and just as racism

was at the centre of Nazi policies in general, it was also at the centre of Nazi policies toward women" ("Anti-Natalism," 113). See also the following seminal works in this field: Renate Bridenthal, Atina Grossmann, and Marion Kaplan, eds., *When Biology Became Destiny: Women in Weimar and Nazi Germany* (New York: Monthly Review Press, 1984); Claudia Koonz, *Mothers in the Fatherland: Women, the Family, and Nazi Politics* (New York: St. Martin's, 1984); Bock, *Zwangssterilisation.* For an excellent overview of some of the salient arguments in this ongoing debate, see Adelheid von Saldern, "Victims or Perpetrators? Controversies about the Role of Women in the Nazi State," in *Nazism and German Society, 1933–1945,* ed. David F. Crew (London: Routledge, 1994); Atina Grossmann, "Feminist Debates about Women and National Socialism," *Gender and History* 3 (1991): 350–58.

7. Wilhelm Stuckart and Hans Globke, *Kommentare zur deutschen Rassengesetzgebung,* vol. 1 (Munich: Beck, 1936), 5.

8. S. Friedländer, *Nazi Germany and the Jews,* 148–49.

9. As cited in S. Friedländer, *Nazi Germany and the Jews,* 150.

10. Ibid.

11. As *Hitler's Forgotten Victims* demonstrates, many Blacks suffered persecution at Nazi hands, and some Blacks were interned in camps throughout the Reich. Nevertheless, it remains unclear to what extent Blacks and particularly Afro-Germans who were not children of the occupation were persecuted as Blacks rather than on the basis of other broader categorizations—for example, as asocials, politicals, or prisoners of war.

12. S. Friedländer, *Nazi Germany and the Jews,* 204.

13. This tendency supports Saul Friedländer's assertion that the "separateness and the compatibility of both the specific anti-Jewish and the general racial and eugenic trends were at the very center of the Nazi system. The main impetus for the Nuremberg Laws and their applications was anti-Jewish; but the third law could without difficulty be extended to cover other racial exclusions, and it logically led to the additional racial legislation of the fall of 1935. The two ideological trends reinforced each other" (*Nazi Germany and the Jews,* 155). Nevertheless, the situation of Afro-Germans in the Third Reich also tested the extent to which the comprehensiveness of Nazi racial policy could be achieved in reality.

14. Oguntoye, for example, cites the oral testimony of her Afro-German interview partners, who recall both their own sense of the threat of sterilization and one case of an acquaintance of African heritage who was sterilized. The grounds for his sterilization remain unclear. See Oguntoye*, Eine Afro-Deutsche Geschichte,* 138; Opitz, Oguntoye, and Schultz, *Farbe bekennen,* 65–84.

15. At the suggestion of Harry Sharp, a prison doctor in Jeffersonville, Indiana, the state of Indiana passed a 1907 sterilization law directed at "hardened criminals," rapists, and the mentally handicapped. The state of Washington passed similar legislation in 1909, and the passage of sterilization laws followed shortly in several other states (Noakes, "Nazism and Eugenics," 80).

16. Noakes, "Nazism and Eugenics," 87.

17. Bock, "Anti-Natalism," 120.

18. Ibid., 115.

19. Ibid., 114. Bock has undertaken some of the most extensive statistical analysis of the demographics of Nazi sterilization and remains a cornerstone of the scholarship on this topic. Her analysis serves as an important secondary source for this chapter.

20. Bock, "Anti-Natalism," 116.

21. Bock, *Zwangssterilisation,* 238, 303.

22. Hans Hauck, interview. "Ich habe mit fünfzehn Jahren angefangen zu lernen, auf der Eisenbahn. Das mußte genehmigt werden vom Vormundschaftsgericht. . . . Auf meiner Arbeit habe ich kaum Zurücksetzung erfahren. Ich wußte nur, daß ich beispielsweise nie Beamter werden könnte. . . . Wegen der Herkunft. Ich war ja nicht Arier. . . . Ja, das hat man mir gesagt. . . . Natürlich wollte ich immer sein. Ich wollte immer blaue Augen haben und blonde Haare. Ich habe mir als Kind die Haare mit Zuckerwasser glatt gemacht, weil die doch, auf den Bildern hast du gesehen, die waren doch rubbelig. . . . Das ging ja nur nicht. . . . Als ich denken konnte, [als ich mir] über meine Herkunft, über mein Wesen im klaren war. . . . Da war alles zu spät. Hitler war schon an der Regierung und während meiner Lehrzeit bin ich 1936 sterilisiert worden. [Ich] wurde vorgeladen bei der Staatspolizei mit meiner Großmutter. [Ich] wurde in einer Pseudo-Gerichtsverhandlung dazu verurteilt, [und bin] sterilisiert worden. . . . Ich war doch Waise. Hätte meine Mutter jetzt wieder geheiratet. . . . Da waren die Kinder nicht mehr registriert beim Vormundschaftsgericht. Und bei dieser Registrierung war das ganz leicht zu kriegen. Und da sind noch fünf andere mit mir sterilisiert worden. . . . Nach dem Urteil wurden wir sofort verladen und ins Krankenhaus [gebracht] und da wurde am nächsten Tag operiert, und nach 10 Tagen wurde ich entlassen. Und da habe ich auf der Arbeit gestanden. Die wurden verständigt auf der Eisenbahn. Und mir wurde das auch mitgeteilt. Ich durfte ja nicht heiraten, kein deutsches Mädchen heiraten. Das war klar. Spielt unter den Nürnberger Gesetzen."

23. Bock, *Zwangssterilisation,* 354. See also Pommerin, *"Sterilisierung der Rheinlandbastarde";* Georg Lilienthal, "'Rheinlandbastarde,' Rassenhygiene, und das Problem der rassenideologischen Kontinuität," *Medizinhistorisches Journal* 15 (1980): 426–36.

24. "Ein andere wesentlicher Grund für unsere Rasseverschlechterung liegt in der Vermischung mit den für uns fremden Rassen. Da gilt es zunächst noch ein Überbleibsel der Schwarzen Schmach am Rhein auszumerzen. Diese Mulattenkinder sind entweder durch Gewalt entstanden oder aber die weiße Mutter war eine Dirne. In beiden Fällen besteht nicht die geringste moralische Verpflichtung gegenüber dieser fremdrassigen Nachkommenschaft. Etwa 14 Jahre sind inzwischen vergangen; wer von diesen Mulatten noch lebt, wird nun in das zeugungsfähige Alter eintreteten, es bleibt also nicht mehr viel Zeit zu langen Erörterungen. Mögen Frankreich und andere Staaten mit ihren Rassefragen fertig werden wie sie wollen, für uns gibt es nur eins: Ausmerzung von allem Fremden, ganz besonders in diesen durch brutale Gewalt und Unmoral entstandenen Schäden. So stelle ich als Rheinländer die Forderung auf: Sterilisierung aller Mulatten, die uns die Schwarze Schmach am Rhein hinterlassen hat! Diese Maßnahme muß

Notes to Pages 75–77 **249**

innerhalb der nächsten zwei Jahre durchgeführt sein, sonst ist es zu spät, und noch in Jahrhunderten wird sich diese Rasseverschlechterung geltend machen. Mit der gesetzlichen Verhinderung einer Verheiratung mit Rassefremden wird sich nichts erreichen lassen, denn was nicht auf legalem Wege möglich ist, geschieht illegitim" (Hans Macco, *Rasseprobleme im Dritten Reich* [Berlin: P. Schmidt, 1933], 13f, as cited in Pommerin, *"Sterilisierung der Rheinlandbastarde,"* 43).

25. "Aus allen Listen ging in jedem Falle hervor, daß die Vorstellung des Reichsministeriums des Innern, wenigstens die meisten Mischlingskinder marokkanischer Herkunft wegen der angeblichen geistigen Minderwertigkeit zum Kreis der unter das 'Gesetz zur Verhütung erbkranken Nachwuchses' fallenden Personen rechnen und somit sterilisieren zu können, sich nicht erfüllte. . . . Da es aber galt, die vielfach beschworenen Gefahren für Deutschland durch die Vermischung mit diesem 'artfremden Blut' abzuwenden, mußte ein anderer Lösungsweg für die Sterilisierung der Mischlingskinder gefunden werden" (ibid., 61).

26. The results of the study were published in 1937 under the title "Über Europäer-Marokkaner- und Europäer-Annamiten-Kreuzungen," in *Zeitschrift für Morphologie und Anthropologie* 36 (Stuttgart: E. Nägele, 1937), 311–29.

27. "Da aus naheliegende Gründen vor vielen Müttern die fremdrassige Abstammung ihrer Kinder verschweigen . . . und sich deswegen einer genauen Ermittlung entzieht, da ferner erfahrungsgemäß die Mischlinge oft einen fast rein europäischen Typ zeigen und daher auch von dem Rassenfachmann nicht ohne weiteres aus der deutschen Bevölkerung herausgefunden werden können. Dies gilt insbesondere auch für Mischlinge, die von solchen weißen Franzosen gezeugt wurden, die selbst afrikanischem Blute entstammen und die das französische Volk schon heute in recht beachtlicher Zahl durchsetzen" (Prussian Ministry of the Interior to the Foreign Office, 28 March 1934, reprinted in Pommerin, *"Sterilisierung der Rheinlandbastarde,"* 96).

28. "Da nun in Frankreich schon heute Millionen Farbige vorhanden sind und bei der geringen Geburtlichkeit des französischen Volkes die Mischlinge vielleicht schon in 4–5 Generationen die Hälfte des Volkskörpers ausmachen werden, besteht die offensichtliche Gefahr, daß sich die rassischen Unterschiede in den deutsch-französischen Grenzgebieten im Laufe der Zeit durch die Vermehrung der Marokkanerabkömmlinge mehr und mehr verwischen werden, und daß der heutige, rassebedingte schützende Grenzwall sich einebnet" (ibid., 98).

29. "Zweifellos kann dieser Gefahr mit weitgehender Aussicht auf Erfolg eine zielbewußte Bevölkerungspolitik entgegengestellt werden . . . da sie zur Zeit die einzigen Maßnahmen zu sein scheinen, zu denen gegriffen werden kann. Denn wenn von verschiedenen Seiten eine Unfruchtbarmachung der in den obersten Altersklassen bald fortpflanzungsfähig werdenden Mischlinge empfohlen wird, so muß dem entgegen gehalten werden, daß nach den Vorschriften des Gesetzes zur Verhütung erbkranken Nachwuchses eben nur diejenigen Mischlinge unfruchtbar gemacht werden können, die im Sinne des Gesetzes erbkrank sind. . . .

Immerhin dürfte auf Grund der bisherigen Untersuchungsergebnisse anzunehmen sein, daß namentlich unter den Mischlingen marokkanischer Herkunft eine größere Zahl erblich Minderwertiger ist, auf die das Gesetz vom 14

Juli 1933 ohne weiteres anwendbar ist. Wenn die zuständige Dienststellen daher angewiesen werden, bei Durchführung dieses Gestezes ihr besonders Augenmerk auf jene Mischlinge zu richten, so darf erwartet werden, daß eine nicht unerhebliche Zahl dieser unerwünschten Keimträger im Rahmen eines schon bestehenden Gesetzes von der Fortpflanzung ausgeschaltet werden kann" (ibid., 98–99).

30. The SBR was composed of a mixture of top elites drawn from the NSDAP, the NS administration (in particular, the Ministry of the Interior), the academic and scientific communities, and most significantly, leading figures in the field of racial hygiene. Members included Alfred Ploetz, arguably the father of racial hygiene; Friedrich Burgdörfer, editor of *Politische Biologie;* Walther Darré, Reich Farmers' Führer; Hans F. K. Günther, a leading racial anthropologist; Charlotte von Hadeln, the second in command of the Deutsche Frauenfront; Ernst Rüdin, director of the Kaiser Wilhelm Institute for Genealogy, in Munich; Paul Schultze-Naumberg, a member of the Reichstag; Gerhard Wagner, head of the Nazi Physicians League; and Baldur von Schirach, head of the Hitler Youth. The committee's chair was Arthur Gütt, head of public health affairs in the Ministry of the Interior, and subsequent members included Fritz Lenz, Alfred Ploetz's protégé and editor of the *Archive für Rassen- und Gesellschaftsbiologie;* Heinrich Himmler; and industrialist Fritz Thyssen (Proctor, *Racial Hygiene,* 95).

31. The following discussion is drawn from Pommerin's summary of the meetings of AG II of the SBR, as documented in "Niederschrift über die Sitzung der Arbeitsgemeinschaft II des Sachverständigenbeirats für Bevölkerungs- und Rassenpolitik am 11. März 1935," zu IV f 423/1079, in Inland I Partei; Sterilisierung der Rheinlandbastarde 84/4 1934–42, Politisches Archiv, Auswärtiges Amt, Bonn (Pommerin, *"Sterilisierung der Rheinlandbastarde,"* 71).

32. Pommerin, *"Sterilisierung der Rheinlandbastarde,"* 72.

33. "Sterilisierungen sollten entweder freiwillig oder zwangsweise aufgrund des Gesetzes vom 14. Juli 1933 oder illegal auf freiwilligem Wege durchgeführt werden" (ibid., 77).

34. "Es ist bedauerlich, daß Deutschland heute noch nicht über den verschwiegenen und zuverlässigen Apparat verfügt, um in solchen Sonderfällen stillschweigend aus völkischem Verantwortungsbewußtsein unbemerkt Rechtsbrüche zu begehen" (Pommerin, 72).

35. Pommerin, 78.

36. Pommerin emphasizes, "Eugenic abortions were against the law but were conducted in practice by the Bureau of Health on the basis of an appropriate order from the Führer. However, although the usual abortion commission was not involved in this illegal procedure, the judgment of a legal agency was required: the Genetic Health Courts or at least the evaluation of one of the experts in the Genetic Health Court. An evaluating agency was also consulted for the sterilization of the Negro bastards, since mere appearance was not enough to warrant a judgment" (*"Sterilisierung der Rheinlandbastarde,"* 73). See also Bock, *Zwangssterilisation,* 354.

37. Pommerin, 77.

38. In addition to Hauck's testimony quoted in this chapter, Pommerin,

"Sterilisierung der Rheinlandbastarde," 78–84, gives several examples of the often quite elaborate and complicated circumstances under which individual children were sterilized.

1. Jonathan Boyarin, *Remapping Memory: The Politics of Timespace* (Minneapolis: University of Minnesota Press, 1994), 23

2. Ibid., 25.

3. Ibid.

4. Ibid., 26.

5. Popular Memory Group, "Popular Memory: Theory, Politics, Method," in *The Oral History Reader,* ed. Robert Perks and Alistair Thomson (New York: Routledge, 1998), 75–86.

6. Halbwachs, *On Collective Memory,* 40.

7. My analysis of my interview partners' memory narratives constitutes a further level of reconstruction, through my insertion of them into the larger context of the history of the Third Reich.

8. Young, *Writing and Rewriting.*

9. Because of the status of these narratives as oral historical accounts constituted through dialogical interviews, the temporality of my informants' testimony takes on another dimension. On the one hand, the testimony is shaped in important ways by the historical moment in which these interviews occurred— specifically, postreunification Germany, when the Federal Republic had to contend directly with the realities of the multicultural politics that resulted from decades of postwar migration. On the other hand, my presence as a participant in the conversations out of which these narratives emerged is also significant because of my role as an interviewer posing questions that shaped the ultimate structure and, to some extent, the content of my informants' narratives. As an African-American, my presence and subjective participation in these exchanges was often actively solicited by my informants and thus had a direct impact on these narratives. The role of an interviewer as an an interlocutor in the oral history interview has been theorized for some time, both by oral historians and by critical ethnographers and perhaps most notably by feminist oral historians and ethnographers. My point is to note, if only briefly for the moment, that the temporality and dialogicality of these memory narratives have quite specific implications in this study. Some of these implications will be discussed at length in chapter 5 with respect to how they might be read to reflect important questions of diasporic relation.

1. See Judith Butler, *Bodies That Matter: On the Discursive Limits of "Sex"* (New York: Routledge, 1993), 2–16.

2. Hauck, interview. Original German versions of the longer, unedited interview excerpts quoted in chapters 3, 4, and 5 appear in the appendix. All excerpts

were translated by the author. Many of the German-language excerpts cited in these chapters appear to contain typographical and grammatical errors. This is due in part to the fact that they were taken from verbatim transcriptions of these interviews in which my informants spoke in their local vernacular. In addition, both of my interview partners periodically spoke in their regional dialects during the interview. These errors, colloquialisms, and idioms have not been corrected in the transcripts to convey the most accurate and authentic version of their utterances. The close readings of these narratives undertaken in each of these chapters were constructed using the original German. English translations have been inserted in this publication for the benefit of readers who do not understand German.

3. Arno Klönne, *Jugend im Dritten Reich: Die Hitler-Jugend und ihre Gegner* (Düsseldorf: Diederichs, 1982), 34.

4. The Hitler Youth had been in existence since 1926.

5. Hauck's use of indirect negation closely parallels a similar narrative strategy that Gwendolyn Etter-Lewis describes as "suppressed discourse." In *My Soul Is My Own: Oral Narratives of African American Women in the Professions* (New York: Routledge, 1993), Etter-Lewis defines suppressed discourse as a form of oral self-censorship that most often appears as the modification of natural speech to disguise meaning or diminish the impact of a particular situation or event. Etter-Lewis argues that suppressed discourse is central to interpreting African-American women's oral narratives. As she points out, sociolinguistic theory demonstrates that social inequities are reflected in language. In the same way, Etter-Lewis maintains that "the racism and sexism that has characterized African-American women's lives is manifest in language used by and about them" (*My Soul,* 180–81). Similarly, an analysis of Hauck's use of indirect negation reveals a submerged dimension of his narrative.

6. Patricia Hill Collins, *Black Feminist Thought: Knowledge, Consciousness and the Politics of Empowerment* (New York: Routledge, 1990), 11.

7. Michelle Maria Wright, "Others-from-Within from Without: Afro-German Subject Formation and the Challenge of a Counter-Discourse," *Callaloo* 26, no. 2 (2003).

8. *Mein Kampf,* as cited in Klönne, *Jugend,* 56.

9. Hauck, interview.

10. Karen Fields, "What One Cannot Remember Mistakenly," in *History and Memory in African American Culture,* ed. Genevieve Fabre and Robert O'Meally (Oxford: New York, 1994), 158–59.

11. In excerpt B, Hauck explains that he obtained this appointment through his membership in the Hitler Youth (as well as through the close friendship he developed with his Hitler Youth leader). But Hauck attributes his access to such a socially accepted position particularly to his uniform. Hauck's references in this passage to the role of the uniform and to his membership in the Hitler Youth thus go beyond the level of mere appearance.

12. See Lyotard, *The Differend,* 56–57, as cited in S. Friedländer, "Memory," 13.

13. The exact date of Hauck's sterilization is unclear, as he specifies two differ-

ent dates in the course of the interview. In excerpt A, he states 1935, while in two other places he refers to 1936 (see chapter 1 and excerpt C). It is quite plausible that Hauck's sterilization occurred sometime between these dates, as they are consistent with other events mentioned by Hauck in connection with his sterilization. For example, he states that he began his job at the railroad at age fifteen and describes returning to his job at the railroad immediately following his sterilization; because he would have turned fifteen in August 1935, this puts the sterilization in late 1935 or early 1936. This time frame would be consistent with the legal sterilizations carried out under the NS sterilization law, the majority of which occurred in 1934 and 1935.

14. Hauck, interview; emphasis added. This quotation is an edited version of this interview passage. Here Hauck's statements regarding his entrance into the Wehrmacht appear without the author's interview questions. I have chosen to use this version of his statements because the focus of my analysis in the following section is on the content (rather than the context) of these statements.

15. Ibid.

16. It is unclear what role Hauck's sterilization and his non-Aryan or African heritage played in his being declared unfit for military duty (*wehrunwürdig*) because he does not state the specific reasons given for this judgment. When questioned indirectly on this subject, Hans explains that he was permitted to work but not allowed to serve in the military; he does not offer any direct explanation of the circumstances leading to this decision. In excerpt C, he mentions that proof of Aryan purity was usually required for acceptance into the military. It can only be assumed that Hauck's failure to meet this criterion would have sufficed to earn him the label *wehrunwürdig*. Interestingly, he makes no mention at this point of either his fears or the practical consequences of his being rejected for active duty. This is an interesting contrast to excerpt C, in which the fear of this process plays a central role for Hauck, eventually leading to his attempted suicide. Yet Hauck makes no mention of his suicide attempt in this earlier passage, quoted in excerpt B, despite the fact that it was the decisive event that led to or perhaps even enabled his induction into the army in 1942.

17. Hauck, interview.

18. Ibid.

19. Some of the most important works on the idea of positionality in the field of feminist theory are Teresa De Lauretis, ed., *Feminist Studies, Critical Studies* (Bloomington: Indiana University Press, 1986); de Lauretis, *Technologies;* Linda Alcoff, "Cultural Feminism versus Post-Structuralism: The Identity Crisis in Feminist Theory," *Signs* 13 (1988): 405–36; Caren Kaplan, "Deterritorializations: The Rewriting of Home and Exile in Western Feminist Discourse," *Cultural Critique* 6 (1987): 187–98. Leslie Adelson also offers a comprehensive and critical evaluation of the implications of the various theoretical formulations of positionality for German identity in *Making Bodies, Making History: Feminism and German Identity* (Lincoln: University of Nebraska Press, 1993).

20. Adelson, *Making Bodies, Making History,* 64.

21. Biddy Martin and Chandra Mohanty, "Feminist Politics: What's Home

Got to Do with It?" in *Feminist Studies, Critical Studies,* ed. Teresa de Lauretis (Bloomington: Indiana University Press, 1986), 196.

22. Adelson, *Making Bodies, Making History,* 64.

23. De Lauretis, *Technologies,* 26.

24. Ibid.

25. Hauck's comments in excerpt F underline this point: "I never listened to [the soldiers]. I'm German and was so, contrary to what Hitler thought, or the Nazis. I'm German, even [in Russia]."

CHAPTER 4

1. In our interview, Jansen states that her birth father was Momolu Massaquoi, grandfather of Hans Massaquoi, author of *Destined To Witness: Growing Up Black in Nazi Germany* (New York: William Morrow, 1999). Despite the fact that they reportedly lived in proximity of one another in Hamburg, Jansen was unaware of his presence there during her youth. Although many interesting parallels, distinctions, and contradictions might be drawn from a comparative analysis and more extensive research of their respective life histories, unfortunately such an analysis exceeds the scope of this book.

2. Fasia Jansen, interview by author, Oberhausen, Germany, 2 February 1992.

3. Ibid.

4. Joseph Walk, ed., "Gesetz gegen die Überfüllung deutscher Schulen und Hochschulen vom 25.5.1933 and the 2.Verordnung zur Durchführung des Gesetzes gegen die Überfüllung deutscher Schulen und Hochschulen vom 25.4.1933," in *Das Sonderrecht für die Juden im NS-Staat* (Heidelberg: Muller Juristischer, 1981), 17–18.

5. Ibid., 19.

6. "Die Zulassung von Zigeunerkindern, die die deutsche Staatsangehörigkeit nicht besitzen und demgemäß nicht schulpflichtig sind, ist grundsätzlich abzulehnen. Soweit aus der Tatsache, daß diese Kinder nicht beschult sind, der öffentlichen Sicherheit und Ordnung Gefahren erwachsen, wird es Sache der Polizeiverwaltung sein, mit entsprechenden Maßnahmen, gegebenfalls mit Ausweisung gegen diese Elemente einzuschreiten.

Bei Zigeunerkindern, die die deutsche Staatsangehörigkeit besitzen und daher schulpflichtig sind, wird eine grundsätzliche Ablehnung der Aufnahme in die öffentlichen Volksschulen nicht angängig sein. Da die Zahl der Zigeunerkinder in der Regel hierfür nicht ausreicht, wird es auch nicht möglich sein, für sie besondere Schulen einzurichten. Soweit solche Kinder in sittlicher oder sonstiger Beziehung für ihre deutschblütigen Mitschüler eine Gefahr bilden, können sie jedoch von der Schule verwiesen werden. In solchen Fällen wird es sich empfehlen, die Polizeibehörde entsprechend zu benachrichtigen.

Bei der Behandlung von Negermischlingen ist nach den gleichen Grundsätzen zu verfahren. Dieser Erlaß ist nicht zu veröffentlichen" ("Runderlass des

Reichsministers für Wissenschaft, Erziehung und Volksbildung vom 22.3.1941," "Zulassung von Zigeunern und Negermischlingen vom Besuch öffentlicher Volksschulen," reprinted in Wolfgang Wippermann, *Das Leben in Frankfurt zur NS-Zeit,* vol. 2, *Die nationalsozialistische Zigeunerverfolgung* [Frankfurt: W. Kramer, 1986], 101; emphasis added). Although originally issued on 15 June 1939, this directive was not made public until 22 March 1941, as stipulated in the order itself, "at the request of certain subordinate agencies [*nach Anfragen einzelner nachgeordneter Behörden*]." See also Wippermann, *Das Leben in Frankfurt,* 42–46.

7. As was also the case with the Law against the Overcrowding of German Schools, the differentiation between citizens and noncitizens of Germany is noteworthy. Although this is only a formal distinction in the directive for gypsies and Afro-Germans, the explicit desire to avoid diplomatic difficulties in the school law echoes similar motivations that would shape Nazi social policy regarding African immigrants living in Germany during the Third Reich. The Nazis' future imperialist aims in Africa led to the development of an overtly instrumental policy of functionalization and containment of African citizens in Germany. Such diplomatic concerns did not play a role in the Third Reich's treatment of Afro-German citizens such as Jansen and Hauck. For a more extensive analysis of Nazi policies toward Germany's African immigrant community, see Campt, Grosse, and Lemke Muniz de Faria, "Blacks, Germans, and the Politics of Imperial Imagination."

8. Jansen, interview, 2 February 1992.

9. Burleigh and Wippermann, *Racial State,* 46.

10. "Als nicht arisch gilt, wer von nichtarischen, insbesondere jüdischen Eltern oder Großeltern abstammte. Es genügte, wenn ein Elternteil oder ein Großelternteil nicht arisch ist. Dies ist insbesondere dann anzunehmen, wenn ein Elternteil oder ein Großelternteil der jüdischen Religion angehört hat" ("Erste Verordnung zur Durchführung des Gesetzes zur Wiederherstellung des Berufsbeamtentums," Stuckart and Globke, *Kommentare,* 260).

11. Marianne Sigg, *Das Rassenstrafrecht in Deutschland in den Jahren 1933–1945 unter besonderer Berücksichtigung des Blutschutzgesetzes* (Aarau, Switz.: H. R. Sauerländer, 1951), 34–35. See also Burleigh and Wippermann, *Racial State,* 45.

12. "Bei der Entscheidung der Frage, welche rassischen Erfordernisse erfüllt werden müssen, um das Reichsbürgerrecht zu erlangen, ist folgendes zu beachten:

a) Grundsätzlich sollen nur Staatsangehörige deutschen oder artverwandten Blutes das Reichsbürgerrecht erlangen (§ 2). Das deutsche Volk setzt sich aus Angehörigen verschiedener Rassen (der nordischen, fälischen, westischen, dinarischen, ostischen und ost-baltischen Rasse) und ihren Mischungen untereinander zusammen. Das danach im deutschen Volk vorhandene Blut ist *deutsches Blut.*

Dem deutschen Blute artverwandt ist das Blut derjenigen Völker, deren rassische Zusammensetzung der deutschen verwandt ist. Das ist durchweg der Fall bei den geschlossen in Europa siedelnden Völkern und denjenigen ihrer Abkömmlinge in außereuropäischen Erdteilen, die sich artrein erhalten haben.

Der Begriff 'deutsches oder artverwandtes Blut' tritt an die Stelle des bisher üblichen Begriffs 'arische Abstammung.' Personen deutschen und Personen artverwandten Blutes werden unter der Bezeichnung 'deutschblütig' zusammengefaßt; vgl. Runderlaß vom 26. November 1935 (MbliB.S. 1429), Abs. 2f, unten S. 151 ff.

b) *Artfremdes Blut* ist alles Blut, das nicht deutsches Blut noch dem deutschen Blut verwandt ist. Artfremden Blutes sind in Europa regelmäßig nur Juden (s. unten Bem. c) und Zigeuner. Artfremde erhalten das Reichsbürgerrecht grundsätzlich nicht.

c) Insbesondere werden die staatsangehörigen *Juden* nicht Reichsbürger. Der Kreis der Personen, die als Juden vom Erwerb des Reichsbürgerrechts ausgeschlossen sind, bestimmt sich nach §5 der Ersten B.z. RbürgG. Danach ist kraft seines Blutes Jude, wer von mindestens drei der Rasse nach volljüdischen Großeltern abstammt; ferner gilt kraft Gesetzes als Jude der staatsangehörige jüdische Mischling ersten Grades, der sich selbst durch Zugehörigkeit zur jüdischen Religionsgemeinschaft oder durch Verheiratung mit einem Juden zum Judentum bekannt hat oder der diesem auf Grund einer Bestimmung seiner Eltern angehört; dies wird angenommen, wenn der Mischling aus einer Ehe mit einem Juden stammt, die nach Inkrafttreten des Blutschutzgesetzes- zulässiger oder unzulässigerweise (vgl. unten Bem. 6 zu §1 BlSchG.)—geschlossen ist, oder wenn er aus dem außerehelichen Verkehr mit einem Juden stammt und nach dem 31. Juli 1936 außerehelich geboren wird. Im einzelnen vgl. die Bem. zu §5 der Ersten B. z. RbürgG. Mischlinge zweiten Grades oder deutschblütige Personen gelten auch dann nicht als Juden, wenn sie der jüdischen Religionsgemeinschaft angehören. Eine Ausnahme von diesem Grundsatz gilt nur insoweit, als es sich um die rassische Einordnung ihre Enkel handelt; insoweit bestimmt §2 Abs. 2 Satz 2 und §5 Abs. 1 Satz 2 der Ersten B.z. RbürgG., daß ein Großelternteil ohne weiteres als volljüdisch gilt, wenn er der jüdischen Religionsgemeinschaft angehört hat. Vgl. im einzelnen die Bem. zu §2 und 5 der Ersten B. z. RbürgG.

d) Außer den Personen artfremdes Blutes gehören auch die aus Verbindungen deutschblütiger und artfremder Personen hervorgegangenen *Mischlinge* nicht zu den Personen deutschen oder artverwandten Blutes. Diese Mischlinge können aber auch nicht zu den Artfremden gerechnet werden. Der Mischling hat deutsche und fremde Erbmasse. Die gesetzliche Behandlung der Mischlinge geht daher von der Erkenntnis aus, daß sie weder dem deutschen noch dem artfremden Blute wesensgleich sind. Wer Mischling ist, ist durch §2 Abs. 2 der Ersten B. z. RbürgG. nur für Personen mit jüdischem Bluteinschlag ausdrücklich geregelt; jüdischer Mischling ist danach, wer von einem oder zwei der Rasse nach volljüdischen Großeltern abstammt; wer mehr als zwei volljüdische Großeltern besitzt, ist Jude; wer keinen volljüdischen Großelternteil hat, wird grundsätzlich als deutschblütig behandelt und nicht mehr zu den Mischlingen gezählt, auch wenn er einen geringfügigen jüdischen Bluteinschlag aufweisen sollte. Die gleichen Grundsätze, wie sie für die rassische Einordnung als jüdischer Mischling gelten, müssen auch für die Einordnung als sonst artfremder Mischling zugrunde gelegt werden.Wenn auch nach §2 den Mischlingen an sich das Reichsbürgerrecht nicht zusteht, da dieses auf die Staatsangehörigen deutschen oder artverwandten Blutes beschränkt ist, so trägt doch §2 Abs. 1 der Ersten B. z. BürgG. der biologischen Tatsache, daß der Mischling mindestens zur Hälfte deutsche Erbmasse hat, dadurch Rechnung, daß den staatsangehörigen jüdischen Mischlingen auch das vorläufige Reichsbürgerrecht verliehen worden ist.

e) Welcher Rasse eine Person angehört, läßt sich niemals ohne weiteres nach ihrer Zugehörigkeit zu einem bestimmten Volke oder einer bestimmten Völkergruppe beurteilen, sondern kann immer nur aus ihren persönlichen rassebiologischen Merkmalen entnommen werden" ("Erläuterungen zum §2 des Reichsbürgergergesetzes," in Stuckart and Globke, *Kommentare,* 55–57).

13. "Eine Ehe soll ferner nicht geschlossen werden, wenn aus ihr eine der Reinerhaltung des deutschen Blutes gefährdende Nachkommenschaft zu erwarten ist" ("Erste Verordnung zur Ausführung des Gesetzes zur Schutze des deutschen Blutes," in Stuckart and Globke, *Kommentare,* 132). Stuckart was *Staatssekretär* of the Ministry of the Interior, responsible for constitution and law and one of the primary authors of the Nuremberg Laws. Globke was *Ministerialrat* of the Ministry of the Interior, in charge of racial name changes.

14. "Ob ein Ehehindernis nach § 6 vorliegt, wird sich meist aus den von den Verlobten vor dem Aufgebot gemäß Runderlaß vom 26. November 1935 . . . beizubringenden urkundlichen Nachweisen ihrer Abstammung (Geburtsurkunde, Heiratsurkunde ihrer Eltern, in Zweifelsfällen weiterer Urkunden) ergeben. Es kommen jedoch auch Fälle vor, in denen sich aus den beigebrachten Urkunden ausreichend sichere Feststellungen nicht treffen lassen. Man denke z.B. an den Fall, daß ein Verlobter offenbar einen Einschlag artfremden Blutes, z.B. von Negerblut, aufweist, ohne daß sich aus den Urkunden Anhaltspunkte dafür ergeben, woher dieser Bluteinschlag stammt. In der Regel werden in diesen Fällen uneheliche Geburten eine Rolle spielen, bei denen der Erzeuger des unehelichen Kindes nicht festgestellt ist, es sei in diesem Zusammenhang an die Negerbastarde aus der Zeit der Rheinlandbesetzung erinnert, bei denen die Feststellung des Erzeugers wegen der französischen Gesetzgebung über die unehelichen Kinder vielfach auf Schwierigkeiten stieß" (Stuckart and Globke, *Kommentare,* 136).

15. See also "Runderlaß vom 26. November 1935," in Stuckart and Globke, *Kommentare,* 153, and their commentaries to paragraph 3 of the "Erste Verordnung zur Durchführung des Ehegesundheitsgesetz," *Kommentare,* 195.

16. Burleigh and Wippermann also contend that it was seen neither as necessary nor as opportune to publicize the persecution of "alien races" or the "racially less valuable" through formal legislation (*Racial State,* 50).

17. Indeed, this tendency continues into the secondary literature on this subject. For example, commenting on the 1939 directive to prohibit Sinti and Roma as well as Blacks of mixed heritage from attending German schools, Wippermann interprets this reference to "Negermischlinge" as referring exclusively to the children of the Rhineland occupation (*Das Leben in Frankfurt,* 45 n.68).

18. "1) Anspruch auf Entschädigung nach diesem Gesetz hat, wer in der Zeit vom 30. Januar 1933 bis zum 8. Mai 1945 (Verfolgungszeit) wegen seiner gegen den Nationalsozialismus gerichteten politischen Überzeugung, aus Gründen der Rasse, des Glaubens oder der Weltanschauung (Verfolgungsgründe) durch natio-

nalsozialistische Gewaltmaßnahmen verfolgt worden ist und hierdurch Schaden an Leben, Körper, Gesundheit, Freiheit, Eigentum, Vermögen oder in seinem beruflichen und wirtschaftlichen Fortkommen erlitten hat (Verfolgter). . . .

(3) Nationalsozialistische Gewaltmaßnahmen sind solche Maßnahmen, die auf Veranlassung oder mit Billigung einer Dienststelle oder eines Amtsträgers des Reiches oder eines Landes oder einer sonstigen Körperschaft, Anstalt oder Stiftung des öffentlichen Rechtes oder der NSDAP oder ihrer Gliederungen oder angeschlossenen Verbände aus den Verfolgungsgründen gegen den Verfolgten gerichtet worden sind. Es wird vermutet, daß solche Maßnahmen gegen den Ver- folgten gerichtet worden sind, wenn dieser zu einem Personenkreis gehörte, den in seiner Gesamtheit die deutsche Regierung oder die NSDAP durch die Maßnah- men vom kulturellen und wirtschaftlichen Leben Deutschlands auszuschließen beabsichtigte" (Sigg, *Das Rassestrafrecht,* 39).

19. "Eine *rassische Verfolgung liegt* also *vor,* wenn schon die Tatsache, daß jemand einer bestimmten Rasse zugerechnet wurde, genügte, ihn unabhängig von charackterlichen Eigenschaften, Stellung und Beruf, Ansehen und Vorleben nachteiligen Maßnahmen auszusetzen, denen andere nicht unterworfen waren. Die rassische Verfolgung richtet sich somit gegen eine bestimmte Gruppe als Gesamtheit und gegen den Einzelnen nur als Angehörigen dieser Gesamtheit. . . . Der Wortlaut 'aus Gründen der Rasse' ist weiter als der 'wegen seiner Rasse'. Wenn der Gesetzgeber den engeren Wortlaut nicht verwendet hat, so hat er damit zum Ausdruck bringen wollen, daß entschädigungsberechtigt derjenige sein soll, der zwar nicht selbst einer vom NS bekämpften angeblichen Rasse angehörte, aber wegen seiner Beziehungen zu diskriminierten Personen durch ns [*sic*] Maßnahmen verfolgt und geschädigt worden sein kann. . . . Auch der nach § 5 Abs. 2 der Ersten VO vom BlSchG *gemaßregelte arische Partner* ist 'aus Gründen der Rasse' ver- folgt" (Ingeborg Becker, Harald Huber, and Otto Küster, *Bundesentschädigungs- gesetz: Kommentare* [(Berlin: Vahlen, 1955)], 47).

20. "Als Schaden im beruflichen und wirtschaftlichen Fortkommen im Sinne von §25 Abs. 1 gilt auch der Schaden, den der Verfolgte in seiner beruflichen oder vorberuflichen Ausbildung durch Ausschluß von der erstrebten Ausbildung oder durch deren erzwungene Unterbrechung erlitten hat" (Becker, Huber, and Küster, *BEG Kommentare,* 515). The particularly devastating impact of such discrimina- tion for individuals in the arts is emphasized in the explication of this clause: "Diese Schäden, die insbesondere junge Menschen, vor allem rassisch Verfolgte und unter ihnen besonders stark die seit in Deutschland verbliebener sogenannten Mischlinge durch die hybriden ns. Rassevorstellungen erlitten haben, sind beson- ders tiefgreifend. Dies gilt vor allem für Berufe, die ihrem Träger nicht nur bloßer Broterwerb sind, sondern denen noch etwas von Berufung innewohnt, wie vielfach—aber nicht immer und erst recht nicht ausschließlich—akademischen und künstlerischen Berufen" (516).

21. "Voraussetzung für die Entschädigung ist, wie immer, daß der Geschädigte aus den Gründen des §1 Abs. 1 und 2 verfolgt worden ist" (Becker, Huber, and Küster, *BEG: Kommentare,* 520).

22. Wippermann, *Das Leben in Frankfurt,* 8.

23. Angela Vogel's comprehensive study *Das Pflichtjahr für Mädchen. National-sozialistische Arbeitseinsatzpolitik im Zeichen der Kriegswirtschaft* (Frankfurt a.M.: Peter Lang, 1997) provides important historical background for understanding Jansen's account of her work in Rothenburgsort. Jansen explains that her duties in the barracks kitchen were work required of her as part of her Nazi *Pflichtjahr* (required year of service). Vogel notes that as of 1 January 1939, the *Pflichtjahr* was extended to all unmarried German girls under the age of 25 who had not been employed prior to 1 March 1938 (153). The extension of the *Pflichtjahr* was made in preparation for war and intended to increase available labor within the Reich. With the onset of war, German girls were required for their year of service to work not only in the countryside or in homes, but also for the war industry, where German girls provided cheap labor in addition to that supplied by inmates of concentration and labor camps (65). In her account of her *Pflichtjahr* in Rothenburgsort, Jansen implicitly distinguishes her status there from that of *Zwangsarbeit* or forced labor. Although it is difficult to establish the exact nature of Jansen's work requirements, it is useful in this context to differentiate between three specific categories of labor in the Third Reich that might at times be seen to overlap: *Zwangsarbeit, Arbeitsdienst,* and the *Pflichtjahr.* In cases like Jansen's, the distinctions between these categories often tended to blur. *Zwangsarbeit* was a putative act of terror and coercion. *Arbeitsdienst/Dienstverpflichtung* was a requirement of citizens of the Reich. Although it was required, however, it was nevertheless viewed as a voluntary act. Vogel argues that the *Arbeitsdienst* was intended to shift the value of work away from the idea of paid labor toward a conception of work without monetary remuneration utilized as an ideological and pedagogical tool. She discusses four primary features of *Arbeitsdienst:* ideological indoctrination, sacrifice, racial purity, and voluntary participation. In contrast, Vogel explains that the *Pflichtjahr* was considered a form of *Notstandsarbeit* (emergency labor), which distinguished it from *Arbeitsdienst* in that it lacked the central component of ideological indoctrination (244).

24. Jansen, interview, 2 February 1992.

25. Ruth Frankenberg, *White Women, Race Matters: The Social Construction of Whiteness* (Minneapolis: University of Minnesota Press, 1993), 43–44.

26. Jansen, interview, 2 February 1992.

27. Jansen's brief description of the egg is a particularly compelling example of this. Her remarks describing how her friend miraculously managed to bring an egg to the barracks in Rothenburgsort is a little detail that emphasizes her continued contact with the center even while on the margins.

28. My thanks to Michelle Rosenthal for this insightful point.

29. As stated earlier, Jansen's stepfather and mother were active members of the Communist Party in Hamburg throughout her youth. Elsewhere in the interview, she describes herself as the equivalent of a "red-diaper baby," raised in this political context from her early childhood. Throughout her postwar adult life, Jansen was a committed member of the Party and a full-time political activist engaged in numerous social movements. Thus, she would probably have found such a leftist political context familiar and comfortable, not only because of her postwar political involvement but also because of her childhood experiences.

30. See, for example, the biographies of Doris Reiprich and Erika Ngambi ul Kuo, "Our Father Was Cameroonian, Our Mother, East Prussian, We Are Mulattos," in *Showing Our Colors,* ed. Opitz, Oguntoye, and Schultz, 56.

31. Jansen, interview, 2 February 1992.

32. The text of Jansen's nomination for the award read: "Fasia Jansen is a singer and composer with a highly sensitive political and social consciousness. Her horrible experiences in her childhood and youth in the work camp of Neuengamme, where, as a 14 year old girl, she was required to serve as an 'alien worker,' did not leave her bitter. On the contrary, they motivated her to energetically fight for social concerns and struggle against abuses and social injustice." [*Fasia Jansen ist Liedermacherin und Sängerin mit einem hochsensiblen politischen, sozialen Bewußtsein. Ihr furchtbaren Kindheits- und Jugenderfahrungen im Außenlager Neuengamme, in das sie als 14 jährige 'Fremdarbeiterin' Mädchen zwangsverpflichtet wurde, ließen sie nicht verbittern, sondern veranalaßten sie vielmehr, sich mit ganzer Kraft für gesellschaftliche Belange, gegen Mißstände und soziale Ungerechtigkeiten einzusetzen.*] My thanks to Ellen Dietrich for providing the author with this information.

CHAPTER 5

1. James Clifford, "Diasporas," *Cultural Anthropology* 9 (1994): 302.

2. Brown, "Black Liverpool," 297.

3. William Safran, "Diasporas in Modern Societies: Myths of Homeland and Return," *Diaspora* 1 (1991): 84, as cited in Clifford, "Diasporas," in *Routes: Travel and Translation in the Late Twentieth Century* (Cambridge: Harvard University Press, 1997), 248.

4. Clifford, "Diasporas," 302.

5. Brah, *Cartographies,* 180.

6. See most notably Hall, "Cultural Identity," 222–37; and "Race, Articulation and Societies Structured in Dominance," in *Black British Cultural Studies: A Reader,* ed. Houston A. Baker, Manthia Diawara, and Ruth Lindeborg (Chicago: University of Chicago Press, 1996), 16–60; Gilroy, *"There Ain't No Black in the Union Jack";* Gilroy, *Black Atlantic;* Gilroy, *Small Acts.* In addition, see Kobena Mercer, *Welcome to the Jungle: New Positions in Black Cultural Studies* (New York: Routledge, 1994); Barnor Hesse, *Unsettled Multiculturalisms: Diaspora, Entanglements, Transruptions* (New York: Zed Books, 2000); and Hesse, "Black to the Front" (1993).

7. My discussion draws significantly on Brown, "Black Liverpool," which offers a masterful reading of Gilroy's diaspora discourse. Brown's insightful critique of Gilroy's work is required reading for any student of African diaspora studies.

8. Gilroy, *"There Ain't No Black in the Union Jack,"* 156. Brent Edwards offers an insightful reading of some of the tensions that exist within Gilroy's work, between his notion of diaspora and his concept of the "black Atlantic." Edwards's careful parsing of Gilroy's description of Black culture being "actively made and

remade" and his use of the metaphor of "raw material" offers an interesting counterpoint to my own reading of diaspora in this chapter. See Edwards, "Uses of Diaspora," 60–64.

9. Ibid., 152.

10. Brown, "Black Liverpool," 294.

11. Ibid., 298.

12. Ibid., 291.

13. Gilroy, *Small Acts,* 131.

14. Carol Aisha Blackshire-Belay, "Historical Revelations: The International Scope of African Germans Today and Beyond," in *The African-German Experience: Critical Essays,* ed. Blackshire-Belay, 120–21.

15. Audre Lorde, "Foreword to the English Language Edition," in *Showing Our Colors,* ed. Opitz, Oguntoye, and Schultz, xiii.

16. Ibid., vii.

17. Ibid., x.

18. Opitz, Oguntoye, and Schultz, *Showing Our Colors,* xxii.

19. Brown, "Black Liverpool," 298.

20. As Brown asserts, "power asymmetries may be identified in the ways black American cultural products are differently absorbed, translated, and utilized within the individual black European communities into which they travel" ("Black Liverpool," 297).

21. Edwards, "Uses of Diaspora," 46.

22. Ibid., 64.

23. Ibid., 66.

24. *Encyclopedia of Violence, Peace, and Conflict* (San Diego: Academic Press, 1999).

25. Jansen, interview, 2 February 1992.

26. Ibid.

27. Hauck, interview.

28. My reference to *cultural knowledge* is intended to go beyond a participatory notion of experience, conceived either as the subjective apprehension or retrospective interpretation of events. Rather, *cultural knowledge* refers to both individual lived experiences and the cognition of or reflection on the collective experiences of a cultural group. The term also includes the historical knowledge or consciousness of the past experiences of this group.

29. Hauck, interview.

BIBLIOGRAPHY

PRIMARY SOURCES

Archival Sources

Records of the Reichskommissar für die besetzten rheinischen Gebiete, Bundes-archiv Berlin, Abteilung I/1755, Bestandssignatur 16.02, no. 48, Baüdl, Bundes-archiv Abteilung Potsdam, Germany.

Oral Sources

Hauck, Hans. Interview by author (in German). Dudweiler, Germany, 20 April 1992.

Jansen, Fasia. Interview by author (in German). Oberhausen, Germany, 2, 4 February 1992.

SECONDARY SOURCES

Adelson, Leslie. *Making Bodies, Making History: Feminism and German Identity.* Lincoln: University of Nebraska Press, 1993.

Alcoff, Linda. "Cultural Feminism versus Post-Structuralism: The Identity Crisis in Feminist Theory." *Signs* 13 (1988): 405–36.

Alexander, Claire E. *The Art of Being Black: The Creation of Black British Youth Identities.* Oxford: Clarendon, 1996.

Althusser, Louis, and Etienne Balibar. *Reading Capital.* London: Verso, 1979.

Anderson, Benedict. *Imagined Communities: Reflections on the Origin and Spread of Nationalism.* London: Verso, 1991.

Arendt, Hannah. *Eichmann in Jerusalem: A Report on the Banality of Evil.* New York: Viking, 1964.

Arendt, Hannah. *The Origins of Totalitarianism.* New York: Harcourt Brace Jovanovich, 1973.

Assmann, Jan, and Tonio Hölscher. *Kultur und Gedächtnis.* Frankfurt am Main: Suhrkamp, 1988.

Ayim, May. *Blues in schwarz-weiss: Gedichte.* Berlin: Orlanda Frauenverlag, 1995.

Ayim, May. *Grenzenlos und Unverschämt.* Berlin: Orlanda Frauenverlag, 1997.

Ayim, May. *Nachtgesang.* Berlin: Orlanda Frauenverlag, 1997.

Back, Les, and Anoop Nayak, eds. *Invisible Europeans? Black People in the "New Europe."* Handsworth, Birmingham: All Faiths for One Race (AFFOR), 1993.

Bade, Klaus J., ed. *Deutsche im Ausland, Fremde in Deutschland: Migration in Geschichte und Gegenwart.* Munich: C. H. Beck, 1992.

Baker, Houston A., Manthia Diawara, and Ruth H. Lindeborg, eds. *Black British Cultural Studies: A Reader.* Chicago: University of Chicago Press, 1996.

Bartov, Omer. "Defining Enemies, Making Victims: Germans, Jews, and the Holocaust." *American Historical Review* 103 (1998): 771–816.

Bauche, Ulrich, Heinz Bruedigam, Ludwig Eiber, and Wolfgang Weidey, eds. *Arbeit und Vernichtung: Das Konzentrationslager Neuengamme, 1938–1945.* Katalog zur ständigen Ausstellung im Dokumentenhaus der KZ-Gedenkstaette Neuengamme, Aussenstelle des Museums für Hamburgische Geschichte. Hamburg: VSA, 1986.

Bauman, Zygmunt. *Modernity and the Holocaust.* Ithaca: Cornell University Press, 1989.

Blackshire-Belay, Carol Aisha, ed. *The African-German Experience: Critical Essays.* Westport, CT: Praeger, 1996.

Bock, Gisela. "Anti-Natalism, Maternity, and Paternity in National Socialist Racism." In *Nazism and German Society, 1933–1945,* ed. David F. Crew. New York: Routledge, 1994.

Bock, Gisela. *Zwangssterilisation im Nationalsozialismus: Studien zur Rassenpolitik und Frauenpolitik.* Opladen: Westdeutscher, 1986.

Boyarin, Jonathan. *Remapping Memory: The Politics of Timespace.* Minneapolis: University of Minnesota Press, 1994.

Brah, Avtar. *Cartographies of Diaspora: Contesting Identities.* New York: Routledge, 1996.

Bridenthal, Renate, Atina Grossmann, and Marion Kaplan, eds. *When Biology Became Destiny: Women in Weimar and Nazi Germany.* New York: Monthly Review Press, 1984.

Bridenthal, Renate, Claudia Koonz, and Susan Stuard, eds. *Becoming Visible: Women in European History.* Boston: Houghton Mifflin, 1987.

Brodersen, Uwe, ed. *Gesetze des NS-Staates: Dokumente eines Unrechtssystems.* Paderborn: Ferdinand Schoningh, 1982.

Brown, Jacqueline. "Black Liverpool, Black America, and the Gendering of Diasporic Space." *Cultural Anthropology* 13 (1998): 291–325.

Bryan, Beverley, Stella Dadzie, and Suzanne Scafe. *The Heart of the Race: Black Women's Lives in Britain.* London: Virago, 1985.

Burleigh, Michael. *The Third Reich: A New History.* New York: Hill and Wang, 2000.

Burleigh, Michael, and Wolfgang Wippermann. *The Racial State: Germany 1933–1945.* New York: Cambridge University Press, 1991.

Butler, Judith. *Bodies That Matter: On the Discursive Limits of "Sex."* New York: Routledge, 1993.

Campt, Tina. "African German/African American—Dialogue or Dialectic? Reflections on the Dynamics of 'Intercultural Address.'" In *The African-Ger-*

man Experience: Critical Essays, ed. Carol Aisha Blackshire-Belay. Westport, CT: Praeger, 1996.

Campt, Tina. "Afro-German Cultural Identity and the Politics of Positionality: Contests and Contexts in the Formation of a German Ethnic Identity." *New German Critique* 58 (1993): 109–26.

Campt, Tina, and Pascal Grosse. "'Mischlingskinder' in Nachkriegsdeutschland: Zum Verhältnis von Psychologie, Anthropologie und Gesellschaftspolitik nach 1945." *Psychologie und Geschichte* 6 (1994): 48–78.

Campt, Tina, Pascal Grosse, and Yara-Colette Lemke Muniz de Faria. "Black Germans and the Politics of Imperialist Imagination, 1920–1960." In *The Imperialist Imagination: German Colonialism and Its Legacy,* ed. Sara Lennox, Sara Friedrichsmeyer, and Susanne Zantop. Ann Arbor: University of Michigan Press, 1998.

Clifford, James. "Diasporas." *Cultural Anthropology* 9 (1994): 302–38.

Clifford, James, and George Marcus, eds. *Writing Culture: The Poetics and Politics of Ethnography.* Berkeley: University of California Press, 1986.

Crew, David F., ed. *Nazism and German Society, 1933–1945.* New York: Routledge, 1994.

Davies, F. James. *Who Is Black? One Nation's Definition.* University Park: Pennsylvania State University Press, 1991.

Davison, Robert Barry. *Black British: Immigrants to England.* London: Oxford University Press for the Institute of Race Relations, 1966.

Debrunner, Hans. *Presence and Prestige, Africans in Europe: A History of Africans in Europe before 1918.* Basel: Basler Afrika Bibliographien, 1979.

De Lauretis, Teresa, ed. *Feminist Studies, Critical Studies.* Bloomington: Indiana University Press, 1986.

De Lauretis, Teresa. *Technologies of Gender.* Bloomington: Indiana University Press, 1987.

Dhaliwal, Amarpal K. "Reading Diaspora: Self-Representational Practices and the Politics of Reception." *Socialist Review* 4 (1995): 13–43.

Douglas, Mary. *Purity and Danger: An Analysis of the Concepts of Pollution and Taboo.* New York: Routledge, 1991.

Drake, St. Clair. "Diaspora Studies and Pan-Africanisms." In *Global Dimensions of the African Diaspora,* ed. Joseph Harris. Washington, DC: Howard University Press, 1992.

Du Bois, W. E. B. *The Souls of Black Folk.* 1903; New York: Bantam, 1989.

Edwards, Brent Hayes. "The Uses of Diaspora." *Social Text* 66 (2001): 44–73.

Ehmann, Annegret. "From Colonial Racism to Nazi Population Policy: The Role of the So-Called Mischlinge." In *The Holocaust and History: The Known, the Unknown, the Disputed, and the Reexamined,* ed. Michael Berenbaum and Abraham J. Peck, 115–33. Bloomington: Indiana University Press in association with the U.S. Holocaust Memorial Museum, 1998.

El-Tayeb, Fatima. *Schwarze Deutsche: Der Diskurs um "Rasse" und nationale Identität, 1890–1933.* Frankfurt am Main: Campus, 2001.

Essner, Cornelia. "Zwischen Vernunft und Gefühl: Die Reichstagsdebatten von

1912 um koloniale 'Rassenmischehe' und 'Sexualität.'" *Zeitschrift für Geschichtswissenschaft* 45 (1997): 503–19.

Etter-Lewis, Gwendolyn. *My Soul Is My Own: Oral Narratives of African American Women in the Professions.* New York: Routledge, 1993.

Fanon, Frantz. *Black Skin, White Masks.* Trans. Charles Lam Markmann. New York: Grove, 1967.

Fanon, Frantz. *The Wretched of the Earth.* Intro. Jean-Paul Sartre, trans. Constance Farrington. 1967; New York: Grove Weidenfeld, 1991.

Felman, Shoshana, and Dori Laub. *Testimony: Cries of Witnessing in Literature, Psychoanalysis, and History.* New York: Routledge, 1991.

Ferguson, James, and Akhil Gupta. "Beyond 'Culture': Space, Identity, and the Politics of Difference." *Cultural Anthropology* 7 (1992): 6–23.

Foucault, Michel. *The History of Sexuality,* vol. 1, *An Introduction.* Trans. Robert Hurley. New York: Vintage, 1980.

Frankenberg, Ruth. *White Women, Race Matters: The Social Construction of Whiteness.* Minneapolis: University of Minnesota Press, 1993.

Fremgen, Gisela. *Und wenn du dazu noch schwarz bist: Berichte schwarzer Frauen in der Bundesrepublik.* Bremen: Edition CON, 1984.

Friedlander, Henry. *The Origins of Nazi Genocide: From Euthanasia to the Final Solution.* Chapel Hill: University of North Carolina Press, 1995.

Friedländer, Saul. *Memory, History, and the Extermination of the Jews of Europe.* Bloomington: Indiana University Press, 1993.

Friedländer, Saul. *Nazi Germany and the Jews.* New York: HarperCollins, 1997.

Friedländer, Saul, ed. *Probing the Limits of Representation: Nazism and the "Final Solution."* Cambridge: Harvard University Press, 1992.

Frisch, Michael. *A Shared Authority: Essays on the Craft and Meaning of Oral and Public History.* Albany: State University of New York Press, 1990.

Fryer, Peter. *Black People in the British Empire: An Introduction.* London: Pluto, 1988.

Fryer, Peter. *Staying Power: The History of Black People in Britain.* London: Pluto, 1984.

Gates, Henry Louis, ed. *Race, Writing, and Difference.* Chicago: University of Chicago Press, 1986.

Gilman, Sander. "Black Bodies, White Bodies: Toward an Iconography of Female Sexuality in Late Nineteenth-Century Art." In *Race Writing and Difference,* ed. Henry Louis Gates Jr. Chicago: University of Chicago Press, 1986.

Gilman, Sander. *Difference and Pathology: Stereotypes of Sexuality, Race, and Madness.* Ithaca: Cornell University Press, 1985.

Gilman, Sander. *On Blackness without Blacks: Essays on the Image of the Black in Germany.* Boston: G. K. Hall, 1982.

Gilroy, Paul. *Against Race: Imagining Political Culture beyond the Color Line.* Cambridge: Belknap Press of Harvard University Press, 2000.

Gilroy, Paul. *Between Camps: Race, Identity, and Nationalism at the End of the Colour Line.* London: Allen Lane/Penguin, 2000.

Gilroy, Paul. *The Black Atlantic: Modernity and Double Consciousness.* Cambridge: Harvard University Press, 1993.

Gilroy, Paul. *Small Acts: Thoughts on the Politics of Black Cultures.* New York: Serpent's Tail, 1998.

Gilroy, Paul. *"There Ain't No Black in the Union Jack": The Cultural Politics of Race and Nation.* Chicago: University of Chicago Press, 1991.

Gluck, Sherna Berger, and Daphne Patai, eds. *Women's Words: The Feminist Practice of Oral History.* New York: Routledge, 1991.

Goldberg, David Theo, ed. *Anatomy of Racism.* Minneapolis: University of Minnesota Press, 1990.

Goulbourne, Harry, ed. *Black Politics in Britain.* Aldershot: Avebury, 1990.

Grele, Ronald. *Envelopes of Sound: The Art of Oral History.* New York: Praeger, 1991.

Grewal, Inderpal. *Home and Harem: Nation, Gender, Empire, and the Cultures of Travel.* Durham, NC: Duke University Press, 1996.

Grewal, Inderpal. "The Postcolonial Ethnic Studies and the Diaspora: The Contexts of Immigrant/Migrant Cultural Studies in the U.S." *Socialist Review* 4 (1995): 45–74.

Grewal, Inderpal, and Caren Kaplan, eds. *Scattered Hegemonies: Postmodernity and Transnational Feminist Practices.* Minneapolis: University of Minnesota Press, 1994.

Grewal, Shabnam, Jackie Kay, Liliane Landor, Gail Lewis, and Pratibha Parmar, eds. *Charting the Journey: Writings by Black and Third World Women.* London: Sheba Feminist Publishers, 1988.

Grimm, Reinhold, and Jost Hermand, eds. *Blacks and German Culture: Essays.* Madison: University of Wisconsin Press for Monatshefte, 1986.

Grosse, Pascal. "Eugenik und Kolonialismus: Zum Verhältnis von Wissenschaft und Gesellschaftspolitik im Kaiserreich, 1885–1914." Ph.D. diss., Free University of Berlin, Germany, 1997.

Grosse, Pascal. *Kolonialismus, Eugenik und bürgerliche Gesellschaft in Deutschland, 1850–1918.* Frankfurt am Main: Campus, 2000.

Grosse, Pascal. "Kolonialismus und das Problem der 'Rassenmischung' in Deutschland: Zur Geschichte der anthropologischen Psychologie 1920–1940." In *Psychologie im soziokulturellen Wandel—Kontinuitäten und Diskontinuitäten,* ed. Siegfried Jäger, Irmgard Staeuble, Lothar Sprung, and Horst-Peter Brauns. Frankfurt am Main: Peter Lang, 1995.

Grossmann, Atina. "Feminist Debates about Women and National Socialism." *Gender and History* 3 (1991): 350–58.

Grosz, Elizabeth A. *Volatile Bodies: Toward a Corporeal Feminism.* Bloomington: Indiana University Press, 1994.

Gruner, Wolf, Horst Kahrs, Dieter Maier, and Tatiana Brustin-Berenstein. *Arbeitsmarkt und Sondererlass: Menschenerwertung, Rassenpolitik und Arbeitsamt.* Beiträge zur Nationalsozialistischen Gesundheits- und Sozialpolitik 8. Berlin: Rotbuch, 1990.

Halbwachs, Maurice. *Das Gedächtnis und seine sozialen Bedingungen.* Frankfurt: Luchterhand, 1985.

Halbwachs, Maurice. *On Collective Memory.* Ed., trans., and intro. Lewis A. Coser. Chicago: University of Chicago Press, 1992.

Hall, Stuart. "Cultural Identity and Diaspora." In *Identity: Community, Culture, Difference,* ed. Jonathan Rutherford. London: Lawrence and Wishart, 1990.

Hall, Stuart. "Minimal Selves." In *Black British Cultural Studies: A Reader,* ed. Houston A. Baker Jr., Manthia Diawara, and Ruth H. Lindeborg. Chicago: University of Chicago Press, 1996.

Hall, Stuart. "The Question of Cultural Identity." In *Modernity and Its Futures,* ed. Stuart Hall, David Held and Tony McGrew. Oxford: Polity, 1992.

Hartman, Geoffrey. *The Longest Shadow: In the Aftermath of the Holocaust.* Bloomington: Indiana University Press, 1996.

Hartman, Geoffrey, ed. *Holocaust Remembrance: The Shapes of Memory.* Cambridge: Blackwell, 1994.

Herbert, Ulrich. *Geschichte der Ausländerbeschäftigung in Deutschland, 1880 bis 1980: Saisonarbeiter, Zwangsarbeiter, Gastarbeiter.* Berlin: Dietz, 1986.

Hesse, Barnor. "Reviewing the Western Spectacle: Reflexive Globalization through the Black Diaspora." In *Global Futures: Migration, Environment, and Globalization,* ed. Avtar Brah, Mary Hickman, and Maírtín Mac an Ghaille. London: Macmillan, 1999.

Hilberg, Raul. *The Destruction of the European Jews.* New York: Holmes and Meier, 1983.

Hintrager, Oskar. *Südwestafrika in der deutschen Zeit.* Munich: R. Odenbourg, 1955.

Hiro, Dilip. *Black British, White British: A History of Race Relations in Britain.* London: Grafton, 1991.

Hirsch, Martin, Diemut Majer, and Jürgen Meinck, eds. *Recht, Verwaltung und Justiz im Nationalsozialismus: Ausgewählte Schriften, Gesetze und Gerichtsentscheidungen von 1933–45.* Cologne: Bund, 1984.

Hitler's Forgotten Victims: Black Survivors of the Holocaust. Directed by David Okuefuma and produced by Moise Shewa. 59 min. Afro-Wisdom Productions, United Kingdom, 1997.

Hodges, Carolyn. "The Private/Plural Selves of Afro-German Women and the Search for a Public Voice." *Journal of Black Studies* 23 (1992): 219–34.

Hügel-Marshall, Ika. *Invisible Woman: Growing up Black in Germany.* Trans. Elizabeth Gaffney. New York: Continuum, 2001.

Hutton, Patrick H. *History as an Art of Memory.* Hanover, NH: University Press of New England, 1993.

James, Selma, ed. *Strangers and Sisters: Women, Race, and Immigration.* Bristol, Eng.: Falling Wall, 1985.

Kaienburg, Hermann. *Das Konzentrationslager Neuengamme, 1938—1945.* In cooperation with the KZ-Gedenkstaette Neuengamme. Bonn: Dietz, 1997.

Kaienburg, Hermann. *"Vernichtung durch Arbeit": Der Fall Neuengamme.* Bonn: Dietz, 1990.

Kaplan, Caren. "Deterritorializations: The Rewriting of Home and Exile in Western Feminist Discourse." *Cultural Critique* 6 (1987): 187–98.

Kershaw, Ian. *The Nazi Dictatorship: Problems and Perspectives of Interpretation.* 3d ed. London: E. Arnold, 1993.

Kesting, Robert. "Forgotten Victims: Blacks in the Holocaust." *Journal of Negro History* 77 (1992): 30–36

Klönne, Arno. *Jugend im Dritten Reich: Die Hitler-Jugend und ihre Gegner.* Düsseldorf: Diederichs, 1982.

Koonz, Claudia. *Mothers in the Fatherland: Women, the Family, and Nazi Politics.* New York: St. Martin's, 1987.

Kron, Stefanie. *Fürchte Dich nicht Bleichgesicht: Perspektivenwechsel zur Literatur Afro-Deutscher Frauen.* Muenster: Unrast, 1996.

Langer, Lawrence. *Holocaust Testimonies: The Ruins of Memory.* New Haven: Yale University Press, 1991.

Lavie, Smadar, and Ted Swedenburg, eds. *Displacement, Diaspora, and Geographies of Identity.* Durham, NC: Duke University Press, 1996.

Lebzelter, Gisela. "Die 'Schwarze Schmach': Vorurteile—Propaganda—Mythos." *Geschichte und Gesellschaft* 11 (1985): 37–58.

Lee, A. Robert, ed. *Other Britain, Other British: Contemporary Multicultural Fiction.* London: Pluto, 1995.

Lemke Muniz de Faria, Yara-Colette. *Zwischen Fürsorge und Ausgrenzung: Afrodeutsche Besatzungskinder im Nachkriegsdeutschland.* Berlin: Metropol, 2002.

Lennox, Sara, Sara Friedrichsmeyer, and Susanne Zantop, eds. *The Imperialist Imagination: German Colonialism and Its Legacy.* Ann Arbor: University of Michigan Press, 1998.

Lester, Rosemarie K. *Trivialneger: Das Bild des Schwarzen im westdeutschen Illustriertenroman.* Stuttgart: Akademischer Verlag H.-D. Heinz, 1982.

Lilienthal, Georg. "'Rheinlandbastarde,' Rassenhygiene und das Problem der rassenideologischen Kontinuität." *Medizinhistorisches Journal* 15 (1980): 426–36.

Lüsebrink, Hans-Jürgen. "'Tirailleurs Sénégalais' und 'Schwarze Schande'—Verlaufsformen und Konsequenzen einer deutsch-französischen Auseinandersetzung (1910–1926)." In *"Tirailleurs Sénégalais": Zur bildlichen und literarischen Darstellung afrikanischer Soldaten im Dienste Frankreichs,* ed. Janos Riesz and Joachim Schultz. Frankfurt: Lang, 1989.

Lyotard, Jean-François. *The Differend: Phrases in Dispute.* Trans. Georges Van Den Abbeele. Minneapolis: University of Minnesota Press, 1988.

Majer, Dietmut. *"Fremdvölkische" im Dritten Reich: Ein Beitrag fur nationalsozialistischen Rechtssetzung und Reditspraxis in Verwaltung und Justiz unter besonderer Berücksichtigung der eingegliederten Ostgebiete und des Generalgouvernement.* Boppard am Rhein: Boldt, 1981.

Mangin, Charles. *La Force Noire.* Paris: Hachette, 1910.

Mankekar, Purnima. "Reflections on Diasporic Identities: A Prolegomenon to an Analysis of Political Bifocality." *Diaspora* 3 (1994): 349–71.

Marks, Sally. "Black Watch on the Rhine: A Study in Propaganda, Prejudice, and Prurience." *European Studies Review* 13 (1983): 297–334.

Martin, Biddy, and Chandra Mohanty. "Feminist Politics: What's Home Got to Do with It?" In *Feminist Studies, Critical Studies,* ed. Teresa de Lauretis. Bloomington: Indiana University Press, 1986.

Martin, Peter. *Schwarze Teufel, Edle Mohren: Afrikaner in Bewußtsein und Geschichte der Deutschen.* Hamburg: Junius, 1993.

Mason-John, Valerie, ed. *Talking Black: Lesbians of African and Asian Descent Speak Out.* New York: Cassell, 1995.

Maß, Sandra. "Die 'Schwarze Schmach': Der Diskurs über die afrikanischen Kolonialsoldaten im Rheinland, 1919–1925." Master's thesis, University of Bochum, 1998.

Massaquoi, Hans J. *Destined to Witness: Growing up Black in Nazi Germany.* New York: W. Morrow, 1999.

Massey, Dorinne. *Space, Place, and Gender.* Minneapolis: University of Minnesota Press, 1994.

McBride, David, Leroy Hopkins, and C. Aisha Blackshire-Belay, eds. *Crosscurrents: African Americans, Africa, and Germany in the Modern World.* Columbia, SC: Camden House, 1998.

Mercer, Kobena. *Black Film, British Cinema.* London: Institute of Contemporary Arts, 1988.

Mirza, Heidi Safia, ed. *Black British Feminism: A Reader.* New York: Routledge, 1997.

Morel, Edmund Dene. *The Horror on the Rhine.* London: n.p., 1921.

Morley, David, and Kuan-Hsing Chen. *Stuart Hall: Critical Dialogues in Cultural Studies.* New York: Routledge, 1996.

Mueller-Hill, Benno. *Murderous Science: Elimination by Scientific Selection of Jews, Gypsies, and Others, Germany 1933–1945.* Trans. George Fraser. New York: Oxford University Press, 1988.

Nelson, Keith L. "'The Black Horror on the Rhine': Race as a Factor in Post–World War I Diplomacy." *Journal of Modern History* 42 (1970): 606–27.

Niethammer, Lutz, ed. *Lebenserfahrung und kollektives Gedächtnis: Die Praxis der "Oral History."* Frankfurt am Main: Syndikat, 1985.

Niethammer, Lutz, and Alexander von Plato, eds. *"Wir kriegen jetzt andere Zeiten": Auf der Suche nach der Erfahrung des Volkes in nachfaschistischen Ländern.* Vol. 3 of *Lebensgeschichte und Sozialkultur im Ruhrgebiet, 1930–1960.* Berlin: Dietz, 1985.

Noakes, Jeremy. "Nazism and Eugenics: The Background to the Nazi Sterilization Law of 14 July 1933." In *Ideas into Politics: Aspects of European History, 1880–1950,* ed. R. J. Bullen, H. Pogge von Strandmann, and A. B. Polonsky. Totowa, NJ: Barnes and Noble, 1984.

Nora, Pierre. "Between Memory and History: *Les Lieux de Mémoire.*" In *History and Memory in African-American Culture,* ed. Genevieve Fabre and Robert O'Meally. Oxford: Oxford University Press, 1994.

Oakley, Ann. "Interviewing Women: A Contradiction in Terms." In *Doing Feminist Research,* ed. Helen Roberts. New York: Routledge and Kegan Paul, 1981.

Oguntoye, Katharina. *Eine Afro-Deutsche Geschichte: Zur Lebenssituation von Afrikanern und Afro-Deutschen in Deutschland von 1884 bis 1950.* Berlin: Hoho Verlag Christine Hoffmann, 1997.

Okihiro, Gary. "Oral History and the Writing of Ethnic History." In *Oral History: An Interdisciplinary Anthology,* ed. David Dunaway and Willa Baum. Nashville, TN: American Association for State and Local History in cooperation with the Oral History Association, 1984.

Opitz, May, Katharina Oguntoye, and Dagmar Schultz, eds. *Farbe bekennen: Afro-deutsche Frauen auf den Spuren ihrer Geschichte.* Berlin: Fischer, 1986.

Opitz, May, Katharina Oguntoye, and Dagmar Schultz, eds. *Showing Our Colors: Afro-German Women Speak Out.* Trans. Anne Adams. Foreword by Audre Lorde. Amherst: University of Massachusetts Press, 1992.

Passerini, Luisa. *Autobiography of a Generation: Italy 1968.* Trans. Lisa Erdberg. Foreword by Joan Wallach Scott. Hanover, NH: University Press of New England, 1996.

Passerini, Luisa. *Fascism in Popular Memory: The Cultural Experience of the Turin Working Class.* Trans. Robert Lumley and Jude Bloomfield. New York: Cambridge University Press, 1987.

Passerini, Luisa. "Memory: Résumé of the Final Session of the International Conference on Oral History, Aix-en-Provence, 26 September, 1982." Reprinted in *History Workshop Journal* 15 (1983): 195–96.

Peukert, Detlev J. K. *Inside Nazi Germany: Conformity, Opposition, and Racism in Everyday Life.* Trans. Richard Deveson. New Haven: Yale University Press, 1987.

Pommerin, Reiner. *Sterilisierung der Rheinlandbastarde: Das Schicksal einer farbigen deutschen Minderheit, 1918–1937.* Düsseldorf: Droste, 1979.

Popular Memory Group. "Popular Memory: Theory, Politics, Method." In *The Oral History Reader,* ed. Robert Perks and Alistair Thomson. New York: Routledge, 1998.

Portelli, Alessandro. *The Death of Luigi Trastuilli and Other Stories: Form and Meaning in Oral History.* Albany: State University of New York Press, 2001.

Prescod-Roberts, Margaret, and Norma Steele. *Black Women: Bringing It All Back Home.* Bristol, Eng.: Falling Wall, 1980.

Proctor, Robert. *Racial Hygiene: Medicine under the Nazis.* Cambridge: Harvard University Press, 1988.

Reed, Alan, ed. *The Fact of Blackness: Frantz Fanon and Visual Representation.* Seattle: Bay Press, 1996.

Reinders, Robert. "Racialism on the Left: E. D. Morel and the 'Black Horror on the Rhine.'" *International Review of Social History* 12 (1968): 1–28.

Riesz, Janos, and Joachim Schultz, eds. *"Tirailleurs Sénégalais": Zur bildlichen und literarischen Darstellung afrikanischer Soldaten im Dienste Frankreichs.* Frankfurt: Lang, 1989.

Rushdie, Salman. "Imaginary Homelands. " In Rushdie, *Imaginary Homelands: Essays and Criticism 1981–1991*. London: Granta, 1991.

Schüler, Anja. *The 'Horror on the Rhine': Rape, Racism, and the International Women's Movement*. John F. Kennedy Institute for American Studies Working Paper 86/1996. Berlin: Freie Universität Berlin, 1996.

Schütt, Peter. *"Der Mohr hat seine Schuldigkeit getan . . .": Gibt es Rassismus in der Bundesrepublik?—Eine Streitschrift*. Dortmund: Weltkreis, 1981.

Scott, Joan. "Experience." In *Feminists Theorize the Political,* ed. Judith Butler and Joan Scott. New York: Routledge, 1992.

Sigg, Marianne. *Das Rassestrafrecht in Deutschland in den Jahren 1933–1945 unter besonderer Berücksichtigung des Blutschutzgesetzes*. Aarau, Switz.: H. R. Sauerländer, 1951.

Smith, Helmut Walser. "The Talk of Genocide, the Rhetoric of Miscegenation: Notes on Debates in the German Reichstag Concerning Southwest Africa, 1904–14." In *The Imperialist Imagination: German Colonialism and Its Legacy,* ed. Sara Friedrichsmeyer, Sara Lennox, and Susanne Zantop. Ann Arbor: University of Michigan Press, 1998.

Sofsky, Wolfgang. *The Order of Terror: The Concentration Camp*. Trans. William Templer. Princeton: Princeton University Press, 1997.

Stuckart, Wilhelm, and Hans Globke. *Kommentare zur deutschen Rassengesetzgebung*. Vol. 1. Munich: Beck, 1936.

Thelen, David, ed. *Memory and American History*. Bloomington: Indiana University Press, 1990.

Thimm, Karin, and DuRell Echols. *Schwarze in Deutschland: Protokolle*. Munich: Piper, 1973.

Tucker, William. *The Science and Politics of Racial Research*. Urbana: University of Illinois Press, 1994.

Van der Veer, Peter. "Introduction: The Diasporic Imagination." In *Nation and Migration: The Politics of Space in the South Asian Diaspora,* ed. Peter van der Veer. Philadelphia: University of Philadelphia Press, 1995.

von Saldern, Adelheid. "Victims or Perpetrators? Controversies about the Role of Women in the Nazi State." In *Nazism and German Society, 1933–1945,* ed. David F. Crew. New York: Routledge, 1994.

Walk, Joseph, ed. "Gesetz gegen die Überfüllung deutscher Schulen und Hochschulen vom 25.5.1933 and the 2. Verordnung zur Durchführung des Gesetzes gegen die Überfüllung deutscher Schulen und Hochschulen vom 25.4.1933." In *Das Sonderrecht für die Juden im NS- Staat*. Heidelberg: Muller Juristischer, 1981.

Weindling, Paul. *Health, Race, and German Politics between National Unification and Nazism, 1870–1945*. Cambridge: Cambridge University Press, 1989.

Weingart, Peter, Jürgen Kroll, and Kurt Bayertz. *Rasse, Blut und Gene: Geschichte der Eugenik und Rassenhygiene in Deutschland*. Frankfurt am Main: Suhrkamp, 1988.

Westwood, Sallie. "Gendering Diaspora: Space, Politics, and South Asian Masculinities in Britain." In *Nation and Migration: The Politics of Space in the*

South Asian Diaspora, ed. Peter van der Veer. Philadelphia: University of Philadelphia Press, 1995.

White, E. Frances. "Africa on My Mind: Gender, Counterdiscourse, and African American Nationalism." In *Words of Fire: An Anthology of African-American Feminist Thought,* ed. Beverly Guy-Sheftall. New York: Norton, 1995.

Wildenthal, Lora. *German Women for Empire, 1884–1945.* Durham, NC: Duke University Press, 2001.

Wildenthal, Lora. "Race, Gender, and Citizenship in the German Colonial Empire." In *Tensions of Empire: Colonial Cultures in a Bourgeois World,* ed. Frederick Cooper and Ann Laura Stoler. Berkeley: University of California Press, 1997.

Wippermann, Wolfgang. *Das Leben in Frankfurt zur NS-Zeit.* Vol. 2, *Die national-sozialistische Zigeunerverfolgung.* Frankfurt: W. Kramer, 1986.

Wright, Michelle Maria. "Others-from-Within from Without: Afro-German Subject Formation and the Challenge of a Counter-Discourse." *Callaloo* 26, no. 2 (2003): 296–305.

Young, James Edward. *Writing and Rewriting the Holocaust: Narrative and the Consequences of Interpretation.* Bloomington: Indiana University Press, 1988.

Zantop, Susanne. *Colonial Fantasies: Conquest, Family, and Nation in Precolonial Germany, 1770–1870* . Durham, NC: Duke University Press, 1997.

INDEX

Abel, Wolfgang, 75
absent meaning, 16
Adelson, Leslie, 127
African-American community, 4; as dominant model, 195, 196, 202; hegemony of, 177–79, 203, 210; as outsider within, 102–3; privilege of, 175–76
African-American cultural context, 183, 201–8; blackness and, 202, 205, 206; German identity and, 205–6, 207; interracial marriage and, 203–4, 205
African diaspora, 4, 7–8, 187–90; African consciousness and, 174–76; intercultural address, 170, 187–88, 190–92; interpellative exchanges, 182–83, 189–90. *See also* diasporic relations
African-German Experience, The (Blackshire-Belay, ed.), 4
African soldiers. *See* French colonial (Black) troops
Afro-German movement, 8. *See also* Black Germans; Rhineland Bastards
Alcoff, Linda, 127
Algerian heritage, 25, 96. *See also* heritage
alien blood (*artfremdes Blut*), 143–45
Althusser, Louis, 9, 10
American Medical Association, 70
anti-Semitism, 64, 65, 143, 165
army experience. *See* Wehrmacht experience

Aryan ancestry, 112, 143–44; defined, 50, 149; proof of, 116, 117, 130, 253n. 16
assimilation, 98. *See also* belonging
Ayim, May, 103

Bartov, Omer, 62
Bastardfrage, 77. *See also* Rhineland Bastards
Bauman, Zygmunt, 148
belonging, 107, 108, 114, 136, 199; diasporic relations and, 172, 173, 180. *See also* assimilation; community
"Between Memory and History" (Nora), 12–13
Beveridge, Ray, 58–59, 61, 244n. 51
biological value, 71. *See also* body, memory and
Black America. *See* African-American community
Black British cultural studies, 8, 172
Black Britons, 193
Black communities, African diaspora and, 23, 168–84, 193, 202–3; African-American hegemony/privilege, 175–76, 177–79; Afro-Germans, 170, 174–76, 179–81; belonging and, 172, 173, 180; borrowing and, 172–73; commonalities and, 176, 177; diasporic asymmetries, 174–81; difference, *décalage* and, 181–82, 208; identity and, 176, 177, 179, 183; intercultural address and, 183–84; links between, 8, 168–71; memory and,